DOCUMENTS OF LIBERTY
FROM EARLIEST TIMES TO UNIVERSAL SUFFRAGE

Documents of
Liberty

from earliest times to universal suffrage

Henry Marsh

David & Charles : Newton Abbot

ISBN 0 7153 5313 6

Set in Garamond
and printed in Great Britain
by Bristol Typesetting Company Limited
for David & Charles (Publishers) Limited
South Devon House Newton Abbot Devon

Contents

Note on the Texts and Translations used

The texts and translations of all the documents quoted (with the exception of the Remonstrance to Aethelred, Magna Carta, and the Representation of the People Acts of 1918, 1928 and 1969) are taken from *Select Documents of English Constitutional History* edited by Professor G. B. Adams and Professor H. M. Stephens (Macmillan, New York, 1901).

The Remonstrance to Aethelred is taken from the *Anglo-Saxon Chronicle,* the original language being Anglo-Saxon. For those documents of which the originals were either Latin or Norman-French, the following are the sources of the translations, showing the abbreviations used in the lists of documents quoted, given at the end of each chapter :

G & H — Translated by Henry Gee and W. J. Hardy in *Documents Illustrative of English Church History*

C — Translated by Professor Cheyney in *Translations and Reprints* (University of Pennsylvania)

AS — Translated by Adams and Stephens in *Select Documents of English Constitutional History* (Macmillan, New York, 1901)

R — Translated by Riley in *The Annals of Roger de Hoveden* (slight changes by AS)

SR — Translated in the Statutes of the Realm

S — Translated by Bishop Stubbs, author of *Constitutional History* and *Select Charters*

The translation of Magna Carta is reproduced, with the permission of the British Museum, from their publication on The Great Charter.

The Representation of the People Acts of 1918, 1928 and 1969 are reproduced with the permission of Her Majesty's Stationery Office.

For all the statutes after 1429 the standard regnal references are shown.

Foreword

THE aim of this book is to trace the growth of representative government from the days when Britain's bishops and great landowners sat in the *Witan* (or council) of the Anglo-Saxon kings, to the introduction of universal suffrage in the present century. I have done this by reproducing, in part or in full, the texts of the most important British documents upon which, directly or indirectly, political liberty in Britain and many parts of the world has been built up.

Even the most famous of these are now but rarely read; nor is it generally realised that they are merely the peaks of an extensive range whose foothills lie hidden in the mist of early history. Nowadays there is an increasing consciousness, to be found in many nations, of the need to defend the individual's rights against the growing power of the state, and it seems opportune to recall these charters and statutes. They show how the basic liberties of the British people have been enlarged and safeguarded from generation to generation, and how ancient is the people's right to participate in the processes of government.

I have linked these documents by means of a simple historical narrative, showing how each came about. It has latterly been fashionable to write history in terms of broad social development without detailed references to individual reigns, but I have reverted to the older mode of telling the story in terms of the kings and queens themselves. This is because monarchs were once supreme and rights and liberties have grown out of a continuous dialogue between sovereign and subjects. The personalities, views and attitudes of the individual sovereigns have therefore had a great influence in this context.

Although the theme of the book is the growth of democracy in England, and ultimately in Britain, the story has a far wider relevance. Many other nations have inherited the rights which were obtained at

7

Runnymede, in the councils and parliaments held at Oxford and other cities, and finally in Westminster.

As two thousand years ago the rulers of the Roman Empire dreamed of a world where all nations should share in citizenship of the Eternal City, and should have in their own lands assemblies and senates which typified Roman methods of government, the British people felt their hard-won liberties and rights to participate in government could be transplanted. The common citizenship has vanished; but, as over a period of three or four centuries British people crossed the oceans of the world, establishing new communities in every continent, their forms of government have indeed been planted and have blossomed in many lands.

When the thirteen British colonies in North America declared their independence in 1776, they laid down that 'governments are instituted among Men, deriving their just powers from the consent of the governed . . .' In so doing they were consciously echoing the words of the Great Charter which King John had sealed 561 years before. In this he had undertaken that no tax 'may be levied in our kingdom without its general consent . . .' The constitution which the newly independent states drew up in 1787 was to a large extent the formal statement of those rights and liberties which had been fought for in Britain in days gone by. 'From the unwritten British constitution came many ideas and principles,' to quote a US Information Service booklet, *The United States of America*. The equality of all men before the law, with equal rights to the law's protection, and those further rights laid down by the first ten amendments to the American Constitution (such as the freedom of religious worship, of speech, and of the press) were foreshadowed to some extent in the documents surveyed in this book. The third amendment, guaranteeing that troops shall not be quartered in private homes without the owners' consent, comes directly out of urgent arguments and discussions pursued in England in the preceding century.

Later, as other colonies of British people became independent, further nations derived their constitutions from the various documents of liberty. Canada, whose origins as a nation lie in a Royal Proclamation of 1763, is also the heir to the rights and liberties that were established in Britain. The gothic-style Parliament buildings in Ottawa are a symbol of the shared heritage.

The six colonies which had developed across the world in Australia became an independent commonwealth in 1900. The Australian Constitution, set up by an Act of the Westminster parliament, again is based on the British experience. For example, we shall see how in 1407, long before anyone in Europe even dreamed of a great continent in the southern seas, the English House of Commons won the right to initiate money bills, and ensured that the House of Lords should not be able to take similar steps. In Australia it was taken as a matter of course that the House of Representatives alone, and not the Senate, could originate 'laws appropriating revenue or moneys', or imposing taxation. In the same way, it was laid down that the powers, privileges and immunities of the Senate and of the House of Representatives, and of the members and committees of each house, should be 'those of the Commons House of Parliament of the United Kingdom' until anything to the contrary should be declared by the Australian Parliament.

New Zealand's history shows even closer parallels. The most dramatic of these is that the constitution of New Zealand, like that of the United Kingdom, is not embodied in any one enactment or formally related series of enactments. As the New Zealand official Year Book (1908) stated, 'New Zealand's constitutional law is derived from a number of varied sources, and . . . our constitution is the sum total of these. In other words, our constitution is of the British type . . . constitutional conventions or usages play as large a part in the working of the New Zealand Parliament as they do in the United Kingdom; the institution of Cabinet here, for example, rests on no other basis . . . In all essential respects the New Zealand Constitution is, therefore, the same in content as the British'.

Nor is it only to nations of British stock that the constitutional ideas of the United Kingdom have been carried. In the new countries in Asia and in Africa, where once the British people governed, and to which they took their ideas of government by consent and of the rule of law, parliaments have been set up which are broadly modelled upon the Parliament of Westminster. These nations accordingly have a share in Britain's history, and the origins of their institutions go back to the cities and villages of thirteenth-century England. Men and women in the sunny lands of Asia, in the highlands and plains of Africa, sit in assemblies based on the ideas of Simon de Montfort, Earl of Leicester, who died fighting in defence of those ideals, over 700 years ago on an English battlefield.

All these assemblies recognise Westminster as their exemplar, however widely local needs and local traditions may cause them to diverge. India, for example, declared that the privileges of her parliament, and of its members and committees should be the same of those of the United Kingdom parliament, unless they were later modified by statute.

Article 105 (Clause 3) of India's Constitution stated:

> In other respects, the powers, privileges and immunities of each House of Parliament, and of the members and the committees of each House, shall be such as may from time to time be defined by Parliament by law, and, until so defined, shall be those of the House of Commons of the Parliament of the United Kingdom, and of its members and committees, at the commencement of this Constitution.

It is not only in the English-speaking world that the British example has had influence. The French Revolution, and the aspirations towards liberty, equality and brotherhood upon which it was based, owed much to the fact that many Frenchmen had looked with envy at the growing freedom in eighteenth-century Britain. Voltaire is only one example of those who were influenced by events across the channel. He spent three years in England (1726–9) and was greatly struck by the extent of toleraton in England and by the ready acceptance of radical thought and personal eccentricity. He drew a contrast between these matters and the closely controlled society of France in a work he published in 1733, *Lettres philosophiques sur les Anglais*. This book, which had a great influence in France, described and praised English attitudes, and through that device attacked the lack of freedom in pre-revolutionary France. In the nineteenth and twentieth centuries, as the old absolute monarchies of Europe collapsed, the British example was not without influence on the new forms of government which replaced them.

British society has managed to combine continuity with change. The continuity is exemplified by its institutions. Parliament has a continuous history of over 700 years and its roots lie in the Witan of the Anglo-Saxon kings more than 1,300 years ago. The crown is still worn by a descendant of William the Conqueror and of the Anglo-Saxon kings who preceded him. Yet useful changes have evolved, and the years to come will no doubt bring further changes—some trivial and some radical. The past teaches us that such changes, if they are to be sociologically profitable, will be based upon an unchanging desire for personal liberty within a lawful and orderly society, and for participation by the governed in the processes of government. And all must be done within an institutional framework that provides for stability without stagnation, and radical change without the destruction of a peaceful environment.

H.M.

CHAPTER I

Saxon and Norman Kings
(from earliest times to 1135)

T HE methods whereby England is governed have for centuries been dominated by two paradoxes. Firstly, some of the people have for generations claimed the right to a say in government, and the movement towards a widely based democracy is very ancient. Yet in theory the crown and not the people is the repository of sovereign power. Secondly, although the constitution has never been reduced to writing, the people's liberties depend upon, and have been gradually enlarged by, a series of written documents.

Democracy—the right of the governed to participate in government —developed very early in England. True, not until the nineteenth century were most men, nor until the twentieth century were all men and women, allowed to elect their legislators, but the origins of these processes are to be found a thousand years earlier, when Saxon kings consulted their bishops and great landowners (the thanes) in the *Witan Gemoot* or Wise Men's Meeting.

This pattern continued after the Norman Conquest, save that it was now French barons rather than Saxon thanes who sat in the king's council, balancing the king's demands against their own interests. It was from their estates that farm produce, and later money, was taken by the king for the defence and government of the realm. Since it was they who paid, they began to consider that they should be consulted as of right, and not merely by the king's favour. The concept of no taxation without representation is far more ancient than the slogan which embodies it.

Gradually these rights seeped downwards through society as each class saw with envy the growing privileges of those above it. The process was hastened by that questioning of authority and of those in power which has for so long kept governments in England alert and adaptable.

The growth of liberty was usually achieved within an unchanging social structure. Throughout the continuous and often radical changes there has (with the brief exception of Cromwell's commonwealth) been no departure from the theory that society is organised under a king in whom all authority is vested and whose powers are total. All laws are his, all punishment is carried out in his name, all restraints of liberty or appropriation of property are matters for his decision and execution. Total obedience to the sovereign is the nexus which binds society together, giving it both stability and adaptability. Loyalty to society is simplified and given an added warmth when expressed as loyalty to a person; particularly to one whom hereditary greatness raises above political ambition, and who by tradition must serve all sections of the community, rich and poor alike. It is at least arguable that this is preferable to situations in which ambitious men may be corrupted by adulation or seduced from wisdom by the need to generate popularity.

Experience, compromise, and a reluctance to break too harshly with the past, have gradually modified the application of the royal power which in theory is still supreme. The affairs of the country have always been (and still are) run on this theory, but the crown's subjects have always expected the sovereign to consult them as to how he should exercise this supreme authority. Moreover, the subjects have periodically asked the sovereign to acknowledge that they too possessed rights which were not to be invaded. Verbal promises were not enough, and the subjects requested the sovereign to record in writing his recognition of their rights and his undertaking not to diminish them.

The conception of one sovereign individual is as ancient as the nation itself, and so is the belief that he has duties as inescapable as his powers. First among these has been his responsibility to act only in consultation with at least some of his subjects. In the assemblies where this took place, it was rare for his authority to be openly questioned or brutally diminished. Demands were expressed as prayers, and requests as petitions. The bent knee, the low bow, the reiteration of expressions of obedience, have accompanied each remonstrance and all claims for concessions from crown to subject.

Very early the king's signature was sought as a record of such concessions. This conception of documents binding a king may have arisen from the fact that English kings had for centuries written down the laws by which their subjects were constrained. These laws (dating back thirteen hundred years) were the simple and minimum rules enabling men to live in orderly communities. They dealt with such everyday matters as straying cattle, the theft of horses, the keeping of one's word, and wounding or murdering a man. They recognised that the liberty of each involved the placing of constraint upon all; and that the rights of even great men had to be defined and limited if society were to be stable and order maintained.

It followed that the man at the apex of the state had himself to accept some restraints. But lest these should seem, by reducing his authority, to reduce that of the community which he personified, they were made to appear as being granted by the good grace of the king himself. All the concessions he was forced to cede were shown as acts of majestic and spontaneous generosity. Political stability was esteemed above mere political victory. Thus although many documents of liberty were obtained by a show of force or threat of disobedience, the threats were usually expressed in the language of humility and obedience.

An early example is to be found during the reign of King Aethelred II which began with great promise in AD979. He died thirty-seven weary years later, unlucky, unsuccessful and unloved, earning no better reward for all his long labours and bloody campaigns than the mocking nickname of 'The Unready'.

During his reign, Danish and Viking armies were harrying the land, giving the English no respite. But Aethelred was not condemned because of his military defeats; nor because he tried to buy off the invaders with money. He was derided because he never rose above the events by which he was beleaguered. With England's coasts open to the landings of ruthless sea-rovers, with her towns and fields devastated by merciless armies, no one expected the miracle of total success, but all looked for that dignity and resolution, which had been so splendidly shown by Alfred and many of his successors. Aethelred was judged by the standards of his ancestors whose prowess had matched the stubborn character of their people. And by those standards he had failed.

In 1013 London fell to Swein, the Danish leader and (as the *Anglo-Saxon Chronicle* tells us) 'At this time nothing went right for this nation, neither in the south nor in the north.' The queen fled to France and Aethelred followed her shortly before Christmas.

In the new year the king's councillors met to discuss what should be done. All agreed that they should send a REMONSTRANCE TO AETHELRED declaring, says the *Anglo-Saxon Chronicle,* that 'no lord was dearer to them than their rightful lord, if only he would govern his kingdom more justly than he had done in the past'. In addition to this mixed expression of loyalty and grievance, there was a blunt summons to him to appear before the Witan. He did not come himself but sent his son Edward with a message promising 'that he would be a gracious lord to them, and would remedy each one of the things which they all abhorred, and everything should be forgiven that had been done or said against him, on condition that they all unanimously and without treachery returned to their allegiance.'

The king's message as reported in the *Anglo-Saxon Chronicle* begins with a phrase normally used as a greeting in letters, 'He bade greet all his people', so that it was almost certainly delivered in writing. Accordingly this brief message can be taken as the first recorded document of liberty in English history.

It set a style for the future. First, the king's subjects in summoning the king, used humble words. Next they were demonstrating their right of remonstrance and their right to demand that bad government should cease and their grievances find redress. Finally the king, in acknowledging these rights, maintained his position as sovereign by formally demanding a return to allegiance, and the Witan was content that he should do so.

Later, when the Normans conquered England in 1066 the institution of kingship was fundamentally changed. In Anglo-Saxon England the king was viewed with respect rather than adulation, and his power neither endowed him with divine qualities nor relieved him from human duties.

In France, where the Normans had lived for six or seven generations, the monarchy had developed differently. Charles, King of the Franks (AD768–814), had revived the ideas and much of the splendour of the Roman Empire. He sought to restore the Europe of the Caesars and invested the throne of France with imperial glory. He was acclaimed as *Carolus Magnus* (Charles the Great) and is known to history as Charlemagne.

The power he bestowed upon the French crown did not survive him but much of the splendour remained. His authority had run far beyond his frontiers; that of his successors declined until the kings of France were less powerful than the dukes and counts who were their vassals. The sceptre of France remained an object of veneration but ceased to be an instrument of effective force.

Duke William of Normandy, a vassal of France, had won the crown of England with the help of his feudal army and he could now look across the Channel to the king of France, his former lord, as an equal.

14

He was determined that no vassal of his should ever rise to royalty, as he had done. His resolve was reinforced by the example of King Harold Godwinson against whom he had fought at Hastings. Harold had once been merely Earl of Wessex. Under King Edward the Confessor, who preferred the quiet cloisters to the council chamber or the battlefield, Harold had advanced to greatness until, brushing aside the heirs of the blood, he attained the throne of England.

Accordingly King William competely restructured English society. Previously, although kings of England had been lords of all their subjects, each subject owed a duty to the lord immediately above him. Great men could call up their tenants to form armies which might fight battles other than the king's. In practice, the traditional accept- ance of the king's authority had prevented abuse, but William had seen in France how this system could work to the king's mischief. So, some twenty years after his conquest of England, he summoned to Salisbury all who held their lands directly from him, barons and churchmen alike, together with their principal tenants. He commanded each to take an oath of allegiance to himself, swearing to obey the king first and their own lords after.

To the English, for whom loyalty to one's immediate lord was the supreme social virtue, the Oath of Salisbury was revolutionary. Yet William had done his new country a great service. Because of this oath, the English feudal system developed differently from its Con- tinental counterparts. The power of the king was assured and the growth of a strong central government made possible.

The doctrine that all land belonged to the king, with the barons holding their estates from him as tenants-in-chief in return for military service, led to a simple system of taxation. On the death of a tenant- in-chief the heir had to pay the king for the right to become tenant- in-chief in his turn. When the church held land a similar price, on the death of a bishop or abbot, was exacted from the new incumbent.

Nor were these death duties the only imposts introduced by the Norman kings. The crown's permission was needed before a tenant- in-chief could give a daughter in marriage and the practice grew for the king to make a charge for such permission. Similar charges were made when a tenant's widow remarried. Moreover the king could select the new husband, so that his power now invaded areas of private and personal liberty.

Under the Saxon kings, there had been fixed fines for most offences, but under the Norman kings some crimes involved the forfeiture of all

15

a man's money. This was intolerable to the English landowners. They remembered how King Alfred had collected the ancient laws of several English kingdoms and, after consulting his Witan, had set down the best of them to be the laws of his own realm. To the extent (admittedly limited) to which the Witan represented his subjects, Alfred's laws were therefore legislation by consultation and consent. Succeeding kings had reaffirmed them, and the laws of King Edward the Confessor were based upon them. They symbolised not only the crown's authority but the subjects' rights and dignity.

To the Norman barons, and certainly to their sons, the growing demands of the crown were also intolerable. The theory governing the ownership of land had become a pretext for heavy taxes on inheritance, on marriage, on the estates of the dead, and upon the church. They saw their personal wealth, as well as their personal power, being skilfully diminished. The grievances of the two parties, Norman and English, acted as a unifying force and accelerated the assimilation of the Normans into English society.

There existed an instrument, created by the English and not discarded by the Norman kings, through which the aggrieved landowners could make their voices heard. This was the Witan, with whose counsel and consent Anglo-Saxon kings had for centuries been accustomed to govern. In theory all the great landowners were members of this body, now known as the Grand Council. With such wide membership it could not easily meet. A few tenants-in-chief were therefore selected by the king to form a working sub-committee known as the *Curia Regis*, the King's Council. The Grand Council itself became a place of general discussion (in Norman-French a place of *parlement*), while the *Curia Regis* became a group of advisers and ministers. Members of the *Curia* were the king's nominees, and therefore did his bidding, but inevitably they represented the class to which they belonged and their fellow landowners could talk to them as they could not talk to the king; meanwhile the Grand Council, though it seldom met, kept alive the Anglo-Saxon tradition that kings governed in consultation with some at least of their subjects.

Twenty-one years after his victory at Hastings, William died. His dukedom of Normandy he left to his eldest son Robert, and his kingdom of England to his younger son, William, nicknamed Rufus. Rufus was well served by his justiciar, Flambard, Bishop of Durham. Feudal dues were harshly levied. To the duties on inheritance and on the marriage of heiresses, new fines were added. On the deaths of bishops the cathedral thrones were left vacant so that the king might enjoy the revenues as long as was possible and sometimes longer than was decent.

Early in his reign some of the Norman barons rose against him. Rufus, remembering that he was king of all England and not merely of the Norman barons, summoned Englishmen to his aid. In the words of the *Anglo-Saxon Chronicle* he 'promised them the best laws which there had ever been in this land. He banned every unjust tax, and gave to men their forests and their hunting rights.' Later the king broke his promises even though the English 'came to the help of their lord their king.'

Then the king's brother, Robert Duke of Normandy, made war against him. Invasion and civil war added to the king's expenses and consequently to taxation. When he died in 1100, shot mysteriously by an arrow in the shadowed depths of the New Forest, the *Anglo-Saxon Chronicle* recorded that he had been cruel in his government, had followed the advice of wicked counsellors, exploiting the people through unjust taxes. He had 'claimed to be every man's heir—priest or layman.'

Rufus was succeeded by his younger brother Henry, nicknamed *Beauclerc*, the scholar. The council seized the opportunity offered by the shock of William's sudden death and by the new king's urgent need for their support. A charter redressing the grievances of the kingdom was drawn up within nine days of Rufus's death. At his coronation in London the new king swore before the altar to abolish all injustices, and signed the charter, known as the Coronation Charter. The following is the text:

THE CORONATION CHARTER OF HENRY I

In the year of the incarnation of the Lord, 1101, Henry, son of King William, after the death of his brother William, by the grace of God, king of the English, to all faithful, greeting:

1. Know that by the mercy of God, and by the common counsel of the barons of the whole kingdom of England, I have been crowned king of the same kingdom; and because the kingdom has been oppressed by unjust exactions, I, from regard to God, and from the love which I have towards you, in the first place make the holy church of God free, so that I will neither sell nor place at rent, nor, when archbishop, or

bishop, or abbot is dead, will I take anything from the domain of the church, or from its men, until a successor is installed into it. And all the evil customs by which the realm of England was unjustly oppressed will I take away, which evil customs I partly set down here.

2.   If any one of my barons, or earls, or others who hold from me shall have died, his heir shall not redeem his land as he did in the time of my brother, but shall relieve it by a just and legitimate relief. Similarly also the men of my barons shall relieve their lands from their lords by a just and legitimate relief.

3.   And if any one of the barons or other men of mine wishes to give his daughter in marriage, or his sister or niece or relation, he must speak with me about it, but I will neither take anything from him for this permission, nor forbid him to give her in marriage, unless he should wish to join her to my enemy. And if when a baron or other man of mine is dead, a daughter remains as his heir, I will give her in marriage according to the judgment of my barons, along with her land. And if when a man is dead his wife remains, and is without children, she shall have her dowry and right of marriage, and I will not give her to a husband except according to her will.

4.   And if a wife has survived with children, she shall have her dowry and right of marriage, so long as she shall have kept her body legitimately, and I will not give her in marriage, except according to her will. And the guardian of the land and children shall be either the wife or another one of the relatives as shall seem to be most just. And I require that my barons should deal similarly with the sons and daughters or wives of their men.

5.   The common tax on money which used to be taken through the cities and counties, which was not taken in the time of King Edward, I now forbid altogether henceforth to be taken. If any one shall have been seised, whether a moneyer or any other, with false money, strict justice shall be done for it.

6.   All fines and all debts which were owed to my brother, I remit, except my rightful rents, and except those payments which had been agreed upon for the inheritance of others or for those things which more justly affected others. And if any one for his own inheritance has stipulated anything, this I

18

remit, and all reliefs which had been agreed upon for rightful inheritances.

7. And if any of my barons or men shall become feeble, however he himself shall give or arrange to give his money, I grant that it shall be so given. Moreover, if he himself, prevented by arms, or by weakness, shall not have bestowed his money, or arranged to bestow it, his wife or his children or parents, and his legitimate men shall divide it for his soul, as to them shall seem best.

8. If any of my barons or men shall have committed an offence he shall not give security to the extent of forfeiture of his money, as he did in the time of my father, or of my brother, but according to the measure of the offence so shall he pay, as he would have paid from the time of my father backward, in the time of my other predecessors; so that if he shall have been convicted of treachery or of crime, he shall pay as is just.

9. All murders moreover before that day in which I was crowned King, I pardon; and those which shall be done henceforth shall be punished justly according to the law of King Edward.

10. The forests, by the common agreement of my barons, I have retained in my own hand, as my father held them.

11. To those Knights who hold their land by the cuirass, I yield of my own gift the lands of their demesne ploughs free from all payments and from all labour, so that as they have thus been favored by such a great alleviation, so they may readily provide themselves with horses and arms for my service and for the defence of my kingdom.

12. A firm peace in my whole kingdom I establish and require to be kept from henceforth.

13. The law of King Edward I give to you again with those changes with which my father changed it by the counsel of his barons.

14. If any one has taken anything from my possessions since the death of King William, my brother, or from the possessions of any one, let the whole be immediately returned without alteration, and if any one shall have retained anything thence, he upon whom it is found will pay it heavily to me. Witnesses Maurice, bishop of London, and Gundulf, bishop, and William, bishop-elect, and Henry, earl, and Simon, earl,

and Walter Giffard, and Robert de Montfort, and Roger Bigod, and Henry de Port, at London, when I was crowned.

Note that this document opened with a greeting as had King Aethelred's message which we have already noticed. Like the charters of Anglo-Saxon kings it was witnessed by members of the council— two bishops, one bishop-elect, two earls and four lesser landowners— who by witnessing the king's signature became as it were sureties for his compliance. Besides echoing the past, this charter provided a pat-tern for posterity. Future kings were to sign similar undertakings. As the prototype of other and greater documents it merits a more important place in history than it has generally been accorded. It has been over-shadowed by a later charter, sealed by King John, of which it was the exemplar.

The first clause re-affirmed the ancient right of the Witan to elect kings, for in it Henry acknowledged that he had been crowned on the advice of the barons of the whole kingdom. (The *Anglo-Saxon Chronicle* confirms that on the death of Rufus 'those counsellors who were near at hand elected his brother Henry to be king.') What had been ancient convention was hardening into a known and indisputable rule. The same clause made the church free of inheritance duty, and the king undertook not to continue the exploitation of church property.

Most of the other clauses dealt with grievances in the matter of duties and taxation, and the men who benefited would chiefly have been the great Norman landowners. But other clauses were drafted with the interests of Henry's Saxon subjects specifically in mind. Clauses 5, 8, 9 and 13 restored the laws of Edward the Confessor which had become a symbol of English rights and liberties. The only amendments permitted (clause 13) were those which William the Conqueror had made with the counsel of his barons. This recognised the immensely important principle that laws could not be changed except through the processes of consultation and consent.

Clause 12 formally called into being the king's peace, a conception that had been steadily growing during the Anglo-Saxon period. A disturbance of the peace was not only an offence against the persons aggrieved thereby but an affront to the king himself, and the royal power would be deployed against the wrongdoer. The crown was responsible for the maintenance of a peaceful environment within which men could go about their business undisturbed by violence. This conception remains to this day the basis of law and order within the realm.

Henry's son, Prince William, was drowned in 1120 in a shipwreck in the English Channel. Deprived of a male heir, Henry named his daughter Matilda as his successor, but when he died in 1135 the council, exercising its now established right of election, would have none of her, choosing instead Stephen, Henry's nephew and a grandson of the Conqueror. Stephen was required to give an undertaking to maintain the laws of King Edward the Confessor in the following brief charter which he executed in 1135, the year of his accession, in London:

THE CHARTER OF KING STEPHEN—1135

Stephen, by the grace of God, king of the English, to the justices, sheriffs, barons, and all his ministers and faithful French and English, greeting.

Know that I have conceded and by this my present charter confirmed to all my barons and men of England all the liberties and good laws which Henry, King of the English, my uncle, gave and conceded to them, and all the good laws and good customs which they had in the time of King Edward, I concede to them. Wherefore I wish and firmly command that they shall have and hold all those good laws and liberties from me and my heirs, they and their heirs, freely, quietly, and fully; and I prohibit any one from bringing any obstacle, or impediment, or diminution upon them in these matters on pain of forfeiture to me.

Witness William Martel, at London.

This document, in which the new king renewed the undertaking given by Henry to maintain the laws of Edward, indicated the council's desire not to retreat from what they had achieved.

The landowners and churchmen of England were learning how the liberties they held under the crown could be defended and enlarged. In Anglo-Saxon England, kings had not exercised arbitrary power nor acted without the advice and consent of the Witan. The advent of a conqueror as king, whose authority depended upon force of arms, might have put these practices in peril. Henry I's Coronation Charter,

and Stephen's reaffirmation of it, had removed that peril and did much
to ensure the survival and development of government by consent.

DOCUMENTS QUOTED:

1   The Remonstrance to Aethelred—1014 [*Anglo-Saxon Chronicle*]
2   The Coronation Charter of Henry I—1101 [*C*]
3   The Charter of King Stephen—1135 [*C*]

CHAPTER II

Growth of the Grand Council
(1135-1194)

THE rivalry between two candidates for the throne—Stephen chosen by the Grand Council, and Matilda, the nominee of the late king—led inevitably to a civil war which shook the whole structure of English society. The king's peace collapsed. The great landowners, unchecked by the royal power, became tyrants in their own estates. The *Anglo-Saxon Chronicle* reported that all the barons broke their oaths of allegiance to the king, building castles in which to defy him :

> They grievously oppressed the wretched people of this land with forced labour on those castles. And when the castles were built they filled them with devils and evil men. By night and day they took all those who they thought had any wealth, whether men or women. So as to get their gold and silver they imprisoned them and tortured them with indescribable tortures. The martyrs were never tortured worse than they. Men hung them by the feet and smoked them with terrible smoke. They hung them by the thumbs or by the head and hung chain-mail coats from their feet. They tied knotted rope around their heads and twisted these until they cut into the brains . . . I do not know and I cannot tell all the dreadful things nor all the cruelties they inflicted upon the wretched people of this land. This lasted for all the nineteen years that Stephen was king and it grew ever worse and worse . . . You could well travel a day's journey without finding a village inhabited or a field planted. Then corn and meat and cheese and butter were dear, for there was none in the land.

The vicious violence of the barons vividly demonstrated the value of royal power and of the king's peace. The charters of Henry I and of

Stephen, limiting royal authority, were valueless when royal authority decayed. Men saw that liberty, and the right to enjoy one's possessions in peace, ultimately depended upon the king's power.

When Stephen died and Matilda's son (as had been agreed) succeeded him, men turned with eager hope to the new king, Henry II. A great-grandson of William the Conqueror, he had inherited through his mother both the crown of England and the dukedom of Normandy and from his father, Anjou, Maine, Touraine and Brittany. His wife, Eleanor, brought him Aquitaine, Poitou and Auvergne. Except for the county of Toulouse he was lord of all western France.

Like his grandfather the Conqueror, Henry was resolved that within his English kingdom none of his vassals should overshadow him as he overshadowed the King of France. His first task was therefore to hack away the tangled growth of local power which the barons had planted and which had flourished unchecked under Stephen. He ordered the destruction of many of the castles which had been built in those lawless days. He expelled the continental mercenary troops who had been brought to England by the barons. He insisted that only the king should issue money, and closed the many private mints which had been set up.

The power of the crown grew, and people were content. They were in no mood to be critical of a sovereign who was restoring the king's peace and taking power back into the king's hands. It was not only the barons' powers which Henry had to reduce. The church had long insisted that its courts alone could try clerics. Since the harshest sentence of these courts was expulsion from the church, any cleric could go virtually scot-free however heinous his crime. These ecclesiastical courts had diminished the crown's standing as the sole fount of justice, thus endangering the concept of the king's peace. It was this issue that lay behind the tragic quarrel between the king and Thomas à Becket, his chancellor.

In 1164 (the tenth year of Henry's reign) there was issued a document known as The Constitutions of Clarendon. This was an acknowledgement by Becket and his fellow-bishops 'of a certain part of the customs, liberties and dignities of his [the king's] ancestors, that is of King Henry his grandfather, and of others, which ought to be observed and held in the realm.' The document contained sixteen clauses. The first laid down that the king's court should try all cases between laymen, between clergy and laymen, or between clergy, regarding advowson and presentation to churches. Clause 3 provided that the king's justices could enquire into the findings of the church's courts 'to see in what way the matter is there treated. And if the cleric be convicted or shall confess, the Church must no longer protect him.' Thus a convicted cleric could now be tried in the king's courts and the findings of the ecclesiastical courts came under the scrutiny of the king's justices. The church could not become a state within the state.

THE CONSTITUTIONS OF CLARENDON contain two references to 'twelve lawful men' upon whom was laid the duty of declaring the truth in matters before the court. The first is in Clause 6 which laid down that laymen

. . . are not to be accused save by proper and legal accusers and witnesses in the presence of the bishop . . . And if the accused be such that no one wills or dares to accuse them, the Sheriff, when requested by the bishop, shall cause twelve lawful men from the neighbourhood or the town to swear before the bishop that they will show the truth in the matter according to their conscience.

The second reference is in Clause 9 and deals with disputes between laymen and clerics in respect of any tenement 'which the cleric wishes to bring to frank-almoign but the layman to a lay fee.' (Frank-almoign was the transfer of land to the church in return for prayers to be said for the dead.) Such a case was to go for consideration 'to the king's chief justice on the award of twelve lawful men.' Something approaching the jury system was coming to birth and we shall see how it was to develop.

The document was witnessed by many 'magnates and nobles of the realm, as well clerical as lay', so that Henry was associating the Grand Council in his task of rebuilding the king's authority.

His reign was marked by a series of documents known as 'Assizes'—so called because they recorded decisions taken at sittings (Norman-French *asises*) of the council. In that body Henry was seeking the consent of his subjects, and the Assizes are the precursors of Acts of Parliament.

The following is the text of the first of these, The Assize of Clarendon, issued in 1166, two years after The Constitutions of Clarendon, as a result of a further meeting of the council at the same place :

ASSIZE OF CLARENDON—1166

Here begins the Assize of Clarendon, made by King Henry II. with the assent of the archbishops, bishops, abbots, earls and barons of all England.

1. In the first place, the aforesaid King Henry, with the consent of all his barons, for the preservation of the peace and the keeping of justice, has enacted that inquiry should be made through the several counties and through the several hundreds, by twelve of the most legal men of the hundred and by four of the most legal men of each vill, upon their oath that they will tell the truth, whether there is in their hundred or in their vill, any man who has been accused or publicly suspected of himself being a robber, or murderer, or thief, or of being a receiver of robbers, or murderers, or thieves, since the lord king has been king. And let the justices make this inquiry before themselves, and the sheriffs before themselves.

2. And let any one who has been found by the oath of the aforesaid, to have been accused or publicly suspected of having been a robber, or murderer, or thief, or a receiver of them, since the lord king has been king, be arrested and go to the ordeal of water and let him swear that he has not been a robber, or murderer, or thief, or receiver of them since the lord king has been king, to the value of five shillings, so far as he knows.

3. And if the lord of the man who has been arrested or his steward or his men shall have claimed him, with a pledge, within the third day after he has been seised, let him be given up and his chattels until he himself makes his law

4. And when a robber, or murderer, or thief, or receiver of them shall have been seised through the above-mentioned oath, if the justices are not to come very soon into that county where they have been arrested, let the sheriffs send word to the nearest justice by some intelligent man that they have arrested such men, and the justices will send back word to the sheriffs where they wish that these should be brought before them; and the sheriffs should bring them before the justices; and along with these they shall bring from the

hundred and the vill where they have been arrested, two legal men to carry the record of the county and of the hundred as to why they were seised, and there before the justice let them make their law.

5. And in the case of those who have been arrested through the aforesaid oath of this assize, no one shall have court, or judgment, or chattels, except the lord king in his court before his justices, and the lord king shall have all their chattels. In the case of those, however, who have been arrested, otherwise than through this oath, let it be as it has been accustomed and ought to be.

6. And the sheriffs who have arrested them shall bring such before the justice without any other summons than they have from him. And when robbers, or murderers, or thieves, or receivers of them, who have been arrested through the oath or otherwise, are handed over to the sheriffs they also must receive them immediately without delay.

7. And in the several counties where there are no jails, let such be made in a borough or in some castle of the king, from the money of the king and from his forest, if one shall be near, or from some other neighboring forest, on the view of the servants of the king; in order that in them the sheriffs may be able to detain those who have been seised by the officials who are accustomed to do this or by their servants.

8. And the lord king moreover wills that all should come to the county courts to make this oath, so that no one shall remain behind because of any franchise which he has or court or jurisdiction which he had, but that they should come to the making of this oath.

9. And there is to be no one within a castle or without a castle, or even in the honor of Wallingford, who may forbid the sheriffs to enter into his court or his land for seeing to the frank-pledges and that all are under pledges; and let them be sent before the sheriffs under a free pledge.

10. And in cities and boroughs, let no one have men or receive them in his house or in his land or his soc,[1] whom he does not take in hand that he will produce before the justice if they shall be required, or else let them be under a frank-pledge.

11. And let there be none in a city or borough or in a castle or without or even in the honour[2] of Wallingford who

shall forbid the sheriffs to enter into his land or his jurisdiction to arrest those who have been charged or publicly suspected of being robbers or murderers or thieves or receivers of them, or outlaws, or persons charged concerning the forest; but he requires that they should aid them to capture these.

12.   And if any one is captured who has in his possession the fruits of robbery or theft, if he is of bad reputation and has an evil testimony from the public, and has not a warrant, let him not have law. And if he shall not have been publicly suspected on account of the possession which he has, let him go to the water.

13.   And if any one shall have acknowledged robbery or murder or theft or the reception of them in the presence of legal men or of the hundreds, and afterwards shall wish to deny it, he shall not have law.

14.   The lord king wills moreover that those who make their law and shall be absolved by the law, if they are of very bad testimony, and publicly and disgracefully spoken ill of by the testimony of many and legal men, shall abjure the lands of the king, so that within eight days they shall go over the sea, unless the wind shall have detained them; and with the first wind which they shall have afterward they shall go over the sea, and they shall not afterward return into England, except on the permission of the lord king; and then let them be outlawed if they return, and if they return they shall be seised as outlaws.

15.   And the lord king forbids any vagabond, that is a wandering or an unknown man, to be sheltered anywhere except in a borough, and even there he shall be sheltered only one night, unless he shall be sick there, or his horse, so that he is able to show an evident excuse.

16.   And if he shall have been there more than one night, let him be arrested and held until his lord shall come to give securities for him, or until he himself shall have secured pledges; and let him likewise be arrested who has sheltered him.

17.   And if any sheriff shall have sent word to any other sheriff that men have fled from his county into another county, on account of robbery or murder or theft, or the reception of them, or for outlawry or for a charge concerning the forest of the king, let him arrest them. And even if he knows of himself

or through others that such men have fled into his county, let him arrest them and hold them until he shall have secured pledges from them.

18. And let all sheriffs cause a list to be made of all fugitives who have fled from their counties; and let them do this in the presence of their county courts, and they will carry the written names of these before the justices when they come first before these, so that they may be sought through all England, and their chattels may be seised for the use of the king.

19. And the lord king wills that, from the time when the sheriffs have received the summons of the justices in eyre to appear before them with their county courts, they shall gather together their county courts and make inquiry for all who have recently come into their counties since this assize; and that they should send them away with pledges that they will be before the justices, or else keep them in custody until the justices come to them, and then they shall have them before the justices.

20. The lord king moreover prohibits monks and canons and all religious houses from receiving any one of the lesser people as a monk or canon or brother, until it is known of what reputation he is, unless he shall be sick unto death.

21. The lord kind moreover forbids any one in all England to receive in his land or his jurisdiction or in house under him any one of the sect of those renegades who have been excommunicated and branded at Oxford. And if any one shall have received them, he will be at the mercy of the lord king, and the house in which they have been shall be carried outside the village and burned. And each sheriff will take this oath that he will hold this, and will make all his servants swear this, and the stewards of the barons, and all knights and free tenants of the counties.

22. And the lord king wills that this assize shall be held in his kingdom so long as it shall please him.

The first clause shows the development of the jury system through 'twelve lawful men' who were to enquire upon oath as to the guilt of any man accused of crime, before one of the king's justices or a sheriff. Only if this jury found that a case had been made did the accused go for trial by the ordeal by water, a cruel and primitive way of seeking divine guidance in such matters.

The king's power was fortified by Clause 5, based upon the king's wish to profit by fines and forfeiture, rather than to allow local lords to enrich themselves with the penalties inflicted in their local courts. But the effect was to protect the common man from the decisions, sometimes arbitrary and occasionally malicious, of the local lord of the manor.

Detention of accused men or of criminals was also to be a matter for the king who undertook, in Clause 7, to build jails at his own expense. Again this afforded some protection to the common man against imprisonment in the castles of local magnates, as had happened in Stephen's reign.

Local matters dealt with by the sheriffs were to come under the scrutiny of the king's 'justices in eyre'—the travelling judges (so named from a Norman-French word *eire* meaning to travel, as in the phrase knights-errant).

Before the Norman Conquest, kings of England could call upon all free men to serve them in war, and this national army was known as the *fyrd*. Henry II knew that he might expect greater loyalty from such an army than from the feudal levies which could easily be used against the crown, and he accordingly revived the *fyrd*. THE ASSIZE OF ARMS, issued in 1181, defined the weapons which each class of men should keep ready for the king's service. Every tenant with an estate worth a knight's fee, and every free layman who had chattels or revenue worth sixteen marks (a mark being one-third of a pound), should have a coat of mail, helmet, shield and lance. Those worth ten marks were to have a hauberk, an iron helmet and a lance. All other freemen, and all burghers, were to own a mail doublet, an iron helmet and a lance.

The Assize of Arms, while not intended to guarantee the subjects' liberties, must rank with the other documents, for by reviving the *fyrd* Henry II reduced the military basis of feudalism. All free men were now armed in defence of society against the freebooting armies of the wealthy, within the law and under the king's authority.

Few men, remembering the disastrous days of King Stephen, were inclined to complain of the king's increased authority, yet there was some danger that the crown might depart from the principle of government by consent. For example, in 1188 a 10 per cent levy known as the Saladin Tithe was imposed on income and on movable goods, to pay the cost of the Crusades. The document introducing it states boldly: 'This year each one shall give in alms a tenth of his revenue and movables,' with no mention of the advice and consent of bishops and barons. The tax was ordered at the king's mere pleasure without reference to discussions with those who had to bear the burden.

Had Henry II been succeeded by a strong king like himself, the authority of the council would have permanently declined and a royal autocracy might have developed. In fact he was to be followed on the throne by two of his sons in turn : the first an absentee king and the second a luckless one, with consequences that were of vital importance to the future.

Henry had four sons and divided his wide dominions between them. Henry, the eldest, was to become king of England, but died during his father's reign, and the crown of England passed to the second son Richard, Duke of Aquitaine. Richard, nicknamed the Lionheart, reigned for ten years but spent only ten months in his kingdom. He joined the third Crusade to free Jerusalem from the great Mahometan leader Saladin. He quarrelled with his allies, and defeated the armies of Saladin. On his way home he was shipwrecked, made prisoner by the Emperor Henry VI, and released fifteen months later on payment of an enormous ransom. He died, predictably in battle, besieging a castle in France.

His adventures, though romantic in retrospect, were a weary burden on his kingdom which had to pay for his campaigns and his huge ransom. But, with the king abroad, the council and the king's officers were the repositories of authority, so that the danger of royal tyranny diminished. Hubert de Walter, Archbishop of Canterbury and the absent king's Justiciar, wielded the royal power. He could not take for granted the loyalty of his fellow subjects. If he, a subject, could deputise for the absent king, then it was logical that other subjects should wish to share in the responsibilities and powers of government, and the council's authority grew.

In 1194, after a vast sum had been collected for the king's ransom, and after the suppression of a rebellion by John, the king's younger brother, Hubert de Walter ordered an enquiry into all matters concerning peace and justice in the kingdom. The probems were numerous but it is the manner in which the council handled them that is of interest to us today rather than the problems themselves.

It was not the great lords who were to initiate THE GRAND ENQUIRY but four knights from every county. These came from the middle ranks of society, rich enough (as the Assize of Arms has taught us) to ride to war well accoutred but not, like the barons, lords of wide lands and

31

of all the men who dwelt upon their estates. These four knights were then to choose two further knights from every hundred or *wapentake* (the smaller administrative units into which the counties were divided) who in turn were to choose ten others. If in any area there were not sufficient knights, then the number of twelve was to be made up by appointing 'free and lawful men,' so that there was a panel of twelve in each district. The opening paragraph of the document reads:

In the first place, four knights are to be chosen from out of the whole county, who, upon their oaths, are to chose two lawful knights of every hundred and wapentake,[3] and these two are to chose upon their oath ten knights of every hundred or wapentake, or, if there shall not be knights sufficient, free and lawful men, in order that these twelve may together make inquisition on each of the following heads in every hundred or wapentake.

Power and responsibility were now flowing downwards through society. Hubert de Walter was ensuring that the knights and ordinary free men should be involved in organising society and should learn the value of good order and of law.

Two knights from every shire later became an essential component of the council, and members of parliament are their successors at law. Moreover, the appointment of twelve men in every hundred reinforced the conception of a jury. The essence of this was, and still is, that the facts upon which justice was done were to be established not by the great and powerful whom self-interest sometimes misleads; nor by the king's justices whom loyalty to the king and lack of local knowledge might sometimes lead astray, but by twelve local men. Their familiarity with local folk and customs made it likely that they would reach decisions through sound common sense rather that through the too fine logic of legal niceties; while their remoteness from the king's court (and, in the modern context, from the central government), ensured that measure of independence which is essential to true justice.

The document laid down that even the king's officers were not to be immune from scrutiny, nor their actions to go unquestioned. The final clause of the document read:

Also, the inquisition which was to be made relative to the exactions and seizures made by all bailiffs of the king, as well
by the justices as by the sheriffs, constables, and foresters
and their servants, since the time of the first coronation of our
lord king Richard, and why such seizures were made, and by
whom; and relative to all the chattels, gifts, and promises
made on the occasion of seizure of the lands of earl John and
his supporters; and who received the same, and what, and how
much, was deferred by command of Hubert, archbishop of
Canterbury, the king's chief justice.

In spite of the doctrine that all power was the king's, the reality of
power was now moving to the knights and free men. For the latter
were not merely represented on the juries of twelve when the number
of knights was insufficient. Clause 23 laid down that 'the said jurors
shall also upon oath choose from free men as many and such as they
shall think necessary for the performance of the aforesaid business
of our lord the king as to escheats and wardships, in such manner as
may best be done for the advantage of our lord the king.' Ordinary
men were directly participating in running the country and were becoming part of the executive power.

The king's Jewish subjects were not excluded. The lending of
money at interest was forbidden to Christians, so the Jews had become
the moneylenders of Europe. The same document specified 'that all
debts and pledges of Jews are to be enrolled, as also their lands,
houses, rents, and possessions.' Any Jew who failed to register was to
lose all his possessions and 'shall forfeit to our lord the king his
body.' Special places were to be appointed where loans could be made
and recorded in formal agreements. The idea that men should participate in applying laws which affected them was now extended to the
Jews. In places registered for the making of loans 'let two lawful
Christians and two lawful Jews and two lawful Scribes be appointed.'
These were to witness all loan agreements, to act as custodians of the
official copies and to maintain registers of repayments. At a time when
Jews were in most countries considered the enemies of Christendom,
they were in England already participating in legal processes. True,
they were later to suffer disabilities but this early recognition of their
rights redounds to the country's credit.

The simple idea, developed in the Witan of the Saxon kings, that the ruler should consult with his bishops and nobles, had evolved dramatically. Subjects now enforced the laws and, under the final authority of the king's justices, sought out breaches of the law, gave true judgements in cases where their fellows were charged with unlawful actions, and so upheld the king's peace and exercised the king's power.

From all this the villeins were excluded. These men, with neither rights nor possessions, were the poor farm labourers tied to the estates where they worked, granted small plots of land in return for a rent of labour, enjoying little liberty and no political rights. To them the law gave only minimal protection and they were hardly more able to invoke the law than were the farm animals amongst which they laboured. They were not deemed 'lawful men,' that is to say men to whom the law's protection was available.

Thus there were large numbers of folk still deprived of the law's advantages and still dependent upon the caprice of their immediate lords, who stood between them and the king's justice. But they too were in time to gain the status and advantages of 'free and lawful men' and were to inherit all the rights gained by their social superiors.

Notes p 222

DOCUMENTS QUOTED:

1 The Constitution of Clarendon—1164 [*G & H*]
2 Assize of Clarendon—1166 [*C*]
3 Assize of Arms—1181 [*AS*]
4 The Grand Enquiry—1194 [*R*]

CHAPTER III

The Great Charter
(1199-1215)

WHEN King Richard the Lionheart died, his younger brother John, who during his absence had rebelled against him, succeeded to the throne. Taking his kingly duties seriously, John ensured that his justices visited the shires and he himself heard cases during his travels through the kingdom. No doubt the people of England, who for so long had seen nothing of Richard, were glad to have once more a king who was content to maintain the king's peace at home rather than to seek expensive glory under alien skies.

Richard's absence had greatly increased the powers of the people. Barons, knights and free men had to a large extent become the true governors of England, though all was still done in the king's name. John at first neither diminished those powers nor undermined the authority of the council. England enjoyed for a while the advantages of both the old form of government and the new. She had a strong and active king, and also a powerful council, within which the voice of the subjects could be heard, and from which power was to pass to the knights of the shires and to all free men.

Shortly after Richard's death the King of France impudently invaded Normandy, of which John was Duke, and all the other provinces of the English kings. By 1204, five years after John's accession, Normandy, Anjou and Maine were lost. All that remained were the Channel Islands and the province of Gascony.

Then in 1205 Hubert de Walter died and John had to face alone the consequences of his defeats in France. The barons, now deprived of all but their English possessions, were not only made sullen and resentful by the king's defeat, but had now become undoubted Englishmen with no French estates to divide their interest. They became totally involved in the affairs of England and greatly concerned with their rights and position in that kingdom. They, as well

35

as humbler men, were shocked and humiliated by the national defeat. In derision they nicknamed the king 'John Lackland.' Finally, and this was a graver matter than resentment or derision, they had now to pay for his unsuccessful wars. Because of the examples of the past, he could raise the money only with the consent of his subjects—the very people who had mocked his failure and grumbled at the kingdom's shameful defeats.

At first John wisely followed the example of his predecessors and obtained the consent of his subjects to the new taxes. For example, in 1207 a tax of one thirteenth was imposed on both capital and income. The writ announcing this shows that John had summoned his council and had obtained its consent in the customary manner. The copy quoted below is the writ issued for Northamptonshire, appointing by name those men who were to assess that county in the king's name :

WRIT FOR THE ASSESSMENT OF THE THIRTEENTH—1207

The king to all, etc. Be it known that by the common advice and assent of our council at Oxford it was provided, for the defence of our realm and the recovery of our right, and granted that every layman in all England, of whomsoever he may hold, who has rents and chattels in England, should give us in aid from every mark[4] of his annual revenue, twelve pence, and from every mark's worth of every sort of movable chattels which he had on the octave of the Purification of the Blessed Virgin, that is at the time of the council, twelve pence, and thus in proportion more or less. And all the stewards and bailiffs of earls and barons, shall take oath before our justices of the value of the rents and movable chattels of their lords and likewise concerning their own. And every man except the earls and barons shall take oath concerning his own rents and chattels, according as our justices despatched for this purpose shall see to be best suited to our advantage. And if any one shall have been convicted of removing his chattels fraudulently to avoid our profit, or of concealing them in any place, or of putting them in the power of any one else, or of appraising them at less than their value, all his chattels shall be seised for our use free of claims, and he himself shall be put in our prison until he shall be liberated by us. Moreover, let

every hundred in your county be recorded by itself and each
parish in every hundred by itself, so that our justices may
know how to answer for every vill by itself. Moreover, when
our justices shall have made the assessment of this aid of ours
in any hundred, city or vill,[5] they shall immediately cause copy
to be made from their rolls of all the particulars of the aid
assessed, and shall hand over to the sheriff for the collection
of the aid noted in each roll from fortnight to fortnight, with
all speed, and our justices shall keep their own rolls safely in
their possession until they bring them to us. It is also decreed
that all our clerks, and all our justices and their clerks, and
all who shall busy themselves in any of this work, shall swear
that they will do this work faithfully and with all their might,
as it has been set forth, and that for nothing will they neglect
this. Moreover, we command, upon penalties of life and limb,
that every good penny of lawful weight, although it is not new,
shall be accepted both for our use and for that of all others
in our realm. Moreover, for assessing this aid in your county
we send, in our stead, Robert of Berkeley, Richard of Muce-
gros, William of Falaise, Master R. of Gloucester, Walter of
Aura, Adam Fitz-Nigel, etc. And we bid you to be just as
attentive to them in this as to ourselves.

Witness myself at Northampton, the seventeenth day of
February.

This writ finds its place here for the sake of its preamble rather
than its contents, for the opening words show that John was still using
the methods whereby kings of England had for centuries raised money
from their subjects with the latter's consent.

One point in the writ indicates how kingship had changed since
the Norman Conquest. The tax upon 'every layman in all England
of whomsoever he may hold' is referred to as an 'aid'. This was a
term which could be used only in the context of the feudal system.
'Aids' were monies which a tenant paid to his lord to assist him in
certain circumstances. When the lord's eldest daughter was married
his tenants contributed towards the expenses. Similar 'aids' could be
levied if the lord were captured in war, to be released against a ransom. King John was not acting like the pre-Conquest Saxon kings,
raising money for carrying out his public duties. He was demanding
aid as a feudal lord of all England, from every free tenant in the realm.

The new tax inevitably led to discontent. The English landowners, obstinately remembering the traditions of their ancestors, would have recalled how their predecessors had paid the 'feorm' (a contribution, in kind, of ale, corn and other farm produce) for the maintenance of the king's household troops. That was acceptable. But they now stood in the same relationship to the crown as did their poorer tenants to themselves, and this they resented. Three hundred and fifty years later Shakespeare was to refer to a king of England who treated the realm 'like to a tenement or pelting farm'. Thoughts such as these must have smouldered in the minds of the English.

For the Norman barons the situation was equally intolerable. Five or six generations had passed since their ancestors became the swaggering owners of conquered estates in a foreign kingdom. They themselves were now Englishmen with a clear knowledge of their ancient rights and liberties. They required these aids to be levied only after they themselves had been consulted in the customary manner.

There were other and graver matters which led to thoughts of rebellion. Under the feudal system the lands owned by monasteries, abbeys and bishoprics were not the absolute property of the church, but were held of the king. When a bishopric fell empty the king claimed its rents as overlord, until a new bishop was appointed. King John followed this practice and his relations with Pope Innocent III grew strained.

In 1208 the Pope issued an interdict, closing all the churches in England. A year later he excommunicated King John and in 1212 deposed him, calling upon Philip Augustus of France to invade and seize the realm. John, doubtful of the loyalty of his discontented subjects, made his peace with Rome, becoming the Pope's vassal, paying an annual fee of 1,000 marks for his kingdom. In the summer of 1213 the excommunication was lifted and John renewed his coronation oath, swearing to maintain the old laws of King Edward the Confessor.

In August of the same year a council was held in London where it was suggested that King John should be required to confirm Henry I's coronation oath, the text of which has already been quoted (see page 17). But the council's plan came to nothing, for the king left shortly afterwards for France, returning in October 1214 as 'John Lackland'—defeated, dispirited and humiliated.

In January 1215 a deputation of barons waited upon him in London. Ominously they came clad in armour, their mood as warlike as their appearance. They demanded that John sign an undertaking to uphold the ancient liberties of the realm and to reaffirm the laws of Edward, the Coronation Charter of Henry I, and his own coronation oath, which last he had renewed a mere eighteen months before. The reference to the laws of Edward, as well as to Henry I's Coronation Oath, which we have already considered, is significant. Men were not seeking any radical change in the forms of government, but rather a renewal of their old and remembered rights whose roots lay in pre-Conquest England. For the laws of Edward were themselves based on more ancient documents and echoed the laws of King Alfred the Great.

John asked for, and was granted, three months' respite in which to consider these weighty matters. He made full use of the delay, sending messengers to the Pope to seek the latter's support. Further to secure the protection of the church, he took the Cross as a Crusader. By Easter the three months was almost up. The barons assembled at Stamford and marched south-westwards to Northampton and so to Brackley. Thither King John, who was at Wallingford on the Thames, sent Stephen Langton, Archbishop of Canterbury, together with the Earl of Pembroke, to negotiate.

To them the barons presented in writing a renewal of their demands which Langton and Pembroke brought back to John at Wallingford. Then, after long and fruitless negotiations, the barons' army moved south in warlike array, capturing London on 17 May. The king took refuge in his castle at Windsor and talks went on for another month, Langton and Pembroke still acting for the king. With the capital occupied by the rebel army, and the king virtually isolated at Windsor, it says much for the spirit of continuity which has always typified English affairs that the barons sought a reform of the king's practices and not his total overthrow.

On 10 June the two parties met on neutral ground in a green meadow by the tree-lined Thames, midway between the king's castle at Windsor, and London which was now the barons' stronghold. The meadow is still green and still bears the name it bore seven and a half centuries ago, Runnymede. (The name suggests that this was not the first time that councils had been held there; for the first part is an old English word *Runieg,* meaning the Council Island.) After considerable negotiation a document was formulated, briefly listing forty-nine points upon which the king was willing to yield. It bore the heading 'These are the Articles which the Barons require and which the King concedes'.* To it King John attached his seal and upon the basis of that document a formal charter was drawn up.

Although the original heads of agreement recorded that the king

---

* This is the document reproduced on the dust jacket.

conceded the barons' demands, the final document embodied the same paradox which we have noticed in the *Anglo-Saxon Chronicle*'s account of the undertaking given by Ethelred the Unready nearly three centuries earlier to his angry and exasperated Witan. Although King John had been compelled to comply with the wishes of the barons who had risen in armed rebellion against him, the king greets them in the document as his loyal subjects and records that he has acted with their advice. Nothing is done to diminish the apparent authority of the king even in the hour of his humiliation and defeat. The following is the text of Magna Carta, the Great Charter :

MAGNA CARTA—1215

John, by the grace of God King of England, Lord of Ireland, Duke of Normandy and Aquitaine, and Count of Anjou, to his archbishops, bishops, abbots, earls, barons, justices, foresters, sheriffs, stewards, servants, and to all his officials and loyal subjects, Greeting.

Know that before God, for the health of our soul and those of our ancestors and heirs, to the honour of God, the exaltation of the holy Church, and the better ordering of our kingdom, at the advice of our reverend fathers Stephen, archbishop of Canterbury, primate of all England, and cardinal of the holy Roman Church, Henry archbishop of Dublin, William bishop of London, Peter bishop of Winchester, Jocelin bishop of Bath and Glastonbury, Hugh bishop of Lincoln, Walter bishop of Coventry, Benedict bishop of Rochester, Master Pandulf sub-deacon and member of the papal household, Brother Aymeric master of the knighthood of the Temple in England, William Marshal earl of Pembroke, William earl of Salisbury, William earl of Warren, William earl of Arundel, Alan de Galloway constable of Scotland, Warin Fitz Gerald, Peter Fitz Herbert, Hubert de Burgh seneschal of Poitou, Hugh de Neville, Matthew Fitz Herbert, Thomas Basset, Alan Basset, Philip Daubeny, Robert de Roppeley, John Marshal, John Fitz Hugh and other loyal subjects:

(1) First, that we have granted to God, and by this present charter have confirmed for us and our heirs in perpetuity, that the English Church shall be free, and shall have its rights

undiminished, and its liberties unimpaired. That we wish this so to be observed, appears from the fact that of our own free will, before the outbreak of the present dispute between us and our barons, we granted and confirmed by charter the freedom of the Church's elections—a right reckoned to be of the greatest necessity and importance to it—and caused this to be confirmed by Pope Innocent III. This freedom we shall observe ourselves, and desire to be observed in good faith by our heirs in perpetuity.

To all free men of our kingdom we have also granted, for us and our heirs for ever, all the liberties written out below, to have and to keep for them and their heirs, of us and our heirs:

(2)   If any earl, baron, or other person that holds lands directly of the Crown, for military service, shall die, and at his death his heir shall be of full age and owe a 'relief', the heir shall have his inheritance on payment of the ancient scale of 'relief'. That is to say, the heir or heirs of an earl shall pay £100 for the entire earl's barony, the heir or heirs of a knight 100s. at most for the entire knight's 'fee', and any man that owes less shall pay less, in accordance with the ancient usage of 'fees'.

(3)   But if the heir of such a person is under age and a ward, when he comes of age he shall have his inheritance without 'relief' or fine.

(4)   The guardian of the land of an heir who is under age shall take from it only reasonable revenues, customary dues, and feudal services. He shall do this without destruction or damage to men or property. If we have given the guardianship of the land to a sheriff, or to any person answerable to us for the revenues, and he commits destruction or damage, we will exact compensation from him, and the land shall be entrusted to two worthy and prudent men of the same 'fee', who shall be answerable to us for the revenues, or to the person to whom we have assigned them. If we have given or sold to anyone the guardianship of such land, and he causes destruction or damage, he shall lose the guardianship of it, and it shall be handed over to two worthy and prudent men of the same 'fee', who shall be similarly answerable to us.

(5)   For so long as a guardian has guardianship of such land, he shall maintain the houses, parks, fish preserves, ponds, mills, and everything else pertaining to it, from the

revenue of the land itself. When the heir comes of age, he shall restore the whole land to him, stocked with plough-teams and such implements of husbandry as the season demands and the revenues from the land can reasonably bear.

(6)   Heirs may be given in marriage, but not to someone of lower social standing. Before a marriage takes place, it shall be made known to the heir's next-of-kin.

(7)   At her husband's death, a widow may have her marriage portion and inheritance at once and without trouble. She shall pay nothing for her dower, marriage portion, or any inheritance that she and her husband held jointly on the day of his death. She may remain in her husband's house for forty days after his death, and within this period her dower shall be assigned to her.

(8)   No widow shall be compelled to marry, so long as she wishes to remain without a husband. But she must give security that she will not marry without royal consent, if she holds her lands of the Crown, or without the consent of whatever other lord she may hold them of.

(9)   Neither we nor our officials will seize any land or rent in payment of a debt, so long as the debtor has movable goods sufficient to discharge the debt. A debtor's sureties shall not be distrained upon so long as the debtor himself can discharge his debt. If, for lack of means, the debtor is unable to discharge his debt, his sureties shall be answerable for it. If they so desire, they may have the debtor's lands and rents until they have received satisfaction for the debt that they paid for him, unless the debtor can show that he has settled his obligations to them.

(10)   If anyone who has borrowed a sum of money from Jews dies before the debt has been repaid, his heir shall pay no interest on the debt for so long as he remains under age, irrespective of whom he holds his lands. If such a debt falls into the hands of the Crown, it will take nothing except the principal sum specified in the bond.

(11)   If a man dies owing money to Jews, his wife may have her dower and pay nothing towards the debt from it. If he leaves children that are under age, their needs may also be provided for on a scale appropriate to the size of his holding of lands. The debt is to be paid out of the residue, reserving the service due to his feudal lords. Debts owed to persons

others than Jews are to be dealt with similarly.

(12)   No 'scutage' or 'aid' may be levied in our kingdom without its general consent, unless it is for the ransom of our person, to make our eldest son a knight, and (once) to marry our eldest daughter. For these purposes only a reasonable 'aid' may be levied. 'Aids' from the city of London are to be treated similarly.

(13)   The city of London shall enjoy all its ancient liberties and free customs, both by land and by water. We also will and grant that all other cities, boroughs, towns, and ports shall enjoy all their liberties and free customs.

(14)   To obtain the general consent of the realm for the assessment of an 'aid'—except in the three cases specified above—or a 'scutage', we will cause the archbishops, bishops, abbots, earls, and greater barons to be summoned individually by letter. To those who hold lands directly of us we will cause a general summons to be issued, through the sheriffs and other officials, to come together on a fixed day (of which at least forty days notice shall be given) and at a fixed place. In all letters of summons, the cause of the summons will be stated. When a summons has been issued, the business appointed for the day shall go forward in accordance with the resolution of those present, even if not all those who were summoned have appeared.

(15)   In future we will allow no one to levy an 'aid' from his free men, except to ransom his person, to make his eldest son a knight, and (once) to marry his eldest daughter. For these purposes only a reasonable 'aid' may be levied.

(16)   No man shall be forced to perform more service for a knight's 'fee', or other free holding of land, than is due from it.

(17)   Ordinary lawsuits shall not follow the royal court around, but shall be held in a fixed place.

(18)   Inquests of **novel disseisin**,[6] **mort d'ancestor**,[7] and **darrein presentment**[8] shall be taken only in their proper county court. We ourselves, or in our absence abroad our chief justice, will send two justices to each county four times a year, and these justices, with four knights of the county elected by the county itself, shall hold the assizes in the county court, on the day and in the place where the court meets.

(19)   If any assizes cannot be taken on the day of the county court, as many knights and freeholders shall afterwards

remain behind, of those who have attended the court, as will suffice for the administration of justice, having regard to the volume of business to be done.

(20) For a trivial offence, a free man shall be fined only in proportion to the degree of his offence, and for a serious offence correspondingly, but not so heavily as to deprive him of his livelihood. In the same way, a merchant shall be spared his merchandise, and a husbandman the implements of his husbandry, if they fall upon the mercy of a royal court. None of these fines shall be imposed except by the assessment on oath of reputable men of the neighbourhood.

(21) Earls and barons shall be fined only by their equals, and in proportion to the gravity of their offence.

(22) A fine imposed upon the lay property of a clerk in holy orders shall be assessed upon the same principles, without reference to the value of his ecclesiastical benefice.

(23) No town or person shall be forced to build bridges over rivers except those with an ancient obligation to do so.

(24) No sheriff, constable, coroners, or other royal officials are to hold lawsuits that should be held by the royal justices.

(25) Every county, hundred, wapentake, and tithing shall remain at its ancient rent, without increase, except the royal demesne manors.

(26) If at the death of a man who holds a lay 'fee' of the Crown, a sheriff or royal official produces royal letters patent of summons for a debt due to the Crown, it shall be lawful for them to seize and list movable goods found in the lay 'fee' of the dead man to the value of the debt, as assessed by worthy men. Nothing shall be removed until the whole debt is paid, when the residue shall be given over to the executors to carry out the dead man's will. If no debt is due to the Crown, all the movable goods shall be regarded as the property of the dead man, except the reasonable shares of his wife and children.

(27) If a free man dies intestate, his movable goods are to be distributed by his next-of-kin and friends under the supervision of the Church. The rights of his debtors are to be preserved.

(28) No constable or other royal official shall take corn or other movable goods from any man without immediate

payment, unless the seller voluntarily offers postponement of this.

(29)   No constable may compel a knight to pay money for castle-guard if the knight is willing to undertake the guard in person, or with reasonable excuse to supply some other fit man to do it. A knight taken or sent on military service shall be excused from castle-guard for the period of this service.

(30)   No sheriff, royal official, or other person shall take horses or carts for transport from any free man, without his consent.

(31)   Neither we nor any royal official will take wood for our castle, or for any other purpose, without the consent of the owner.

(32)   We will not keep the lands of people convicted of felony in our hand for longer than a year and a day, after which they shall be returned to the lords of the 'fees' concerned.

(33)   All fish-weirs shall be removed from the Thames, the Medway, and throughout the whole of England, except on the sea coast.

(34)   The writ called **precipe**[9] shall not in future be issued to anyone in respect of any holding of land, if a free man could thereby be deprived of the right of trial in his own lord's court.

(35)   There shall be standard measures of wine, ale, and corn (the London quarter), throughout the kingdom. There shall also be a standard width of dyed cloth, russett, and haberject[10], namely two ells within the selvedges. Weights are to be standardised similarly.

(36)   In future nothing shall be paid or accepted for the issue of a writ of inquisition of life or limbs. It shall be given **gratis,** and not refused.

(37)   If a man holds land of the Crown by 'fee-farm'[11], 'socage'[12], or 'burgage'[13], and also holds land of someone else for knight's service, we will not have guardianship of his heir, nor of the land that belongs to the other person's 'fee', by virtue of the 'fee-farm', 'socage', or 'burgage', unless the 'fee-farm' owes knight's service. We will not have the guardianship of a man's heir, or of land that he holds of someone else, by reason of any small property that he may hold of the Crown for a service of knives, arrows, or the like.

(38)   In future no official shall place a man on trial upon

his own unsupported statement, without producing credible witnesses to the truth of it.

(39) No free man shall be seized or imprisoned, or stripped of his rights or possessions, or outlawed or exiled, or deprived of his standing in any other way, nor will we proceed with force against him, or send others to do so, except by the lawful judgement of his equals or by the law of the land.

(40) To no one will we sell, to no one deny or delay right or justice.

(41) All merchants may enter or leave England unharmed and without fear, and may stay or travel within it, by land or water, for purposes of trade, free from all illegal exactions, in accordance with ancient and lawful customs. This, however, does not apply in time of war to merchants from a country that is at war with us. Any such merchants found in our country at the outbreak of war shall be detained without injury to their persons or property, until we or our chief justice have discovered how our own merchants are being treated in the country at war with us. If our own merchants are safe they shall be safe too.

(42) In future it shall be lawful for any man to leave and return to our kingdom unharmed and without fear, by land or water, preserving his allegiance to us, except in time of war, for some short period for the common benefit of the realm. People that have been imprisoned or outlawed in accordance with the law of the land, people from a country that is at war with us, and merchants—who shall be dealt with as stated above—are excepted from this provision.

(43) If a man holds lands of any 'escheat' such as the 'honour' of Wallingford, Nottingham, Boulogne, Lancaster, or of other 'escheats' in our hand that are baronies, at his death his heir shall give us only the 'relief' and service that he would have made to the baron, had the barony been in the baron's hand. We will hold the 'escheat' in the same manner as the baron held it.

(44) People who live outside the forest need not in future appear before the royal justices of the forest in answer to general summonses, unless they are actually involved in proceedings or are sureties for someone who has been seized for a forest offence.

(45) We will appoint as justices, constables, sheriffs, or

other officials, only men that know the law of the realm and are minded to keep it well.

(46) All barons who have founded abbeys, and have charters of English kings or ancient tenure as evidence of this, may have guardianship of them when there is no abbot, as is their due.

(47) All forests that have been created in our reign shall at once be disafforested. River-banks that have been enclosed in our reign shall be treated similarly.

(48) All evil customs relating to forests and warrens, foresters, warreners, sheriffs and their servants, or river-banks and their wardens, are at once to be investigated in every county by twelve sworn knights of the county, and within forty days of their enquiry the evil customs are to be abolished completely and irrevocably. But we, or our chief justice if we are not in England, are first to be informed.

(49) We will at once return all hostages and charters delivered up to us by Englishmen as security for peace or for loyal service.

(50) We will remove completely from their offices the kinsmen of Gerard de Athée, and in future they shall hold no offices in England. The people in question are Engelard de Cigogné, Peter, Guy, and Andrew de Chanceaux, Guy de Cigogné, Geoffrey de Martigny and his brothers, Philip Marc and his brothers, with Geoffrey his nephew, and all their followers.

(51) As soon as peace is restored, we will remove from the kingdom all the foreign knights, bowmen, their attendants, and their mercenaries that have come to it, to its harm, with horses and arms.

(52) To any man whom we have deprived or dispossessed of lands, castles, liberties, or rights, without the lawful judgement of his equals, we will at once restore these. In cases of dispute the matter shall be resolved by the judgement of the twenty-five barons referred to below in the clause for securing the peace (§61). In cases, however, where a man was deprived or dispossessed of something without the lawful judgement of his equals by our father King Henry or our brother King Richard, and it remains in our hands or is held by others under our warranty, we shall have respite for the period commonly allowed to Crusaders, unless a lawsuit had been begun, or an

enquiry had been made at our order, before we took the Cross as a Crusader. On our return from the Crusade, or if we abandon it, we will at once render justice in full.

(53)   We shall have similar respite in rendering justice in connexion with forests that are to be disafforested, or to remain forests, when these were first afforested by our father Henry or our brother Richard; with the guardianship of lands in another person's 'fee', when we have hitherto had this by virtue of a 'fee' held of us for knight's service by a third party; and with abbeys founded in another person's 'fee', in which the lord of the 'fee' claims to own a right. On our return from the Crusade, or if we abandon it, we will at once do full justice to complaints about these matters.

(54)   No one shall be arrested or imprisoned on the appeal of a woman for the death of any person except her husband.

(55)   All fines that have been given to us unjustly and against the law of the land, and all fines that we have exacted unjustly, shall be entirely remitted or the matter decided by a majority judgement of the twenty-five barons referred to below in the clause for securing the peace together with Stephen, archbishop of Canterbury, if he can be present, and such others as he wishes to bring with him. If the archbishop cannot be present, proceedings shall continue without him, provided that if any of the twenty-five barons has been involved in a similar suit himself, his judgement shall be set aside, and someone else chosen and sworn in his place, as a substitute for the single occasion, by the rest of the twenty-five.

(56)   If we have deprived or dispossessed any Welshmen of lands, liberties, or anything else in England or in Wales, without the lawful judgement of their equals, these are at once to be returned to them. A dispute on this point shall be determined in the Marches by the judgement of equals. English law shall apply to holdings of land in England, Welsh law to those in Wales, and the law of the Marches to those in the Marches. The Welsh shall treat us and ours in the same way.

(57)   In cases where a Welshman was deprived or dispossessed of anything, without the lawful judgement of his equals, by our father King Henry or our brother King Richard, and it remains in our hands or is held by others under our warranty, we shall have respite for the period commonly allowed to Crusaders, unless a lawsuit has been begun, or an

enquiry had been made at our order, before we took the Cross as a Crusader. But on our return from the Crusade, or if we abandon it, we will at once do full justice to the laws of Wales and the said regions.

(58) We will at once return the son of Llywelyn, all Welsh hostages, and the charters delivered to us as security for the peace.

(59) With regard to the return of the sisters and hostages of Alexander, king of Scotland, his liberties and his rights, we will treat him in the same way as our other barons of England, unless it appears from the charters that we hold from his father William, formerly king of Scotland, that he should be treated otherwise. This matter shall be resolved by the judgement of his equals in our court.

(60) All these customs and liberties that we have granted shall be observed in our kingdom in so far as concerns our own relations with our subjects. Let all men of our kingdom, whether clergy or laymen, observe them similarly in their relations with their own men.

(61) Since we have granted all these things for God, for the better ordering of our kingdom, and to allay the discord that has arisen between us and our barons, and since we desire that they shall be enjoyed in their entirety, with lasting strength, for ever, we give and grant to the barons the following security:

The barons shall elect twenty-five of their number to keep, and cause to be observed with all their might, the peace and liberties granted and confirmed to them by this charter.

If we, our chief justice, our officials, or any of our servants offend in any respect against any man, or transgress any of the articles of the peace or of this security, and the offence is made known to four of the said twenty-five barons, they shall come to us—or in our absence from the kingdom to the chief justice—to declare it and claim immediate redress. If we, or in our absence abroad the chief justice, make no redress within forty days, reckoning from the day on which the offence was declared to us or to him, the four barons shall refer the matter to the rest of the twenty-five barons, who may distrain upon and assail us in every way possible, with the support of the whole community of the land, by seizing our castles, lands, possessions, or anything else saving only our own person and those of the queen and our children, until they have secured such redress as they have determined upon. Having secured the redress, they may then resume their normal obedience to us.

Any man who so desires may take an oath to obey the commands of the twenty-five barons for the achievement of these ends, and to join with them in assailing us to the utmost of his power. We give public and free permission to take this oath to any man who so desires, and at no time will we prohibit any man from taking it. Indeed, we will compel any of our subjects who are unwilling to take it to swear it at our command.

If one of the twenty-five barons dies or leave the country, or is prevented in any other way from discharging his duties, the rest of them shall choose another baron in his place, at their discretion, who shall be duly sworn in as they were.

In the event of disagreement among the twenty-five barons on any matter referred to them for decision, the verdict of the majority present shall have the same validity as a unanimous verdict of the whole twenty-five, whether these were all present or some of those summoned were unwilling or unable to appear.

The twenty-five barons shall swear to obey all the above articles faithfully, and shall cause them to be obeyed by others to the best of their power.

We will not seek to procure from anyone, either by our own efforts or those of a third party, anything by which any part of these concessions or liberties might be revoked or diminished. Should such a thing be procured, it shall be null and void and we will at no time make use of it, either ourselves or through a third party.

(62) We have remitted and pardoned fully to all men any ill-will, hurt, or grudges that have arisen between us and our subjects, whether clergy or laymen, since the beginning of the dispute. We have in addition remitted fully, and for our own part have also pardoned, to all clergy and laymen any offences committed as a result of the said dispute between Easter in the sixteenth year of our reign and the restoration of peace.

In addition we have caused letters patent to be made for

the barons, bearing witness to this security and to the concessions set out above, over the seals of Stephen, archbishop of Canterbury, Henry archbishop of Dublin, the other bishops named above, and Master Pandulf.

(63) It is accordingly our wish and command that the English Church shall be free, and that men in our kingdom shall have and keep all these liberties, rights, and concessions, well and peaceably in their fulness and entirety for them and their heirs, of us and our heirs, in all things and all places for ever.

Both we and the barons have sworn that all this shall be observed in good faith and without deceit. Witness the above-mentioned people and many others.

Given by our hand in the meadow that is called Runnymede, between Windsor and Staines, on the fifteenth day of June in the seventeenth year of our reign.

Most of the clauses were designed to ensure that the king should not abuse his rights as feudal overlord. The king was not to levy excessive 'reliefs', the sums payable to him when an heir inherited (Clause 2), nor to compel any widow to remarry against her will (Clause 8). All this we have met before. And if Magna Carta had done no more it would have been a charter for the great landowners and nothing else. But it went a great deal further. It gathered together and formulated many of the advances towards freedom which had been outlined in earlier charters or which had gradually come about in practice.

Clause 12 is of great importance. A tenant-in-chief, holding land of the crown for a rent of military service, could commute this into a money-rent, to pay for another man to bear a shield in the king's wars. This shield money—scutage—was a useful source of income to the king. In the past all tenants-in-chief who had not gone on Crusades had been required to pay, and Clause 12 was drafted to remedy the king's abuse of this tax. It laid down that neither scutage nor aid could be levied without general consent. The principle that those who paid should themselves decide questions of taxation was now stated in precise terms. Later kings, as we shall see, tried to ignore this, but from this principle the English people, whether in England or overseas, were never to depart.

The manner in which the king was to obtain the consent of his subjects was laid down in Clause 14. All those who held land of the crown were to be summoned together. The great ones, ecclesiastical and lay, were to be called directly by the king, and the others by the king's sheriffs. Enough time was given to enable all to attend who wished to do so, and this clause shows the transition from Council to Parliament. True, there is as yet no question of election and the qualification is solely one of property. But the system was none the less democratic in essence. The population was small enough, and the tenants-in-chief few enough, for direct democracy (somewhat along the lines of ancient Greece) to be effective at least for the rich.

At Runnymede the rebel barons were concerned with some matters other than feudal dues and were anxious that the royal power should be exercised with moderation. Fines should not be arbitrarily fixed, but should relate to the gravity of the offence (Clauses 20 and 21); no free man should be so severely fined as to lose his means of livelihood (Clause 20). The king's officers should not in the king's name seize property without consent and there should be no tyrannous confiscations (Clauses 28, 30 and 31). Nor should the king or his officers place a man on trial upon their own unsupported statements (Clause 38). Moreover the council achieved the right of compelling the king to dismiss certain of the king's officers (Clause 50), thus foreshadowing the dependence of ministers upon the goodwill of parliament.

From such particular matters the barons moved to the statement of broad rules as to how justice was to be administered. They had in mind no wider aim than to check current abuses, but in fact they laid down principles of government from which the English people have never departed and which other nations have been eager to follow. No free man was to be punished except by the lawful judgement of his equals or by the law of the land (Clause 39). By that simple phrase—'the lawful judgement of his equals'—the king and his judges were prevented from using the courts to oppress their enemies, or to disguise tyranny in the cloak of justice. Trial by jury was thus secured, and it has been demonstrated in modern times how such a system protects the citizen against the tyrannies of governments. Justice can easily be banished from courts where juries are absent. Governments may bring a man into the courts out of fear or envy. Sycophantic judges may try them. But while the verdict of the court is in fact the verdict of a group of ordinary men, independent of judge and ruler, liberty can never be totally extinguished.

Clause 40 was designed to prevent the king and his officers from using the courts as places of profit, or from limiting access to them

to those whom the king favoured. But again a principle was laid down
that was of far greater importance than the checking of a current
abuse. The courts were to be open to all free men and no fees were to
be paid when a man had recourse to them.

The right of the subject freely to leave and re-enter the country was
assured in Clause 42. In times of war this right might be (and in
modern times has been) suspended for the safety of the realm. But,
war apart, the fundamental right to travel overseas was acknowledged.

Finally, by Clause 61 the king was in effect 'bound over' to be of
good behaviour and to maintain the charter. But the theory of his
sovereignty was maintained, since it was he who gave permission for
his subjects, should he break the contract, to assail him.

In short, a document that set out to redress immediate wrongs and
to recall an errant king to the traditional duties of his office, did not
merely revive those of the subject's rights which had been brushed
aside. Its authors, by defining more precisely the ancient liberties of the
kingdom, drew up a statement of fundamental rights which is valid to
this day, and which is still deserving of vigilant defence. The principles which flowed from these definitions, though the Charter is now
without the formal force of law, have remained for centuries a pattern
of liberty. It was invoked from age to age and its main provisions were
renewed in document after document.

Notes p 222

DOCUMENTS QUOTED :

1   Writ for the Assessment of the Thirteenth—1207 [*AS*]
2   Magna Carta—1215 [Reprinted with the permission of the Trustees
    of the British Museum from their publication *Magna Carta.*]

CHAPTER IV

The Growth of Parliament
(1216-1485)

THE Great Charter guaranteed that no taxes should be levied without the general consent of the realm and defined a procedure whereby this should be obtained. But the consent was to be taken only from 'those who hold lands directly of us [the king]'. Thus the sub-tenants (who rented their farms from the great landowners) were still without a voice. It was only when such men entered the Grand Council that this body began to become Parliament as we know it today. The development was swift to take place, and the accident of a monarch's personality was to play a major part.

John died a year after he had sealed the Great Charter. His son, Henry III, was only nine years old. That a child was permitted to succeed demonstrates how far the Crown's power had passed to the King's Council. Three hundred and forty-five years earlier, when King Aethelred I died leaving young sons, the Witan acclaimed his brother Alfred as king, for the realm was beset by the Danes and this was no time for a boy king. Now, secure in his new-won rights, the Council was content for a child to wear the crown of England. They themselves would wield both the sceptre and the sword in his name.

William Marshall, Earl of Pembroke, and Stephen Langton, Archbishop of Canterbury, became Henry's guardians. Anxious to unite the barons behind the new king, Pembroke reaffirmed the Great Charter. He defeated the invading French army at Lincoln and by the time he died, three years after King Henry's accession, England was united, strong, and at peace.

Hubert de Burgh, one of the barons named in the Great Charter, became Justiciar of England. He acted through the King's Council, greatly increasing its power and authority for, governing in the name of an infant king, he had to win the acquiescence of his fellow subjects.

It was not until 1232 when Henry III (now aged twenty-five) dismissed de Burgh that the conflict between the crown and the growing liberties of the subjects again came into the open. Henry, eager to establish his authority, appointed to high office men from his own circle. One was Peter des Roches, his uncle, and the other (a nephew of des Roches) Peter des Riveaux. When the barons in protest refused to attend meetings of the council, Henry had to dismiss both des Riveaux and des Roches. The present convention which through long tradition has acquired the force of law, whereby the monarch's ministers must have the confidence of a majority in the House of Commons, was thus early and faintly foreshadowed. The king's ministers were seen not merely as his personal servants, but had to be representative of and approved by those over whom they exercised authority.

Henry was slow to learn the lesson. He appointed men of his own choice to positions in his own household, and nonentities to the formal offices of state. For ten years or so he thus made his own household the instrument of government. But the barons could neither forget nor renounce all that had been gained, nor could Henry neglect the principles laid down in the Great Charter. An ambition to regain the lost French possessions soon led him into war and for this he needed money. In 1235 he levied a 'scutage' to help pay for his campaigns. The WRIT FOR THE COLLECTION OF SCUTAGE records that

... the earls and barons and all others of our whole realm of England, of their own free will and not as a precedent, have granted us an effectual aid to promote our great undertaking.

The king's subjects were making it clear that their approval had been given on a once-for-all basis. It is significant that Henry was willing to record his subjects' somewhat grudging attitude. He also recorded that they had consented to the tax. For the writ states :

Wherefore provision was made by their advice ...

Nineteen years later, when the wars in France had reached their disastrous conclusion, Henry again required money. He took a dramatic step that went beyond the provision of the Great Charter, Clause 14 of which had laid down that the bishops, abbots, earls and barons should be summoned to give their consent to the levying of aids. In

1254 Henry issued a WRIT OF SUMMONS FOR TWO KNIGHTS OF THE SHIRE TO GRANT AN AID which in addition to the magnates called to Westminster two knights from every shire to discuss what aid they would grant. Something very like the House of Commons was coming to birth. The writ, dated February 1254, summoning the knights of Bedfordshire and Buckinghamshire has survived. It reads :

The king to the sheriff of Bedfordshire and Buckinghamshire, Greeting.

Since the earls and barons and other magnates of our realm have faithfully promised us that they will be in London in three weeks from next Easter, furnished with horses and arms and well equipped to go without any delay to Portsmouth, to come over to Gascony to us, to aid us against the king of Castile who intends to invade our territory of Gascony with a strong force, next summer, we have ordered you to constrain to this all those in your bailiwick[15] who hold lands worth twenty pounds a year from us in chief, or from others who are under age and in our wardship; we straitly command you, that besides all those aforesaid, you cause to come before our council at Westminster on the fifteenth day after Easter next, four lawful and discreet knights from the said counties whom the said counties shall have chosen for this purpose, in place of all and singular of the said counties, that is, two from one county and two from the other, who together with the knights from the other counties whom we have had summoned for the same day, shall arrange what aid they are willing to pay us in our need. And you yourself carefully set forth to the knights and others of the said counties, our need and how urgent is our business, and effectually persuade them to pay us an aid sufficient for the time being; so that the aforesaid four knights at the aforesaid time shall be able to give definite answer concerning the said aid to the aforesaid council, for each of the said counties. We also give you an absolute command that all dues to us in your bailiwick which are in arrears, and ought to be paid to our exchequer before Easter next, or which ought to be paid to the exchequer at the aforesaid Easter, you shall have at the aforesaid exchequer on the fifteenth day after the aforesaid Easter, and you are to know that unless you have the aforesaid debts then and there, we shall not only cause you to be placed under arrest but we shall also cause those dues to be collected from your lands and tenements to your exceeding loss.

Witness Eleanor the queen and Richard earl of Cornwall, at Windsor, the eleventh day of February.

Henry had not taken this step spontaneously but had for some time been under considerable pressures. His sister had married Simon de Montfort, Earl of Leicester. It was de Montfort, notwithstanding his close relationship with the king, who became the leader of the barons in their struggle to ensure that what their fathers had won at Runnymede should not now be lost.

In 1258 the barons and bishops met at Oxford. They discussed the government of the state and the procedures by which the kingdom should be administered. The king's friends called the meeting 'The Mad Parliament', scorning this attempt by mere subjects to regulate the sovereign's powers, but the subjects were resolute and the king for all his scorn could not ignore them. He sent twelve men to speak for him, led by the Bishop of London, and the barons sent the same number.

These twenty-four men produced a written declaration, known as the PROVISIONS OF OXFORD, as to how the realm should be governed. Each of them

. . . swore on the holy Gospels, that he to the honour of God, and to his faith to the king, and to the profit of the realm, will ordain and treat with the aforesaid sworn persons upon the reformation and amendment of the state of the realm. And that he will not fail for gift, nor for promise, for love, nor for hate, nor for fear of any one, nor for gain, nor for loss, loyally to do according to the tenor of the letter which the king and his son have together given for this.

There were then set down the solemn oaths to be taken by the great officers of state. The Chief Justice of England swore:

. . . that he will well and loyally according to his power do that

which belongs to the justiciar of right to hold, to all persons,
to the profit of the king and the kingdom, according to the provision made and to be made by the twenty-four, and by the
counsel of the king and the great men of the land, who shall
swear in these things to aid and support him.

The Chancellor swore a similar oath :

That he will seal no writ . . . without the commandment of
the King and of his Council who shall be present . . . And that
he will seal nothing which may be contrary to the ordinance
which is made and shall be made by the twenty-four or by the
major part . . .

Two vital principles were thus laid down : first that the king's
ministers should act only after receiving the advice or instructions of
the council; and second, that in the event of dispute the king should
not be the final arbiter, but that the will of the majority should prevail.

A procedure was laid down in another clause whereby the king
should no longer nominate his own council, but that the members
should be elected by a sub-committee of four and the election ratified
by a majority vote of the whole body.

The twelve on the king's side have elected out of the twelve
on that of the commonalty the earl Roger the Marshall, and
Hugh Bigot.

And the party of commonalty have elected out of the twelve
who are on the king's side the earl of Warwick and John
Mansel.

And these four have power to elect the council of the king,
and when they have elected them, they shall present them to
the twenty-four; and there, where the greater part of these
agree, it shall be held.

The composition of the sub-committee was carefully devised, each
side (king's men and the barons') selecting two of the opposite party

so as to ensure mutual acceptability and the choice of moderate men.

The following clauses laid down that the officers of state should be appointed for fixed terms, and that they should be accountable to the council :

OF THE CHIEF JUSTICE

Moreover, that a justice be appointed, one or two, and what power he shall have, and that he be only for a year. So that at the end of the year, he answer concerning his time before the king and his council and before him who shall follow him.

OF THE TREASURER, AND OF THE EXCHEQUER

The like of the treasurer. That he too give account at the end of the year. And other good persons are to be placed at the exchequer according to the direction of the aforesaid twenty-four. And there let all the issues of the land come, and in no part elsewhere. And let that which shall be seen to require amendment, be amended.

OF THE CHANCELLOR

The like of the chancellor. That he at the end of the year answer concerning his time. And that he seal nothing out of course by the sole will of the king. But that he do it by the council which shall be around the king.

The last clause of the document was of supreme importance. The council, whether the king summoned them or not, was to meet as a 'parliament' at least three times a year :

It is to be remembered that the twenty-four have ordained that there be three parliaments a year. The first at the octave of Saint Michael. The second the morrow of Candlemas. The third the first day of June, to wit, three weeks before Saint John. To these three parliaments the elected councillors of the king shall come, even if they are not sent for, to see the state of the realm, and to treat of the common wants of the kingdom, and of the king in like manner. And other times in like manner when occasion shall be, by the king's command.

So it is to be remembered that the commonalty elect twelve honest men, who shall come at the parliaments and other times when occasion shall be, when the king or his council shall send for them to treat of the wants of the king and of the kingdom. And that the commonalty shall hold as established that which these twelve shall do. And that shall be done to spare the cost of the commonalty.

There shall be fifteen named by these four, to wit, by the earl Marshall, the earl of Warwick, Hugh Bigot, and John Mansel, who are elected by the twenty-four to name the aforesaid fifteen, who shall be the king's council. And they shall be confirmed by the aforesaid twenty-four, or by the major part of them. And they shall have power to counsel the king in good faith concerning the government of the realm and all things which appertain to the king or to the kingdom; and to amend and redress all things which they shall see require to be redressed and amended. And over the chief justice and over all other people. And if they cannot all be present, that which the majority shall do shall be firm and established.

This provision was often to be ignored by later kings, but it set a precedent to which men turned in later ages. It was the first attempt to make parliament a permanent partner of the crown, and the aspiration set down was ultimately to be fulfilled.

The Provisions of Oxford formalised the conception of a government elected by a majority of chosen representatives to whom it was ultimately responsible. These are still the foundations upon which the structure of parliamentary government is based.

Henry withdrew his approval of the Provisions of Oxford in 1261. Civil war followed and Simon de Montfort, Earl of Leicester, became the effective ruler of England. He summoned a parliament to ratify his authority and, in order to secure wide support, included in it two knights from every shire and two citizens from each borough which had declared for him during the civil war.

This assembly came to be a pattern for all future parliaments. No longer did the magnates alone participate in governing the realm. The middle classes, in the persons of the knights and leading townsmen, now had a part to play. They had acquired rights which they were never afterwards totally to lose.

Simon de Montfort died in battle in 1265 at Evesham, defeated by

King Henry's warlike son Prince Edward. In the hour of his death he may have felt that his achievements had been slight, his success ephemeral, and his brief triumphs as mortal as himself; but his work lived on, in England and in all those other lands for whose assemblies his parliament became the exemplar.

On Henry's death seven years later, his son succeeded him as Edward I. The new king had great military ambitions and sought to subdue Scotland and Wales; abroad he planned to strengthen England's position in her last French possessions. His wars had to be paid for and, because the rights of the taxpayers to be consulted were now firmly rooted, King Edward became increasingly dependent upon parliament.

In 1275, three years after his accession, he summoned his first parliament to Westminster. There were issued the FIRST STATUTES OF WESTMINSTER of which the preamble reads :

These be the acts of king Edward, son to king Henry, made at Westminster at his first parliament general after his coronation, on the Monday of Easter Utas, the third year of his reign, by his council and by the assent of archbishops, bishops, abbots, priors, earls, barons, and the commonalty of the realm, being thither summoned: . . . . . . the king hath ordained and established these acts underwritten, which he intendeth to be necessary and profitable unto the whole realm.

The 'assent' to which we have grown accustomed is now given not only by the leaders of the church and by the earls and barons, but also by 'the commonalty of the realm.' The ideas of de Montfort were being developed by the very prince who had vanquished him and the House of Commons was beginning to take shape.

Since the knights and townsmen had to be selected by each shire and city, a new principle had to be established, that the processes of selection should never be distorted by force or by threat. Article 5 of the Statutes of Westminster therefore read :

And because elections ought to be free, the King commandeth upon great forfeiture, that no man by force of arms, nor by malice, or menacing, shall disturb any to make free election.

Over the centuries which followed, this vital principle, though some-times disregarded, was never forgotten. It represented an ideal which was ultimately to be realised.

Edward I frequently reaffirmed the right of the commonalty to par-ticipate in the crown's decisions. In the autumn of 1295, when Eng-land lay under the threat of a French invasion, he summoned a par-liament and his WRIT OF SUMMONS TO PARLIAMENT addressed to the Sheriff of Northamptonshire survives. The sheriff is enjoined :

. . . to cause two knights from the aforesaid county, two citi-zens from each city in the same county, and two burgesses from each borough, of those who are especially discreet and capable of labouring, to be elected without delay, and to cause them to come to us at the aforesaid time and place.

Two years later, in 1297, the king issued a WRIT OF CONFIRMATION OF CHARTERS in Clause 6 of which he granted not only to the leaders of the church and to the earls and barons, but also 'to all the common-alty of our realm' that he would take no new aids or levy any taxes 'but by the common assent of all the realm, and for the common profit thereof', an important echo of the Great Charter.

By the end of the thirteenth century the basic shape of parliament had been established. The Witan of the Saxon kings had evolved into an assembly that was increasingly representative of the free men of the kingdom, with the 'commonalty of the realm' sitting separately from the prelates and barons. Although the purpose that lay behind this full assembly was originally to implement Clause 14 of the Great Charter, and to provide a means through which consent could be obtained to all new taxation, the results were far wider. Kings, since they now had to rely upon parliament for their revenue, were more and more de-pendent upon their subjects. The sceptre still glittered and the crown was still resplendent; but power was passing almost imperceptibly to the soberly dressed men, wearing neither mitre nor coronet, who came to Westminster on the king's business from all the cities and shires of England, proud of their king's greatness but watchful of their own interests in farm and market place, very conscious and very jealous of their ancient and growing liberties.

Early in the fourteenth century, Edward II, the weak and unfortunate son of the first Edward, succeeded to the throne. After twenty years of bad government, with the king and parliament at loggerheads, parliament finally deposed him, replacing him with his son Edward. THE ARTICLES OF ACCUSATION which parliament issued in January 1327 open tersely and continue brutally :

It has been decided that prince Edward, the eldest son of the king shall have the government of the realm and shall be crowned king, for the following reasons:

1. First, because the king is incompetent to govern in person. For throughout his reign he has been controlled and governed by others who have given him evil counsel, to his own dishonour and to the destruction of holy Church and of all his people, without his being willing to see or understand what is good or evil or to make amendment, or his being willing to do as was required by the great and wise men of his realm, or to allow amendment to be made.

2. Item, throughout his reign he has not been willing to listen to good counsel nor to adopt it nor to give himself to the good government of his realm, but he has always given himself up to unseemly works and occupations, neglecting to satisfy the needs of his realm.

3. Item, through the lack of good government he has lost the realm of Scotland and other territories and lordships in Gascony and Ireland which his father left him in peace, and he has lost the friendship of the king of France and of many other great men.

4. Item, by his pride and obstinacy and by evil counsel he has destroyed holy Church and imprisoned some of the persons of holy Church and brought distress upon others and also many great and noble men of his land he has put to a shameful death, imprisoned, exiled, and disinherited.

5. Item, wherein he was bound by his oath to do justice to all, he has not willed to do it, for his own profit and his greed and that of the evil councillors who have been about him, nor has he kept the other points of his oath which he made at his coronation, as he was bound to do.

6. Item, he has stripped his realm, and done all that he could to ruin his realm and his people, and what is worse, by his cruelty and lack of character he has shown himself incorrigible without hope of amendment, which things are so notorious that they cannot be denied.

The right of parliament to dismiss a king had ancient roots. The *Anglo-Saxon Chronicle* tells us that in the year 755 the West Saxon Witan 'deprived Sigebryht of his kingdom for his unrighteous deeds.' Parliament's reassertion of its almost forgotten powers was highly significant; for parliament no longer spoke only with the voice of the great and privileged; the commoners were beginning to learn the realities of power.

Early in the reign of the new king, Edward III, who was only fifteen when he succeeded, it was agreed that parliament should meet annually. In the same document the system of Justices of the Peace was finally established. The following is an extract from the 1330 STATUTE CONCERNING JUSTICES AND SHERIFFS,

2. Item, it is ordained, that good and discreet persons, other than of the places, if they may be found sufficient, shall be assigned in all the shires of England, to take assizes, juries, and certifications, and to deliver the jails; and that the said justices shall take the assizes, juries, and certifications, and deliver the jails, at the least three times a year, and more often, if need be; also there shall be assigned good and lawful men in every county to keep the peace; and in the said assignments, mention shall be made that such as shall be indicted or taken by the said keepers of the peace, shall not be let to mainprise [bail] by the sheriffs, nor by none other ministers, if they be not mainpernable by the law; nor that such as shall be indicted, shall not be delivered but at the common law. And the justices assigned to deliver the jails shall have power to deliver the same jails of those that shall be indicted before the keepers of the peace; and that the said keepers shall send their indictments before the justices, and they shall have power to enquire of sheriffs, jailers, and others, in whose ward such indicted persons shall be, if they make deliverance, or let to mainprise any so indicted, which be not

mainpernable, and to punish the said sheriffs, jailers, and others, if they do anything against this act.

13.　Item, because divers charters of pardon have been granted of felonies, robberies, and manslaughters, against the form of the statute lately made at Northampton, containing that no man should have such charters out of the parliament, whereby such misdoers have been the more bold to offend; it is enacted, that from henceforth the same statute shall be kept and maintained in all points.

14.　Item, it is accorded that a parliament shall be holden every year once, or more often if need be.

15.　Item, because sheriffs have before this time let hundreds and wapentakes in their bailiwicks to so high ferm*, that the bailiff cannot levy the said ferm, without doing extortion and duress to the people; it is ordained, that the sheriffs shall from henceforth let their hundreds and wapentakes for the old ferm, and not above; and that the justices assigned shall have power to enquire of the said sheriffs, and punish them that shall be found offending against this statute.

The people were now beginning to enjoy participation in almost all aspects of power. The House of Commons gave them an influence upon taxation and thus upon government; through the system of Justices of the Peace they took part in the maintenance of law; while through the jury system they and not the king's justices decided questions of guilt or innocence. But there were many to whom these rights were denied. Not only the villeins and serfs, but many poor free men had no say in selecting the knights of the shires or the burgesses in parliament. Those who were too poor to contribute to the king's revenue had, as then seemed natural, no political powers.

These deprived classes were beginning to see opportunities to obtain for themselves the same rights as they had seen granted to the knights and burgesses. Their ambitions were stimulated by the Black Death, a plague which struck England in 1348. It subsided after twelve appalling months, but there were further outbreaks for the next twenty years. It is hard to know how many died : one person in ten or maybe one in eight.

* The *ferm* was tax on land payable in kind.

Before the advent of the plague, the system of villeinage and serf-dom had aready begun to decay. In return for the land which they tilled, and to which they and their sons were perpetually bound, the villeins and serfs paid a rent of labour, sowing their lords' crops and harvesting them at the proper season. This had disadvantages for lord and villein alike. The rich man could control his labour force only on certain days, and could neither deploy it as he wished nor substantially enlarge it. During the reigns of the first two Edwards, landlords began to free their serfs, charging them money rent and, with that money, to hire free labourers whose services they could command each day of the week. By the turn of the century the number of poor free men was thus enormously increased.

The tragedy of the Black Death savagely reduced the labour force. Rich men, desperate to find workers for their neglected fields, com-peted with one another for the services of the surviving free labourers. Wages rose and the poor began to understand their own value. In every village men whose grandfathers had been serfs saw the possi-bility of acquiring new rights and increased prosperity. They found that they could charge higher and higher prices for the products of their hands. The price of bread rose, of cloth, of furniture and cartage.

Parliament, representing the aristocracy and the middle classes, watched prices soar and understood very little of the reasons. It was sure that greed and obduracy among labouring men could be cured, like any other antisocial activity, by force of law. So in 1349 King Edward III issued AN ORDINANCE CONCERNING LABOURERS AND SERVANTS. It was a pathetic attempt to check economic change by price controls and by penalties. The following are extracts from the copy issued to the Sheriff of Kent :

The king to the sheriff of Kent, Greeting. Because a great part of the people, and especially of workmen and servants, late died of the pestilence, many seeing the necessity of masters, and great scarcity of servants, will not serve unless they may receive excessive wages, and some rather willing to beg in idleness, than by labour to get their living; we, consider-ing the grievous incommodities, which of the lack especially of ploughmen and such laborers may hereafter come, have upon deliberation and treaty with the prelates and the nobles, and learned men assisting us, of their mutual counsel or-dained:

1.   That every man and woman of our realm of England, of what condition he be, free or bond, able in body, and within the age of three score years, not living in merchandise, nor exercising any craft, nor having of his own whereof he may live, nor proper land, about whose tillage he may himself occupy, and not serving any other, if he be required to serve in convenient service, his estate considered, he shall be bounden to serve him which shall so him require; and take only the wages, livery, meed, or salary, which were accustomed to be given in the places where he oweth to serve, the twentieth year of our reign of England, or five or six other common years next before. Provided always that the lords be preferred before others in their bondmen or their land tenants, so in their service to be retained: so that nevertheless the said lords shall retain no more than be necessary for them; and if any such man or woman, being so required to serve, will not do the same, that proved by two true men before the sheriff, bailiff, lord, or constable of the town where the same shall happen to be done, he shall anon be taken by them, or any of them, and committed to the next jail, there to remain under strait keeping, till he find surety to serve in the form aforesaid.

5.   Item, that sadlers, skinners, whitetawers[16], cordwainers, tailors, smiths, carpenters, masons, tilers, boatmen, carters, and all other artificers and workmen, shall not take for their labour and workmanship above the same that was wont to be paid to such persons the said twentieth year, and other common years next before, as afore is said, in the place where they shall happen to work; and if any man take more, he shall be committed to the next jail, in manner as afore is said.

6.   Item, that butchers, fishmongers, hostelers, brewers, bakers, pulters, and all other sellers of all manner of victual, shall be bound to sell the same victual for a reasonable price, having respect to the price that such victual be sold at in the places adjoining, so that the same sellers have moderate gains, and not excessive, reasonably to be required according to the distance of the place from whence the said victuals be carried . . .

67

This was not a document that enlarged men's liberties, but it illustrates the difficult path that was being trodden by the common people on their long journey to freedom.

Two years later there was further legislation, known as the Statute of Labourers. Again there was reference to the pestilence and to the unwillingness of either men or women to take service except at wages double and treble what had previously been current. This statute originated 'by the petition of the commonalty' who had found that servants and labourers were going to the great and wealthy. The House of Commons had taken the initiative and was evidently growing in influence.

Edward III died in 1377. He had won great victories in France, but he must have wondered at the end of his life what he had accomplished. His successes had been purchased at great cost, and taxes had reached an extremely high level. His eldest son, Edward the Black Prince, had died before him and he was therefore succeeded by his grandson Richard II, a boy of ten. As had happened before under a child king, parliament enlarged its powers. It now demanded that the king should be answerable both to the Lords and Commons as to how taxes were spent. In the first year of Richard's reign 'the Lords and Commons of the realms of England perceiving clearly the great peril of the realm' agreed to a tax of one-fifth of all men's possessions in cities and boroughs, and two-fifteenths in the countryside. But in 1377 the Commons, in a PETITION FOR PERSONS TO BE APPOINTED TO SUPERVISE EXPENDITURE, also humbly prayed 'their liege lord and the other lords of Parliament that . . . certain suitable persons shall be appointed by the king to be treasurers or guardians . . .' It was the Commons who made this demand and it was commoners who were appointed: William Walworth and John Philipot, merchants of London. Some argued that it had never been known for accounts to be rendered to anyone else but the king, but the demand of the Commons was granted.

More and more revenue was required and in 1379 parliament agreed to a personal tax upon every free man in the kingdom. Although payment was graded, with earls paying £4, knights 40s, merchants 6s 8d and so on, every married couple and every single man and woman irrespective of their condition had to pay 4d. An earl was far more than 240 times richer than the poorest free labourer so the tax was patently unjust. This was the first time that people were taxed per head or per 'poll'. The POLL TAX was renewed in 1380 and it was laid down that the wealthy should aid the poorer. But the basic injustice remained: the wealthiest was to pay no more than sixty groats and the poorest no less than one groat (4d). This ratio did not reflect the actual differences in incomes and the smouldering resentment of the poor burst into angry flame.

They were in any event on the march. John Wycliffe, one of Oxford's most outstanding scholars, was active in the field of religious and social reform. His followers, the Lollards, preached the radical doctrine that all men were equal with equal rights to economic sufficiency and happiness. John Ball, a priest in Kent, summed up their beliefs in the couplet:

> When Adam delved and Eve span,
> Who was then the gentleman?

Ball was cast into Maidstone prison. The poor of Essex were the first to revolt. The Kentish men, led by Wat Tyler, released Ball, marched on London, burned the palace of the king's uncle, John of Gaunt, seized the Tower of London, and killed both the Archbishop of Canterbury and the King's Treasurer.

Richard, now fourteen, rode out to meet the rebels, and the following day there was a further meeting at Smithfield. Tempers rose and in the affray the Lord Mayor, William Walworth, stabbed Wat Tyler. It seemed as if the young king would be killed by the rebels. Showing great courage he declared that he himself would be their leader, promising to pardon them all. Later he broke his word and many of the rebels, including John Ball, were put to death.

The violence of the peasants' revolt achieved little. But neither the courage of the rebels nor the radical teachings of John Ball are to be disregarded. Both were signs of how thoughts of freedom were stirring among the poor. The ruin of John of Gaunt's palace and the mangled corpse of the Archbishop of Canterbury served as grim warnings to the great and powerful. Massive fortifications and the sanctity of high office had alike failed against the fury of the discontented poor.

Richard II was deposed by John of Gaunt's son who was proclaimed king as Henry IV. His first act was to reaffirm the Great Charter at the special request of the Commons—yet another portent of the growing power of that House. The preamble and the first three clauses of the ACT FOR THE SECURITY OF THE SUBJECT (1399) read as follows:

Henry, by the grace of God, king of England, and of France, and lord of Ireland, to the laud and honour of God, and rever-

ence of Holy Church, for to nourish unity, peace, and concord in all parts within the realm of England, and for the redress and recovery of the same realm, which now of late hath been dangerously put to great ruin, mischief, and desolation; of the assent of the prelates, dukes, earls, and barons, and at the instance and special request of the commons of the same realm, assembled at his parliament holden at Westminster in the feast of St. Faith the Virgin, the first year of his reign, hath caused to be ordained, and established certain ordinances and statutes in form as hereafter followeth.

1. First, that Holy Church have and enjoy all her rights, liberties, and franchises, entirely and without inblemishing; and that the great charter, and the charter of the forest, and other good ordinances and statutes made in the time of his noble progenitors, and not repealed, be firmly holden and kept in all points; and that the peace within this realm be holden and kept, so that all his lawful liege people and subjects may from henceforth safely and peaceably go, come, and dwell, according to the laws and usages of the same realm; and that good justice and even right be done to every person.

2. Item, that no lord spiritual nor temporal nor other person, of what estate or condition that he be, which came with our sovereign lord the king that now is into the realm of England, nor none other persons, whatsoever they be, then dwelling within the same realm, and which came to the king in aid of him to pursue them that were against the good intent of our sovereign lord the king and the common profit of the realm, in which pursuit Richard late king of England the second after the conquest was pursued, taken, and put in ward, and yet remaineth in ward, be impeached, grieved nor vexed, in person nor in goods, in the king's court nor in the court of none other for the pursuit of the said king, taking and withholding of his body, nor for the pursuit of any other, taking of persons and chattels or of the death of a man, or any other thing done in the said pursuit, from the day that the said king that now is arrived, till the day of the coronation of our said sovereign lord king Henry. And the intent of the king is not that offenders, which committed trespasses or other offences out of the said pursuit without special warrant shall be aided or have any advantage of this statute;

but that they be thereof answerable at the common law.

3. Item, whereas the Monday next after the feast of the Exaltation of the Holy Cross, the xxi year of the reign of the said late King Richard, a parliament was summoned and holden at Westminster, and from thence adjourned to Shrewsbury, at which town a certain power was committed by authority of the parliament, to certain persons to proceed upon certain articles and matters comprised in the roll of the parliament thereof made, as by the same roll may appear, in which parliament, and also by authority foresaid, divers statutes, judgments, ordinances, and stablishments were made, ordained, and given erroneously and right sorrowfully; in great disherison[17] and final destruction and undoing of many honorable lords and other liege people of the realm and of their heirs forever: our sovereign lord the king, considering the great mischiefs aforesaid, by the advice and assent of all the lords spiritual and temporal, and of all the commonalty, hath judged the said parliament, holden the said xxi year, and the authority thereof given, as afore is said, with all the circumstances and dependents thereupon to be of no force nor value: and that the same parliament, with the authority aforesaid and all the circumstances and dependents thereupon, be wholly reversed, revoked, voided, undone, repealed, and annulled forever.

Two years later, in January 1401, the vital principle was established that members of parliament should be privileged. The Commons elected Sir Arnold Savage as their spokesman or Speaker, and the following document in which the SPEAKER ASKS FOR THE PRIVILEGES OF PARLIAMENT, records the rights which he obtained from the crown :

Saturday, the twenty-second of January, the commons of the realm presented to the king Sir Arnold Savage as their speaker and procurator in parliament whom the king kindly accepted. And then the said Sir Arnold humbly requested the king, that he might make protestation, that, if he should say anything through ignorance, negligence or in any other way which was not agreed to by his companions or which should be displeasing to the king, or too little through lack of wisdom, or too much through folly or ignorance that the king would excuse him therefor, and that it might be corrected and amended by his said companions: and that the said commons should have their liberty in parliament as they had had before this time; and that this protestation should be recorded in the roll of parliament; which protestation seemed honest and reasonable to the king and he agreed to it. And after that, the said Sir Arnold, in order to have in memory the pronouncement of parliament which was pronounced by the said Sir Wm. Thirning on his own authority, declared in substance before the king and his lords in parliament the reasons for the summons of the said parliament, to his knowledge clearly and briefly. And besides, he prayed our said lord the king on the part of the said commons that on the matters brought before the said commons in this present parliament they should have good advice and deliberation without being suddenly called upon to reply to the most important matters at the end of parliament, as had been done before this time. To which reply was made by the king through the earl of Worcester that it was not the intention of the king to follow this order of action and that he did not imagine any such subtlety, also that they should have good advice and deliberation from time to time as the need demanded.

In the same year parliamentary privilege was further enlarged when the Commons discussed the danger that some of their number might try to curry favour with the king by secretly reporting to him what other members had said. The Rolls of Parliament record a PETITION of 1401 and the KING'S REPLY:

Item, on the same day the said commons showed to our lord the king how on certain matters moved among them, it might happen in the future that certain of their companions, out of complaisance to the king, and for their own advancement should recount to our said lord the king such matters before they had been determined and discussed or agreed upon among the commons, by reason of which the said lord our king might be grievously moved against the said commons or some of them; wherefore they most humbly pray our lord the king, not to receive any such person to recount such matters nor to give him hearing nor any faith nor credence to such a person. To which answer was made by the king that it was his will that the said commons should have deliberation and advice, to discuss and treat of all matters among themselves, in order to bring them to a better end and conclusion, in so far as they know how, for the welfare and honour of himself and of all his realm. And that he would not hear any such person or give him credence, before such matters had been shown to the king, by the advice and with the assent of all the commons, according to the purport of their said prayer.

The request of the commons that they should assent to taxation only after their petitions had been granted, was set out, but not granted by the king.

Item, the same Saturday, the said commons pointed out to our said lord the king, that, as in divers parliaments before this time, their common petitions had not been answered before they had made their grant of some aid or subsidy to our lord the king; therefore they prayed our said lord the king that for the great convenience and comfort of the said commons it should please our lord the king to grant to the said commons that they should be able to learn the responses to their said petitions before any such grant was made. To which response was made that on this matter the king wished to confer with the lords of parliament and to do in regard to it what it should seem best to do with advice of the said lords. And then afterwards, that is to say on the last day of the parliament, response was made that this manner of deed had not been seen nor used in the time of any of his ancestors or predecessors, that they should have any response to their petitions or knowledge of the same before they had taken up and completed all the other business of parliament, be it to make any grant or otherwise. And therefore the king did not wish in any way to change the good customs and usages made and used in former times.

The reign of Henry IV, perhaps because he had been elected king by parliament, is rich in documents bearing witness to the growth of

73

the power of the Commons. In 1406 the Commons protested that in some counties the sheriff appointed the knights of the shire by nomination and not by election. So procedure was laid down whereby the MANNER OF ELECTING KNIGHTS OF THE SHIRE was established :

15. Item, our lord the king, at the grievous complaint of his commons of the undue election of the knights of counties for the parliament, which be sometime made of affection of sheriffs, and otherwise against the form of the writs directed to the sheriff, to the great slander of the counties, and hindrance of the business of the commonalty of the said county; our sovereign lord the king, willing therein to provide remedy, by the assent of the lords spiritual and temporal, and of all the commonalty of the realm in this present parliament, hath ordained and established, that from henceforth the elections of such knights shall be made in the form as followeth; that is to say, that at the next county [court], to be holden after the delivery of the writ of the parliament, proclamation shall be made in the full county of the day and place of the parliament, and that all they that be there present, as well suitors duly summoned for the same cause, as other, shall attend to the election of their knights for the parliament; and then in the full county they shall proceed to the election freely and indifferently, notwithstanding any request or commandment to the contrary; and after that they be chosen, the names of the persons so chosen, be they present or absent, shall be written in an indenture under the seals of all them that did choose them, and tacked to the same writ of the parliament; which indenture, so sealed and tacked, shall be holden for the sheriff's return of the said writ, touching the knights of the shires. And that in the writs of the parliament to be made hereafter, this clause shall be put: and thy election in thy full county made, distinctly and openly, under thy seal and the seals of those who were present at that election, to us in our chancery, at the day and place in the writ contained, certify without delay.

Then in 1407 the king took the views of the Lords on a new aid. The Commons were asked to send a deputation of twelve of their members to confirm this 'most nearly to the purpose of the Lords aforesaid'. The Commons would have none of it, protesting their RIGHT TO INITIATE MONEY BILLS and the following is an extract from the Rolls of Parliament :

Item, on Friday, the second day of December, which was the last day of parliament, the commons came before the king and the lords in parliament and there by command of the king a schedule of indemnity for a certain dispute between the lords and commons was read; and thereupon it was commanded by our said lord the king, that the said schedule be recorded in the roll of parliament; of which schedule the tenor was as follows.—Be it remembered that on Monday the twenty-first day of November, the king our sovereign lord being in the council room within the abbey of Gloucester, there being in his presence the lords spiritual and temporal assembled at this present parliament, there was a discussion among them on the state of the realm and the defence of the same in order to resist the malice of the enemies who on every coast seemed to be harassing the said realm and the faithful subjects of the same, and no man would be able to resist that malice, if for the safe-guard and defence of the said realm, our sovereign lord the king aforesaid had not some notable aid and subsidy granted to him in this present parliament. And thereupon it was demanded of the aforesaid lords by way of question, what aid would be sufficient and needful in this case? To which demand and question the said lords made response severally that considering the necessity of the king on one side and the poverty of his people on the other, a less aid would not suffice than one-tenth and a half from the cities and boroughs, and one-fifteenth and a half from other laymen. And besides, to grant a prolongation of the subsidy on wools, leather, and woolfells, and three shillings on the ton, and twelve pence in the pound, from the feast of St. Michael next coming till the feast of St. Michael in two years then next ensuing. Whereupon, by command of the king our said lord, word was sent to the commons of this present parliament to send before our said lord the king and the said lords a certain number of the members of their company, to hear and to report to their companions that which they should have in command of our lord the king aforesaid. And thereupon the said commons sent to the presence of the king our said lord and the said lords twelve of their companions; to whom, by command of our said lord the king the question aforesaid was declared and the response of the aforesaid lords severally given to it. Which response, it was the will of our said lord the king, they should report to the rest of their companions; also that they should see to it that they conformed most nearly to the purpose of the lords abovesaid. Which report having been made to the said commons, they were greatly disturbed, saying and affirming that this was in great prejudice and derogation of their liberties; and when our said lord the king heard of this, not wishing that anything should be done at present or in time to come, which could in any way turn against the liberty of the estate, for which they were come to parliament, nor against the liberty of the lords aforesaid, willed and granted and declared, with the advice and assent of the said lords, in the following manner. That is to say, that it is lawful for the lords to discuss among themselves assembled in this present parliament, and in every other in time to come, in the absence of the king, concerning the estate of the realm and the remedy needful to it. And that in like manner it is lawful for the commons, on their part, to discuss together concerning the state and remedy aforesaid. Provided always, that the lords on their part and the commons on theirs, make no report to our said lord the king of any grant granted by the commons, and agreed to by the lords, nor of the negotiations of the said grant, before the said lords and commons shall be of one assent and of one accord in the matter, and then in the manner and form customary, that is to say by the mouth of the speaker of the said commons for the time being, to the end that the said lords and commons should have the agreement of our said lord the king. Besides this our said lord the king wills with the assent of the lords aforesaid that the negotiations had as aforesaid in this present parliament neither be treated as an example in time to come, nor be turned to the prejudice or derogation of the liberty of the estate, for which the said commons were now come together, neither in this present parliament nor in any other in time to come. But wills that the said and all other estates be as free as they had been before.

The Commons were now the declared equals of the Lords and no money matters could be decided without their separate consent. The right to initiate money Bills lies with the Commons to this day, and it was the foregoing document which conceded that right to them.

Thus, by King Henry IV's death in 1413 the House of Commons had become an instrument of undoubted power. Holding as it now did power over money bills and the right to examine the accounts of the realm, it was becoming a formidable body. Henceforth no king—though still accepted as exercising sovereign power—could reign without the support of the Commons. As members of parliament were now not nominated but elected, the middle classes were becoming the effective rulers of England. But just as they had acquired powers which were originally the monopoly of the aristocracy, so the poorer free men were beginning to reach towards the same powers for themselves. The gradual enfranchising of the serfs was bringing more and more of the population within the scope of the ancient liberties, and the advance towards universal participation in political power was inevitable.

The seventy years which followed the death of Henry IV opened with martial splendour and with the glories of England's victories over the French. Henry V, once the madcap Prince of Wales, resumed his great-grandfather's wars against France and two years after his accession gained immortal renown on the field of Agincourt.

His reign, which lasted only nine years, was as glorious as it was brief. In 1414, the year after his accession, the Commons made a demand, expressed in terms of deepest humility, that in future no change should be made in any of the petitions which they might submit. All power resided in the king; nevertheless, nothing was to be entered upon the statute book which varied in the least degree from what the Commons had resolved, as laid down in the PETITION OF 1414, THAT THE KING WAS NOT TO ALTER THE PETITIONS OF PARLIAMENT.

Item, be it remembered, that the commons delivered to the king our very sovereign lord, in this present parliament a petition, of which the tenor follows word for word.

Our sovereign lord, your humble and true lieges that have come for the commons of your land, trusting in your great justice that as it hath been ever their liberty and freedom that there should no statute or law be made unless they gave thereto their assent, considering that the commons of your land, the which is and ever hath been, a member of your parliament, have been as well assenters as petitioners, that from this time forth, by complaint of the commons of any mischief, asking remedy by mouth of their speaker for the commons or else by written petition, that there never be any law made thereupon and engrossed as statute and law, neither by addition or by diminution, by no manner of term or terms, the which should change the sentence and the intent asked by the speaker by mouth, or the petitions aforesaid given in writing by the manner aforesaid, without the assent of the foresaid commons. Considering our sovereign lord that it is not in any wise the intent of your commons if it be so that they ask you by speaking or by writing, two things or three or as many as pleases them; but that ever it stand in the freedom of your Highness to grant which of those that please you and to refuse the rest.

REPLY

The king by his especial grace granteth that from henceforth nothing be enacted to the petitions of his commons that be contrary to their asking whereby they should be bound without their assent; saving always to our liege lord his prerogative to grant and deny what him list of their petitions and askings aforesaid.

The humble tone of the message and the condescension of the reply were alike conventional. The facts were simple : the subordinate rights of the subjects to approve taxation had increased to the point where the commoners were now the initiators, and where it was the king who had merely the right of assent.

With the success of the king's wars in France, the Commons were in generous mood. In 1415, the year of Agincourt, they voted a GRANT TO THE KING OF A SUBSIDY FOR LIFE :

. . . to the honour and exaltation of the crown, of its good fame, and to the special comfort of his loyal lieges and to the fear of all his enemies and probably to the perpetual profit of all his realm, to the honour and reverence of God, and for the great affection and entire love that the commons of the realm of England have for our said sovereign lord the king, . . .

The tax took the form of a duty on wool, hides and skins, and was fairly onerous, but with the blood-red cross of St George advancing against the pale lilies of France, the Commons of England were neither grudging nor critical even though, by voting a tax for the king's lifetime, they were reducing his dependence upon them and consequently their own powers.

On the surface all seemed set fair. In a second expedition Henry triumphantly achieved his warlike purposes, was recognised as heir to the French throne and married Katherine, daughter of the French king. A year later, Katherine bore him a son who was christened Henry like his father and grandfather before him. The young prince seemed destined to enjoy a golden future as heir to the two crowns of England and of France.

Nine months later Henry V died in battle and the infant prince was proclaimed as Henry VI of England. The French, with the valiant Harry dead, repudiated the treaty whereby the child king was to inherit the crown of France.

Matters went ill for the English. Joan of Arc inflicted defeats upon them and French hopes revived. The reverses suffer by English arms were followed by a period of social restlessness. One form of this unrest was an increase in the number of those coming to the hustings to elect members of the House of Commons. The growing number of poor free men saw their freedom as an entitlement to join in the processes of election. The wealthier commoners were alarmed that poor men should disturb their dignified deliberations and that peasants should begin to share their power. Accordingly, a decision was taken to allow only those to take part in elections who possessed a certain minimum wealth—FORTY SHILLING FREEHOLDERS:

7. Item, whereas the elections of knights of shires chosen to come to the parliaments of the king, in many counties of England, have now of late been made by very great, and excessive number of people dwelling within the same counties of the which most part was by people of small substance, or of no value, whereof every of them pretended a voice equivalent, as to such elections to be made, with the most worthy

knights and esquires dwelling within the same counties; whereby manslaughters, riots, batteries, and divisions among the gentlemen and other people of the same counties, shall very likely rise and be unless convenient remedy be provided in this behalf: our lord the king, considering the premises, hath provided, and ordained by authority of this present parliament, that the knights of the shires to be chosen within the same realm of England to come to the parliaments hereafter to be holden, shall be chosen in every county, by people dwelling and resident in the same, whereof every one of them shall have free tenement to the value of forty shillings by the year at the least above all charges; and that they which shall be so chosen shall be dwelling and resident within the same counties; and such as have the greatest number of them that may expend forty shillings by year and above, as afore is said, shall be returned by the sheriffs of every county, knights for the parliament, by indentures sealed betwixt the said sheriffs and the said choosers so to be made; and every sheriff of England shall have power, by the said authority, to examine upon the holy evangelists every such chooser, how much he may expend by the year: and if any sheriff return knights to come to the parliament contrary to this ordinance, that the justices of assizes in their sessions of assizes shall have power by the authority aforesaid, thereof to inquire; and if by inquest the same be found before the same justices, and the sheriff thereof be duly attainted, that then the said sheriff shall incur the pain of an hundred pounds to be paid to our lord the king, and also that he have imprisonment by a year, without being let to bail or mainprise; and that the knights for the parliament returned contrary to the said ordinance shall lose their wages. Provided always, that he which cannot expend forty shillings by year as afore is said shall in no wise be chooser of the knights for the parliament; and that in every writ that shall hereafter go forth to the sheriffs to choose knights for the parliament, mention be made of the said ordinances.

The long wars with France (there had been a hundred years of fighting) came to their disastrous end. Joan of Arc was burned as a witch in the gabled market place of Rouen, but this was revenge, not victory.

The soldiers, veterans of long and brutal campaigns, returned to England but not to peace.

Agincourt, and the fighting which followed, held many lessons. First, the nobles and lawnowners learned that in spite of the theory of the king's power and the slow destruction of the feudal system, power still rode with the man who could call up a troop of spears and a company of bowmen. Because the fedual system was decaying, the armies which had fought in France were not like the levies of former days. The growing number of poor free men enabled the rich to raise companies of hired soldiers who owed little loyalty save to their paymasters. The barons once more knew the feeling of power as they rode along the sunny roads of France, commanders of their private armies, able to pillage where they wished, answerable to no man and to no assembly. So the great barons and their private armies came back to an England where a gentle hand held the sceptre and where the crown no longer encircled the bright war-helmet of a royal soldier, for Henry VI was a man more fit for learning than for battle.

For the peasants and poor free men the French campaigns also carried messages of power. They had seen how their long bows could defeat armoured knights (as at Creçy in 1346). The wealthy, who could afford horses and armour, had, since the later Roman Empire, dominated the battlefield and therefore dominated society. But at Agincourt, the English peasants had seen the rich knights of France, mounted proudly upon their tall horses, fall impotently before the swift and relentless arrows of the poor. Six feet of good yew branch, two cheap bowstrings, a fistful of shafts tipped with a pennyworth of iron and guided by a tuft of goose-feather—these had proved more invincible than armour and more powerful than the horses. Perhaps all political power is a reflection of military power. If so, then the power of the aristocracy in England took a mortal wound at Agincourt.

Moreover, the English soldiers had seen their proudest captains defeated by a girl who, like themeslves, was a peasant. If Agincourt had demonstrated that the wealthy were not invincible, Joan of Arc had proved that there was nothing sacred about the authority of the great.

These two conflicting forces—the renewed power of the barons with their lawless companies of mercenaries, and the grim lessons learned by the poor men of England—were to tear the realm apart for many decades.

In 1450 came the rebellion of Jack Cade, self-styled Captain of Kent who trod almost the same path as Wat Tyler and those other rebels some seventy years before, leading his army through Rochester and

Dartford, to Southwark on the outskirts of London. But this was no simple rising of peasants. Jack Cade claimed the proud name of Mortimer. The Mortimers were the descendants of John of Gaunt's elder brother Clarence and therefore senior in the royal line to King Henry, who was the great-grandson of John of Gaunt himself.

Few had questioned the right to the crown of Henry IV or Henry V whose military prowess had won the hearts of their warlike subjects. But Henry VI was another matter. The foundation of King's College, Cambridge, and of his school at Eton were, for many, poor substitutes for the high adventures of his fighting ancestors.

Two years after the return of the armies from France, the Duke of York (a Mortimer on his mother's side) made a bid for the crown. A battle was fought at St Albans and for more than twenty years civil war raged in England. The private armies of the barons eagerly joined in the quarrels of their masters. Those who followed the Duke of York and his sons (for the struggle spanned two generations) sported the white rose of York while those who fought on the side of King Henry VI and his son wore the red rose of Lancaster, the duchy of their ancestor John of Gaunt.

During the long years of the Wars of the Roses the reality of power seemed to have withdrawn from the council chamber and from parliament. The troubled reigns of the Duke of York's son, Edward IV (who took the crown from Henry VI in battle), of poor young Edward V (who was king for three summer months and who died tragically in the Tower of London) and of Richard III (whose name became a byword for villainy) provide no documents for our study.

Then, in 1485, on the field of Bosworth, Richard III was slain, fighting an army raised against him by a Welsh nobleman, Henry Tudor, Earl of Richmond, a distant kinsman.

Henry's mother, Margaret Beaufort, was a great-granddaughter of John of Gaunt so that he could claim descent from Edward III and thus from all preceding kings. Through his father, Edmund Tudor, he was also descended from the former princes of Wales, and he had marched to Bosworth under the ancient standard of the Red Dragon.

Notes p 222

DOCUMENTS QUOTED:

1 Writ for the collection of Scutage—1235 [*AS*]
2 Writ of Summons for Two Knights of the Shire to Grant an Aid—1254 [*AS*]
3 Provisions of Oxford—1258 [*AS*]
4 The First Statutes of Westminster—1275 [*S*]
5 Writ of Summons to Parliament—1295 [*C*]
6 Writ of Confirmation of Charters—1297 [*S*]
7 Articles of Accusation against Edward II—1327 [*AS*]
8 Statute concerning Justices and Sheriffs—1330 [*SR*]
9 An Ordinance concerning Labourers and Servants—1349 [*SR*]
10 Rolls of Parliament—Persons appointed to supervise expenditures —1377 [*AS*]
11 The Poll Tax—1379 [*AS*]
12 An Act for the Security of the Subject—1399 [*SR*]
13 Rolls of Parliament—The Speaker asks for the Privileges of Parliament—1401 [*AS*]
14 Rolls of Parliament—Petition of the Commons and the King's Reply—1401 [*AS*]
15 Rolls of Parliament—The Manner of Electing the Knights of the Shire—1406 [*SR*]
16 Rolls of Parliament—Declaration that the Commons should initiate money Bills—1407 [*AS*]
17 Rolls of Parliament—The King not to alter Petitions of the Commons—1414 [*AS*]
18 Rolls of Parliament—Grant to the King of a Subsidy for Life— 1415 [*AS*]
19 Statute Providing the Electors must be Forty Shilling Freeholders —1429 [*SR*]

CHAPTER V

The Tudors
(1485-1603)

THE victorious Earl of Richmond was acclaimed king on the field of Bosworth and reigned as Henry VII for twenty-four prosperous years.

When the sun set on the trampled field of Bosworth the long day of medieval England was over and the dawn of the new reign was the dawn of a new age. Chaucer had already moulded the English language, Caxton had set up his printing press near Westminster Abbey, and gunpowder had brought new techniques to the arts of war. Within a few years of King Henry's accession a new world in the west had been discovered and men's minds began to range, like the swift and adventurous ships, beyond the confines of old knowledge.

There were new and sometimes conflicting forces shaping men's lives. Printing made possible the wide dissemination of knowledge and the questioning of authority began to grow. If new lands could exist beyond what had always been considered the western edge of the world, then surely many other old beliefs might be untrue. Ancient standards and concepts began to be questioned. For a long while, all this took place in the studies of priests, the halls of the wealthy and perhaps in the ale-houses of the poor. The new forces did not at once intrude into parliament or the council chamber.

Other developments worked in the opposite direction, reinforcing authority and the powers of the strong central government. Siege guns could breach the stoutest walls, and it was the royal power and royal wealth which could best exploit the costly new weapons. So the might of the barons began to crumble as their castles crumbled before the new artillery.

Above all, the Wars of the Roses had made most people anxious to see the king's peace restored, and if this meant a strengthening of the king's powers, they were content.

Parliament confirmed King Henry's royal title, bestowed upon him on the battlefield. They thus reaffirmed that it was not an army, however powerful, which appointed kings of England. Parliament alone could install the monarch and legalise his coronation.

Two years after his accession, King Henry established The Court of Star Chamber, so called after the painted ceiling of the room in Westminster where it held its sessions. This was an attempt by Henry to free himself from the trammels of the safeguards against the royal power.

In this court there was no jury to prevent the political wishes of the king from over-riding justice. Later (notoriously under Charles I) this court became a hated symbol of oppression, but when it was founded, parliament and people accepted it as an instrument by which the king could summarily put down his enemies within the realm, without the delays and problems found in the older courts. The surrender of some of their rights was an acceptable price for the re-establishment of peace.

The political fatigue of the people, as well as the wealth which Henry was able to derive from the fines levied in his own courts, enabled him to govern without regular parliaments, and during the last ten years of his reign, Lords and Commons assembled on only three occasions.

For twenty years there was a pause in the march towards freedom. Security and the rebuilding of all that had been lost during the Wars of the Roses, seemed alone to occupy men's minds. But the lull was temporary and the march was to be resumed.

Henry VII's eldest son Arthur was, as a boy, betrothed to a Spanish princess, Catherine of Aragon. He died before they were married, and his young brother Henry married Catherine in his stead. This marriage was to have great consequences.

At the time of Henry VII's death in 1509, England was in a mood for change. Henry VII had become a remote and forbidding figure, engendering respect rather than affection. The new King, Henry VIII, provided a complete contrast. He was as learned as he was handsome, fond of music and poetry, a great sportsman, as lavish in dress as he was extravagant in living. His gaiety and the free-and-easy manner in which he went among his people earned him the affectionate nickname of Bluff King Hal.

Henry VIII exercised his authority through Thomas Wolsey, a member of King Henry VII's council. In the fifth year of the new reign Wolsey was made Archbishop of York. A year later he became Lord

Chancellor of England, and the Pope made him a Cardinal with the title of Papal Legate.

King Henry's willingness to have the Pope's Legate as Lord Chancellor of England was not the only evidence of his devotion to the Roman Catholic church. Throughout northern Europe there was a growing resentment of the Pope's powers. In Germany, Martin Luther had nailed to the church door in Wittenberg a document criticising the Papal practice of Indulgences, whereby remission of penance was sold for cash. Henry VIII wrote a learned treatise refuting Luther and the Pope gave him the title of *Fidei Defensor* (Defender of the Faith), which is still borne by kings and queens of England and is to be seen on coins to this day.

It was Henry's waywardness rather than any desire for reform that led him to break with the church of Rome, and it was national pride rather than differences of doctrine which drove him on once he had taken the first step. Eighteen years of marriage to Catherine had brought him no son but only a daughter, Mary, the sole heir to the throne. The story is well known : how Henry fell in love with Anne Boleyn ; how he sought from the Pope a divorce on the grounds that his wife Catherine had been not merely betrothed but married to his dead brother Arthur ; how the Pope refused his request ; how the frustrated king angrily dismissed Wolsey from the post of Lord Chancellor ; and how Wolsey was accused of treason, and died awaiting trial.

In the year 1529, a parliament was summoned which was to remain in being for seven years and become known as the Reformation Parliament. In 1532 this Parliament passed an Act abolishing the payment to the Pope of 'annates' which were the sums due when archbishops or bishops were appointed. The act recalled the vast sums which had gone to Rome on this account :

THE CONDITIONAL RESTRAINT OF ANNATES—1532

Forasmuch as it is well perceived, by long-approved experience, that great and inestimable sums of money have been daily conveyed out of this realm, to the impoverishment of the same; and specially such sums of money as the pope's holiness, his predecessors, and the Court of Rome, by long time have heretofore taken of all and singular those spiritual persons which have been named, elected, presented, or postulated to be archbishops or bishops within this realm of England, under the title of annates, otherwise called first-fruits: which annates, or first-fruits, heretofore have been taken of every archbishopric, or bishopric, within this realm, by restraint of the pope's bulls, for confirmations, elections, admissions, postulations, provisions, collations, dispositions, institutions, installations, investitures, orders, holy benedictions, palls, or other things requisite and necessary to the attaining of those their promotions; and have been compelled to pay, before they could attain the same, great sums of money, before they might receive any part of the fruits of the said archbishopric, or bishopric, whereunto they were named, elected, presented, or postulated; by occasion whereof, not only the treasure of this realm has been greatly conveyed out of the same, but also it has happened many times, by occasion of death, unto such archbishops, and bishops, so newly promoted, within two or three years after his or their consecration, that his or their friends, by whom he or they have been holpen to advance and make payment of the said annates, or first-fruits, have been thereby utterly undone and impoverished:

II.   And for because the said annates have risen, grown, and increased, by an uncharitable custom, grounded upon no just or good title, and the payments thereof obtained by restraint of bulls, until the same annates, or first-fruits, have been paid, or surety made for the same; which declares the said payments to be exacted, and taken by constraint, against all equity and justice:

III.   The noblemen, therefore, of the realm, and the wise, sage, politic commons of the same, assembled in this present Parliament, considering that the Court of Rome ceases not to tax, take, and exact the said great sums of money, under the title of annates, or first-fruits, as is aforesaid, to the great damage of the said prelates and this realm; which annates or first-fruits, were first suffered to be taken within the same realm, for the only defence of Christian people against the infidels, and now they be claimed and demanded as mere duty, only for lucre, against all right and conscience: insomuch that it is evidently known, that there has passed out of this realm unto the Court of Rome, since the second year of the reign of the most noble prince of famous memory, King Henry VII, unto this present time under the name of annates,

87

or first-fruits, paid for the expedition of bulls of archbishop-
rics and bishoprics, the sum of eight hundred thousand
ducats, amounting in sterling money, at the least, to eight score
thousand pounds, besides other great and intolerable sums
which have yearly been conveyed to the said Court of Rome,
by many other ways and means, to the great impoverishment
of this realm:

IV. And albeit that our said sovereign the king, and all his
natural subjects, as well spiritual as temporal, be as obedient,
devout, catholic, and humble children of God and Holy
Church, as any people be within any realm christened; yet
the said exactions of annates, or first-fruits, be so intolerable
and importable to this realm, that it is considered and declared, by the whole body of this realm now represented by
all the estates of the same assembled in this present parliament, that the king's highness before Almighty God is bound,
as by the duty of a good Christian prince, for the conservation
and preservation of the good estate and commonwealth of
this his realm, to do all that in him is to obviate, repress, and
redress the said abuses and exactions of annates, or first-
fruits: and because that divers prelates of this realm be now
in extreme age, and in other debilities of their bodies, so that
of likelihood bodily death in short time shall or may succeed
unto them; by reason whereof great sums of money shall
shortly after their deaths be conveyed unto the Court of
Rome, for the unreasonable and uncharitable causes abovesaid, to the universal damage, prejudice, and impoverishment
of this realm, if speedy remedy be not in due time provided:

V. It is therefore ordained, established, and enacted, by
authority of this present parliament, that the unlawful payments of annates, or first-fruits, and all manner contributions
for the same, for any archbishopric or bishopric, or for any
bulls hereafter to be obtained from the Court of Rome, to or
for the aforesaid purpose and intent, shall from henceforth
utterly cease, and no such hereafter to be paid for any archbishopric, or bishopric, within this realm, other or otherwise
than hereafter in this present Act is declared; and that no
manner person nor persons hereafter to be named, elected,
presented, or postulated to any archbishopric, or bishopric,
within this realm, shall pay the said annates, or first-fruits,
for the said archbishopric, or bishopric, nor any other manner

of sum or sums of money, pensions, or annuities for the same, or for any other like exaction, or cause, upon pain to forfeit to our said sovereign lord the king, his heirs and successors, all manner his goods and chattels for ever, and all the temporal lands and possessions of the same archbishopric, or bishopric, during the time that he or they which shall offend, contrary to this present Act, shall have, possess, or enjoy the archbishopric, or bishopric, wherefore he shall so offend contrary to the form aforesaid.

The same act denied that the Pope could excommunicate the king or any other Englishman; and laid down that the king and his subjects could perform all sacraments or ceremonies notwithstanding any papal ban :

XII.   And if that upon the aforesaid reasonable, amicable, and charitable ways and means, by the king's highness to be experimented, moved, or compounded, or otherwise approved, it shall and may appear, or be seen unto his grace, that this realm shall be continually burdened and charged with this, and such other intolerable exactions and demands as heretofore it hath been; and that thereupon, for continuance of the same, our said holy father the pope, or any of his successors, or the Court of Rome, will, or do, or cause to be done at any time hereafter, so as is above rehearsed, unjustly, uncharitably, and unreasonably, vex, inquiet, molest, trouble, or grieve our said sovereign lord, his heirs or successors, kings of England, or any of his or their spiritual or lay subjects, or this his realm, by excommunication, excommengement, interdiction, or by any other process, censures, compulsories[18], ways or means:

XIII.   Be it enacted by the authority aforesaid, that the king's highness, his heirs and successors, kings of England, and all his spiritual and lay subjects of the same, without any scruples of conscience, shall and may lawfully, to the honour of Almighty God, the increase and continuance of virtue and good example within this realm, the said censures, excommunications, interdicts, compulsories, or any of them notwithstanding, minister, or cause to be ministered, throughout this said realm, and all other the dominions or territories belonging or appertaining thereunto, all and all manner of sacraments, sacramentals, ceremonies, or other divine service of Holy Church, or any other thing or things necessary for the health of the soul of mankind, as they heretofore at any time or times have been virtuously used or accustomed to do within the same; and that no manner such censures, excommunications, interdictions, or any other process or compulsories, shall be by any of the prelates, or other spiritual fathers of this region, nor by any of their ministers or substitutes, at any time or times hereafter published, executed, nor divulged, nor suffered to be published, executed, or divulged in any manner of wise.

XIV.   Be it remembered that on the 9th day of July, in the 25th year of the reign of King Henry, the same lord the king, by his letters patent, sealed under his great seal, ratified and confirmed the aforesaid Act, and gave to that Act his royal assent.

But there was no outright rejection of Rome's authority. In Clause XII there is a reference to 'our said holy father the pope . . .'

In 1533 Henry and Anne Boleyn were secretly married. In March (by which time Anne was royally pregnant) Thomas Cranmer, Archbishop of Canterbury, declared the king's marriage to Catherine invalid. To forestall any appeal to the Pope against this, a further Act banned appeals to Rome in suits concerning wills, divorces, and other matters. The opening words formally define the totality of the royal power upon which all constitutional development has been based, and which is still the theory underlying the structure of the state :

ACT IN RESTRAINT OF APPEALS—1533

Where by divers sundry old authentic histories and chronicles, it is manifestly declared and expressed, that this realm of England is an empire, and so hath been accepted in the world, governed by one supreme head and king, having the dignity and royal estate of the imperial crown of the same, unto whom a body politic, compact of all sorts and degrees of people, divided in terms, and by names of spiritualty and temporalty, be bounden and ought to bear, next to God, a natural and humble obedience: he being also institute and furnished, by the goodness and sufferance of Almighty God, with plenary, whole, and entire power, pre-eminence, authority, prerogative and jurisdiction, to render and yield justice, and final determination to all manner of folk, residents, or subjects within this his realm, in all causes, matters, debates, and contentions, happening to occur, insurge, or begin within the limits thereof, without restraint, or provocation to any foreign princes or potentates of the world; the body spiritual whereof having power, when any cause of the law divine happened to come in question, or of spiritual learning, then it was declared, interpreted, and showed by that part of the said body politic, called the spiritualty, now being usually called the English Church, which always hath been reputed, and also found of that sort, that both for knowledge, integrity, and sufficiency of number, it hath been always thought, and is also at this hour, sufficient and meet of itself, without the intermeddling of any exterior person or persons, to declare and determine all such doubts, and to administer all such offices and duties, as to their rooms spiritual doth appertain; for the due administration whereof, and to keep them from corruption and sinister affection, the king's most noble progenitors, and the antecessors of the nobles of this realm, have sufficiently endowed the said Church, both with honour and possessions; and the laws temporal, for trial of property of lands and goods, and for the conservation of the people of this realm in unity and peace, without rapine or spoil, was and yet is administered, adjudged, and executed by sundry judges and ministers of the other part of the said body politic, called the temporalty; and both their authorities and jurisdictions do conjoin together in the due administration of justice, the one to help the other.

This Act, while forbidding any appeal to Rome, could not prevent the Pope from denouncing Cranmer's declaration. So long as the Pope's special authority was accepted, this would have nullified Henry's marriage to Anne. So the king took the final step and banished the Pope's authority from his realm. In 1534 parliament passed an Act declaring the king to be the only supreme head of the Church of England.

Nominally, at any rate, the statute was enacted by the sole authority of parliament and not by the king :

ACT OF SUPREMACY—1534

Albeit the king's majesty justly and rightfully is and ought to be the supreme head of the Church of England, and so is recognised by the clergy of this realm in the Convocations, yet nevertheless for corroboration and confirmation thereof, and for increase of virtue in Christ's religion within this realm of England, and to repress and extirp all errors, heresies, and other enormities and abuses heretofore used in the same: be it enacted by authority of this present Parliament, that the king our sovereign lord, his heirs and successors, kings of this realm, shall be taken, accepted, and reputed the only supreme head in earth of the Church of England, called **Anglicana Ecclesia;** and shall have and enjoy annexed and united to the imperial crown of this realm, as well the title and style thereof, as all honours, dignities, pre-eminences, jurisdictions, privileges, authorities, immunities, profits, and commodities to the said dignity of supreme head of the same Church belonging and appertaining; and that our said sovereign lord, his heirs and successors, kings of this realm, shall have full power and authority from time to time to visit, repress, redress, reform, order, correct, restrain, and amend all such errors, heresies, abuses, offences, contempts, and enormities, whatsoever they be, which by any manner spiritual authority or jurisdiction ought or may lawfully be reformed, repressed, ordered, redressed, corrected, restrained, or amended, most to the pleasure of Almighty God, the increase of virtue in Christ's religion, and for the conservation of the peace, unity, and tranquillity of this realm; any usage, custom, foreign law, foreign authority, prescription, or any other thing or things to the contrary hereof notwithstanding.

The Act of Supremacy had its origins in a wilful and middle-aged king's desire for a young mistress; it was begotten in intrigue; in the cynical rejection of a faithful wife and the callous dismissal of a devoted minister. It was nonetheless destined to enlarge the liberty of England. Englishmen now professed the new form of Christianity, Protestantism, which sought to bring into religion some of the rationality which was developing in other fields. They rejected the doctrine that the elements of the Mass underwent a change of substance to become the actual flesh and blood of Christ. Also, they found it inappropriate to set up images of Christ and the saints, since the proper objects of worship were the eternal God who could not be depicted, and the ineffable mysteries of the Son.

Those Protestants, who identified the older beliefs with the authority of Rome, may have seen the Act as a rejection not merely of the Pope's power but of those ancient ways which had become unacceptable to them. They were to be savagely disappointed. Henry, seeking national independence not heresy, continued to defend orthodox doctrine, punishing those who deviated. Five years after the Act of Supremacy, Henry's Parliament drew up six articles designed to defend the ancient religion :

SIX ARTICLES ACT—1539

Where the king's most excellent majesty is, by God's law, supreme head immediately under Him of this whole Church and congregation of England, intending the conservation of the same Church and congregation in a true, sincere, and uniform doctrine of Christ's religion, calling also to his blessed and most gracious remembrance as well the great and quiet assurance, prosperous increase, and other innumerable commodities, which have ever ensued, come, and followed, of concord, agreement, and unity in opinions, as also the manifold perils, dangers, and inconveniences which have heretofore, in many places and regions, grown, sprung, and arisen, of the diversities of minds and opinions, especially of matters of Christian religion, and therefore desiring that such a unity might and should be charitably established in all things touching and concerning the same, as the same, so being established, might chiefly be to the honour of Almighty God, the very Author and Fountain of all true unity and sincere concord, and consequently redound to the common wealth of this his highness's most noble realm, and of all his loving subjects, and other residents and inhabitants of or in the same; has therefore caused and commanded this his most High Court of Parliament, for sundry and many urgent causes and considerations, to be at this time summoned, and also a synod and Convocation of all the archbishops, bishops, and other learned men of the clergy of this his realm, to be in like manner assembled.

II.   And forasmuch as in the said Parliament, synod and Convocation, there were certain Articles, matters, and questions proponed and set forth touching Christian religion, that is to say:

First, whether in the most blessed Sacrament of the Altar remaineth, after the consecration, the substance of bread and wine, or no.

Secondly, whether it be necessary by God's law that all men should be communicate with both kinds, or no.

Thirdly, whether priests, that is to say, men dedicate to God by priesthood, may, by the law of God, marry after, or no.

Fourthly, whether vow of chastity or widowhood, made to God advisedly by man or woman, be, by the law of God, to be observed, or no.

Fifthly, whether private masses stand with the law of God, and be to be used and continued in the Church and congregation of England, as things whereby good Christian people may and do receive both godly consolation and wholesome benefits, or no.

Sixthly, whether auricular confession is necessary to be retained, continued, used, and frequented in the Church, or no.

III.   The king's most royal majesty, most prudently pondering and considering, that by occasion of variable and sundry opinions and judgments of the said Articles, great discord and variance has arisen, as well amongst the clergy of this his realm, as amongst a great number of vulgar people, his loving subjects of the same, and being in a full hope and trust that a full and perfect resolution of the said Articles should make a perfect concord and unity generally amongst all his loving and obedient subjects, of his most excellent goodness not only commanded that the said Articles should deliberately and advisedly, by his said archbishops, bishops, and other learned men of his clergy, be debated, argued, and reasoned, and their opinions therein to be understood, declared, and known, but also most graciously vouchsafed, in his own princely person, to descend and come into his said High Court of Parliament and council, and there, like a prince of most high prudence and no less learning, opened and declared many things of high learning and great knowledge, touching the said Articles, matters, and questions, for a unity to be had in the same; whereupon, after a great and long, deliberate, and advised disputation and consultation had and made concerning the said Articles, as well by the consent of the king's highness, as by the assent of the lords spiritual and temporal, and other learned men of his clergy in their Convocation, and by the consent of the commons in this present Parliament assembled, it was and is finally resolved, accorded, and agreed in manner and form following, that is to say:

First, that in the most blessed Sacrament of the Altar, by the strength and efficacy of Christ's mighty word (it being spoken by the priest), is present really, under the form of bread and wine, the natural body and blood of our Saviour Jesus Christ, conceived of the Virgin Mary; and that after the consecration there remaineth no substance of bread or wine, nor any other substance, but the substance of Christ, God and man.

Secondly, that communion in both kinds is not necessary **ad salutem**[19], by the law of God, to all persons; and that it is to be believed, and not doubted of, but that in the flesh, under the form of bread, is the very blood; and with the blood, under the form of wine, is the very flesh; as well apart, as though they were both together.

Thirdly, that priests after the order of priesthood received, as afore, may not marry, by the law of God.

Fourthly, that vows of chastity or widowhood, by man or woman made to God advisedly, ought to be observed by the law of God; and that it exempts them from other liberties of Christian people, which without that they might enjoy.

Fifthly, that it is meet and necessary that private masses be continued and admitted in this the king's English Church and congregation, as whereby good Christian people, ordering themselves accordingly, do receive both godly and goodly consolations and benefits; and it is agreeable also to God's law.

95

Sixthly, that auricular confession is expedient and necessary to be retained and continued, used and frequented in the
Church of God.

Like *Magna Carta* which was simply intended to protect rich landowners, the Act of Supremacy had wider results than its authors intended. It banished an overseas authority out of England, and gave
Englishmen the liberty to debate (and sometimes to fight over) the
issue of religion without foreign interference. Despite its selfish
origins and despite the bigotry (sometimes bloody) which later marred
the relationship between Catholic and Protestant, it ultimately made
possible the growth of tolerance throughout the realm. It also revived
the Saxon tradition of the appointment of bishops by the crown with
the advice of the assembly.

The Act, as we have seen, was made in the sole name of parliament
and not in the name of the king. The same parliament sat for seven
years and became a partner of the crown in the nation's affairs.

Hitherto it was during the reigns of boys or of absent, weak or unsuccessful monarchs, or of kings with doubtful claims to the crown,
that the powers of parliament had grown. Not so with Henry VIII; a
strong king was deliberately making parliament joint ruler with himself.

In 1536 Catherine died, lonely and neglected. Ironically, Anne
Boleyn died in the same year at the hands of the public executioner.
She had borne a daughter to Henry, the Princess Elizabeth, so that
there were now two heirs to the throne—Mary, daughter of Catherine,
legitimate only in the eyes of those who rejected the Act of Supremacy;
and Elizabeth who, unless that Act was accepted, was merely a royal
bastard.

In the following year Henry, now undoubtedly a widower, married
his third wife Jane Seymour who gave birth to a son, Edward, and the
succession seemed secure.

In 1547 Henry died—diseased, obese and apparently unsuccessful.
Wars had depleted his treasury, the currency was debased, many of the
personal estates of the crown had been sold to raise cash, while in his
personal life he had met disappointment and tragedy. But his reign in
fact had been one of solid achievement. He had freed England from a
continental authority, had brought parliament and the crown into close
partnership, and had made the monarchy, more than ever before, the
symbol and instrument of national unity and domestic peace.

His son, Edward VI, was only ten years old when he succeeded. During his six years' reign there were no documents to mark the development of liberty. Parliament and the council were preoccupied with other matters. The establishment of the Church of England as a Protestant church was begun, and the designs of Henry VIII to maintain Catholic doctrine were overthrown. The Act of the Six Articles was repealed, Protestant refugees from the continent made welcome, and Cranmer's *Book of Common Prayer* was published. An Act of Uniformity required it to be used in all English churches.

King Edward died in his teens, having first been persuaded to name his cousin Lady Jane Grey as heir to the throne. Poor Jane was the sad victim of her father-in-law's ambitions (she was married to the Duke of Northumberland's son). She reigned for only nine days, and was later beheaded by Mary I.

The people of England, tired of ambitious nobles who had ruled for the boy king, rejoiced to see King Henry's daughter on the throne. She was now thirty-seven, embittered by long years of sorrow, and for her the Church of England was a memorial to her mother's disgrace and her father's selfishness. So long as the new church endured she was in law but a bastard and her half-sister Elizabeth, daughter of Anne Boleyn, the only rightful Tudor.

So Mary had to restore the Pope's authority in England. But parliament was now beginning to reflect public opinion, and Mary, during the first eighteen months of her reign, had to hold three elections before she found a parliament prepared to support her. For six years she strove to bring England back to Rome and for six bloody years she was defied. She married her cousin, King Philip of Spain, into whose Catholic empire she sought to bring her own kingdom. Many hundreds of her protestant subjects, including Cranmer and three other bishops, were burned as heretics. Memory of their fortitude and of Mary's cruelty long survived and did much to advance the cause of Protestantism in the next two centuries. Mary, heedless alike of tradition and of the realities of power, flouted the opinions of her people, disregarded the advice of her council, and by the time of her death the old relationship between crown and people seemed damaged beyond repair. England was no longer esteemed abroad, and it seemed that the brave days of King Henry would never again be equalled.

In fact, they were to be surpassed. When Mary died in 1558 Elizabeth emerged from obscurity and became queen of a torn and divided England. Like Mary, Elizabeth knew that her legitimacy was in doubt. Her right to the throne depended upon the validity of Anne Boleyn's marriage to her father. Archbishop Cranmer, upon whose annulment of Henry's earlier marriage her legitimacy was based, had been burned as a heretic. The Act of Supremacy, the buttress of her parent's marriage, had been repealed. Elizabeth thus had powerful motives to undo all that Mary had done.

Accordingly in the second year of her reign (1559) another ACT OF SUPREMACY was passed in which Elizabeth took the title of Supreme Governor of the church, instead of Supreme Head as her father had done. It was felt that this would cause less offence.

Like her father, she was acutely sensitive to the feelings of her people. She knew that England was tired of religious extremism and of harsh persecutions and accordingly she sought compromise and moderation. The *Prayer Book* was restored but so modified as to make it more acceptable to Roman Catholics. The re-establishment of national pride reinforced the idea of a national church under the sovereign. But such a church had to appeal to all moderate men, Protestant or Roman Catholic. Elizabeth saw that unity could best be achieved by negotiation, not persecution. She and her advisers sought to give as much liberty of worship as was consistent with independence from foreign influence and the politics of the age. For the first seventeen years of her reign no man was executed for his religious beliefs. Later, when some Roman Catholics were put to death, they were sentenced not because of their religion but because they were held to have conspired treasonably against the queen's office and person.

The great monument to this new spirit of conciliation is the Thirty-Nine Articles of the Church of England to be found in *The Book of Common Prayer*. They were a genuine attempt to widen the original Six Articles and to permit men of varying doctrinal convictions conscientiously to come together.

There were of course many who could not accept a central position. On the one side were the various groups of uncompromising Protestants, chief of whom were the Puritans who strove to keep acts of worship completely pure from what they considered as popish taints. On the other side were the unyielding Roman Catholics, whose numbers gradually dwindled as more and more accepted the new Church of England.

Twelve years after Elizabeth's accession the Pope issued a Bull excommunicating her and a harsher attitude towards Roman Catholics was the inevitable result. Within a few years some were executed and to become a Roman Catholic or to convert others was now counted as treason.

It was during this reign that the office of Justice of the Peace became even more important than hitherto. In the COMMISSION OF A JUSTICE OF THE PEACE (1579) the justices were enjoined 'to keep the peace'; to maintain the ordinances regarding labourers, servants, innkeepers, beggars and others; and to uphold the statutes of former kings.

Elizabeth, conscious of her position as sovereign, sought to re-establish the ascendancy of the crown and to diminish the powers of parliament. She drew many matters into the sweep of her own prerogative. The Court of Star Chamber over which her Lord Chancellor presided, assisted by members of her Privy Council, was active. During the forty-four years of her reign there were only thirteen sessions of parliament, each lasting an average of only two or three months. She resisted encroachments by the Commons on what she deemed matters for the crown. She sent members of parliament to the Tower or imprisoned them.

But for all her high-handed actions there was no open conflict between crown and parliament. The glorious successes of her long reign—the defeat of the Armada, the triumphs of English arms, the founding of colonies in North America—generated an affectionate tolerance in her people. Many of the differences between the crown and the people, which her own attitudes had sharply defined, had to be solved after her death at the cost of bloodshed and of civil war. Her reign is marked by at least once document which ran counter to the advance of freedom. In 1566 her Court of Star Chamber issued the following ORDINANCE FOR THE CENSORSHIP OF THE PRESS :

(1566. PROTHERO, 168, 169.)

I.   That no person should print or bring into the realm printed any book against the force and meaning of any ordinance contained in any the statutes or laws of this realm or in any injunctions, letters patents or ordinances set forth by the Queen's authority.

II.   That whosoever should offend against the said ordinances should forfeit all such books, and from thenceforth should never exercise the feat of printing; and to sustain three months' imprisonment.

III.   That no person should sell, bind or sew any such

books, upon pain to forfeit all such books and for every book 20s.

IV. That all books so forfeited should be brought into Stationers' Hall, and all the books so to be forfeited to be destroyed or made waste paper.

V. That it should be lawful for the wardens of the [Stationers'] Company to make search in all workhouses, shops and other places of printers, booksellers and such as bring books into the realm; and all books to be found against the said ordinances to seise and carry to the Hall to the uses above said and to bring the persons offending before the Queen's Commissioners in causes ecclesiastical.

VI. Every stationer, printer, bookseller should enter into several recognisances of reasonable sums of money to her Majesty that he should truly observe all the said ordinances.

Upon the consideration before expressed and upon the motion of the Commissioners, we of the Privy Council have agreed this to be observed and kept. At the Star-Chamber the 29th of June 5, 1566.

Not only did the ordinance seek to reduce the liberty of the subject; it was a breach of the old custom of government by consent for there is no mention of the advice or consent of parliament. It is simply a ruling handed down from the crown itself.

The greatest document of Elizabeth's reign was the COMMISSION FOR THE FREEING OF VILLEINS, issued by her in 1574 to members of her council. Again, it is not a document of consent but an order given by the queen under her Great Seal. One writ appointed Sir William Cecil and Sir Walter Mildmay as Commissioners in the West Country to make all villeins free men:

Elizabeth, by the grace of God . . . to our right trusty and well-beloved counsellor Sir William Cecil and to our trusty and right well-beloved counsellor Sir Walter Mildmay greeting. Whereas divers and sundry of our poor faithful and loyal subjects, being born bond in blood and regardant to divers and sundry our manors and possessions within our realm of England, have made humble suit unto us to be manumised, enfranchised and made free, with their children and sequels.

100

We therefore do name and appoint you two our commissioners and do commit unto you full power to accept to be
manumised, enfranchised and made free, such and so many
of our bondmen and bondwomen in blood with all their children and sequels, their goods, lands, tenements and hereditaments as are now appertaining or regardant to any of our
manors, lands . . . within the said several counties of Cornwall, Devon, Somerset and Gloucester, as to you shall seem
meet, compounding with them for such reasonable fines or
sums of money for the manumission as you and they can
agree: the tenor of which said manumissions . . . shall be in
such order and form as is here in these presents contained.

'Elizabeth, by the grace of God . . . to all whom . . . greeting.
Since from the beginning God created all men free by nature,
while afterward the law of nations placed some under the
yoke of servitude, we believe it to be pious and acceptable to
God and in accordance with Christian charity that those in
villeinage to us, our heirs and successors, subject and bound
in servitude, should be wholly free.

'Know therefore that we, moved by piety have manumitted
and made free, and liberated from every yoke of servitude and
servile condition A. B. C. D. &c. and all and every their issue
thus begotten and to be begotten in the future and every one
of them. Also we give and concede to the aforesaid A. B. C. D.
&c. messuages, lands and also goods, chattels, and whatsoever is owing to them of which they are now seised and
possessed to have, to hold, and to enjoy forever without
rendering to us thenceforward account of any sort by reason
of servitude or servile condition saving to us nevertheless
our free-holds and the hereditaments of the customs, lands,
and tenements of which they are now seised by copy-hold, and
the services, dues . . . to be rendered and done for them, as
well as the dues and services to be rendered to us as supreme
lady of the fief for any free-hold lands . . . of which they are
now seised.'

And our further will and pleasure is that every such bill or
warrant so by you subscribed, shall be a sufficient and immediate warrant to the said lord chancellor for the making
and passing of every such manumission under our great seal
paying only for all manner of fee at the Great Seal 26s. 8d.

Witness ourself at Gorhambury. **Per ipsam reginam.**

So at last it had been formally stated that 'from the beginning God created all men free by nature.' The age-old system of bondage was ended and all Englishmen were now free, with access to and the protection of the law. The liberties which had been slowly won, sometimes for selfish motives by small privileged groups, were now to be inherited by all; and the establishment of true freedom throughout the realm was, however long it might take to achieve, finally assured.

Notes p 222

DOCUMENTS QUOTED:

1 Act of the Conditional Restraint of Annates—1532 [*23 Henry VIII, c. 20*]
2 Act in Restraint of Appeals—1533 [*24 Henry VIII. c. 12*]
3 Act of Supremacy—1534 [*26 Henry VIII. c. 1*]
4 The Six Articles Act—1539 [*31 Henry VIII. c. 14*]
5 Act of Supremacy—1559 [*1 Elizabeth I. c. 1*]
6 The Commission of a Justice of the Peace—1579
7 Ordinance of the Star Chamber for the Censorship of the Press—1566
8 Commission for the Freeing of Villeins—1574

CHAPTER VI

Stuarts and Commonwealth
(1603-1685)

IN 1502, Henry VII's daughter Margaret married King James IV of Scotland. Her son, James V, died in 1542, leaving a daughter, Mary, who was proclaimed Queen of Scots and whose story is well known. Through her mother, Princess Margaret of England, she was cousin to Edward VI, Mary and Elizabeth and—in the absence of any children of those three—was next heir to the English crown. But, being a Catholic, she represented a threat to Protestant England and was a natural focus for Catholic conspiracies. In 1587 she was executed. Mary's son, James VI of Scotland, thus became Elizabeth's heir and succeeded her in 1603 as James I of England. He was the great-great-grandson of the first Tudor, Henry VII, a collateral descendant of Henry VIII and cousin to the great Elizabeth. Unlike any earlier heir, he already had long experience in kingship, having been king in Scotland since he was one year old. He had a formidable reputation for erudition and was a writer of books.

In fact poor James, for all his erudition, was a stupid man. Dazzled by the splendour of his new kingdom, he over-rated his own importance and under-rated that of the English House of Commons. The Scottish parliament had acquired no such powers as its English counterpart and James had reigned as undisputed master of his Scottish realm. He saw no reason why as king of England he should reign differently.

The kingdom was his and the revenues thereof. Thanks to the acts of his predecessors, the church was his and the government thereof. His first parliament must have been a bewildering experience for him. First, there was a dispute over the re-election of the member for Buckinghamshire who, said James, was an outlaw and therefore could not sit. The Commons reminded him of their right to manage their own affairs and agreed to a new election only after James had conceded that right. James fervently believed, in his own words that 'Kings are

103

not only God's lieutenants on earth but even by God Himself they are called gods.' He commented impatiently upon the privileges of his new parliament. The Commons reacted with a statement defending their traditional rights. In this *Apology* the Commons rejected outright the idea that they derived their authority from the grace or favour of the king, stating that :

> Our privileges and our liberties are our right and due inheritance no less than our goods and land.

Then in 1605 came the famous Gunpowder Plot. A group of Catholics resolved to blow up king and parliament together, on 5 November, the date of the state opening. The plot was frustrated and echoes of the country's triumphant relief are to be heard to this day, on misty autumn evenings, in the sound of fireworks and the excited chatter of children.

A wiser man than James would have seized the occasion of his subjects' joy to advance his own popularity. But he continued as before, heedless alike of danger and opportunity.

In the very next year he raised customs duties without consulting parliament. A London merchant, John Bates, refused to pay and the Commons upheld him. But the king's Exchequer Court imprisoned him and James began to appear as a tyrant. Parliament met again in 1610 and an attempt was made to end the dispute by voting an annual income to the king in return for the latter's surrender of all feudal dues. This came to nothing and parliament was dissolved in 1611.

Still short of money, James called his second parliament in 1614, but dissolved it after two months of bickering. For the next seven years he ruled without parliament, raising money as best he might, by selling monopolies and titles for cash down. War and the need for more money forced James to summon another parliament in 1621. Forthwith the new House of Commons began to criticise the king, and particularly his plan to marry his son Prince Charles to a Spanish Catholic princess. James, who had called them merely to vote new taxes, resented this interference and said so. In reply the Commons drew up a document called the Protestation in which they restated their privileges and recalled their right to discuss, with full freedom of speech, any matters which concerned the state. Furious, James dismissed parliament and tore from their records the page containing the Protestation. He also imprisoned Sir Edward Coke, a former chief justice and a great enemy of tyrannous and arbitrary rule.

In 1625 James died. By his total misunderstanding of the subtle relationship in England between king and parliament, he had set Crown and Commons at loggerheads as never before, no longer partners but rivals. His folly and insensitivity had sown the dragon's teeth. It was left to his handsome and proud son, Charles, tragically to reap the harvest of armed conflict.

Charles I was the sad inheritor of many dreary legacies. The tide of England's greatness had woefully ebbed since the glorious days of Elizabeth. Parliament had been exasperated, its traditional loyalty to the crown stretched to breaking point by James's continuous flouting of its ancient rights. A combination of military defeat abroad and resentment against the crown at home had created an explosive situation.

Yet there were possibilities for good available to the new king. The English flag had been planted in America and he now had subjects dwelling across the wide Atlantic. English merchants were active in India and had set up forts and trading centres there. Britain was becoming a world power.

Three months after his accession Charles summoned his first parliament to obtain its assent to such taxes and duties as would enable him to continue the war which England was waging against Spain. The Commons insisted, before voting any money to the king, that he should redress their many grievances. Amongst other matters, suspicious because the king had married a Catholic princess, Henrietta Maria of France, they demanded sterner measures to be taken against the Catholics. Charles would have none of this and dismissed parliament.

For a while he obtained revenue by collecting customs duties without parliament's assent, despite the warning of the Bates case. In the following year he summoned his second parliament, which was as hostile as the first. The Commons impeached his friend Buckingham; and Charles, to save him, dissolved parliament once more.

The wars continued and Charles, in a desperate attempt to bypass parliament, raised money by forced loans. Those who refused to lend money were summarily imprisoned or compelled to contribute to the army's maintenance by having soldiers billeted upon them. Here were two fresh grievances: imprisonment without trial by jury, and the invasion of private houses by the king's soldiers.

Accordingly, when parliament met in 1628 it was in no mood to retreat from its earlier stand that the redress of grievances must precede consent to taxation. Sir Edward Coke, who had (as we have seen) felt the oppression of royal power under James I, was prominent in arranging that parliament's demand should go to the king. This took the

105

form of a petition humbly reminding Charles of those earlier documents, including the Great Charter, which had defined the rights of
the subject and which were as much a part of the king's inheritance
as his royal authority. The Petition of Right was drawn up by both
the Lords and the Commons and submitted to King Charles on
2 June:

THE PETITION OF RIGHT—1628

TO THE KING'S MOST EXCELLENT MAJESTY.

Humbly show unto our Sovereign Lord the King, the Lords
Spiritual and Temporal, and Commons in Parliament assembled, that whereas it is declared and enacted by a statute made
in the time of the reign of King Edward the First, commonly
called **Statutum de tallagio non concedendo**, that no tallage
or aid shall be laid or levied by the King or his heirs in this
realm, without the good will and assent of the Archbishops,
Bishops, Earls, Barons, Knights, Burgesses, and other the freemen of the commonalty of this realm: and by authority of Parliament holden in the five and twentieth year of the reign of
King Edward the Third, it is declared and enacted, that from
thenceforth no person shall be compelled to make any loans to
the King against his will, because such loans were against
reason and the franchise of the land; and by other laws of this
realm it is provided, that none should be charged by any
charge or imposition, called a Benevolence, nor by such like
charge: by which, the statutes before-mentioned, and other
the good laws and statutes of this realm, your subjects have
inherited this freedom, that they should not be compelled to
contribute to any tax, tallage, aid, or other like charge, not
set by common consent in Parliament:
  II. Yet nevertheless, of late divers commissions directed
to sundry Commissioners in several counties, with instructions,
have issued, by means whereof your people have been in
divers places assembled, and required to lend certain sums
of money unto your Majesty, and many of them upon their
refusal so to do, have had an oath administered unto them,
not warrantable by the laws or statutes of this realm, and have

been constrained to become bound to make appearance and give attendance before your Privy Council, and in other places, and others of them have been therefore imprisoned, confined, and sundry other ways molested and disquieted: and divers other charges have been laid and levied upon your people in several counties, by Lords Lieutenants, Deputy Lieutenants, Commissioners for Musters, Justices of Peace and others, by command or direction from your Majesty or your Privy Council, against the laws and free customs of this realm.

III.   And where also by the statute called, 'The Great Charter of the Liberties of England', it is declared and enacted that no freeman may be taken or imprisoned or be disseised of his freehold or liberties, or his free customs, or be outlawed or exiled, or in any manner destroyed, but by the lawful judgment of his peers, or by the law of the land:

IV.   And in the eight and twentieth year of the reign of King Edward the Third, it was declared and enacted by authority of Parliament, that no man of what estate or condition that he be, should be put out of his lands or tenements, nor taken, nor imprisoned, nor disherited, nor put to death, without being brought to answer by due process of law:

V.   Nevertheless, against the tenor of the said statutes, and other the good laws and statutes of your realm, to that end provided, divers of your subjects have of late been imprisoned without any cause showed, and when for their deliverance they were brought before your Justices, by your Majesty's writs of Habeas Corpus, there to undergo and receive as the Court should order, and their keepers commanded to certify the causes of their detainer; no cause was certified, but that they were detained by your Majesty's special command, signified by the Lords of your Privy Council, and yet were returned back to several prisons, without being charged with anything to which they might make answer according to the law.

VI.   And whereas of late great companies of soldiers and mariners have been dispersed into divers counties of the realm, and the inhabitants against their wills have been compelled to receive them into their houses, and there to suffer them to sojourn, against the laws and customs of this realm, and to the great grievance and vexation of the people.

VII.   And whereas also by authority of Parliament, in the

25th year of the reign of King Edward the Third, it is declared and enacted, that no man shall be forejudged of life or limb against the form of the Great Charter, and the law of the land; and by the said Great Charter and other the laws and statutes of this your realm, no man ought to be adjudged to death, but by the laws established in this your realm, either by the customs of the same realm or by Acts of Parliament: and whereas no offender of what kind soever is exempted from the proceedings to be used, and punishments to be inflicted by the laws and statutes of this your realm; nevertheless of late divers commissions under your Majesty's Great Seal have issued forth, by which certain persons have been assigned and appointed Commissioners with power and authority to proceed within the land, according to the justice of martial law against such soldiers and mariners, or other dissolute persons joining with them, as should commit any murder, robbery, felony, mutiny, or other outrage or misdemeanour whatsoever, and by such summary course and order, as is agreeable to martial law, and is used in armies in time of war, to proceed to the trial and condemnation of such offenders, and them to cause to be executed and put to death, according to the law martial:

VIII. By pretext whereof, some of your Majesty's subjects have been by some of the said Commissioners put to death when and where, if by the laws and statutes of the land they had deserved death, by the same laws and statutes also they might, and by no other ought to have been, adjudged and executed:

IX. And also sundry grievous offenders by colour thereof, claiming an exemption, have escaped the punishments due to them by the laws and statutes of this your realm, by reason that divers of your officers and ministers of justice have unjustly refused, or forborne to proceed against such offenders according to the same laws and statutes, upon pretence that the said offenders were punishable only by martial law, and by authority of such commissions as aforesaid; which commissions, and all other of like nature, are wholly and directly contrary to the said laws and statutes of this your realm.

X. They do therefore humbly pray your Most Excellent Majesty, that no man hereafter be compelled to make or yield any gift, loan, benevolence, tax, or such like charge, without common consent by Act of Parliament; and that none be called to make answer, or take such oath, or to give attendance, or be confined, or otherwise molested or disquieted concerning the same, or for refusal thereof; and that no freeman, in any such manner as is before-mentioned, be imprisoned or detained; and that your Majesty will be pleased to remove the said soldiers and mariners, and that your people may not be so burdened in time to come; and that the aforesaid commissions for proceeding by martial law, may be revoked and annulled; and that hereafter no commissions of like nature may issue forth to any person or persons whatsoever, to be executed as aforesaid, lest by colour of them any of your Majesty's subjects be destroyed or put to death, contrary to the laws and franchise of the land.

XI. All of which they most humbly pray of your Most Excellent Majesty, as their rights and liberties according to the laws and statutes of this realm: and that your Majesty would also vouchsafe to declare that the awards, doings, and proceedings to the prejudice of your people, in any of the premises, shall not be drawn hereafter into consequence or example: and that your Majesty would be also graciously pleased, for the further comfort and safety of your people, to declare your royal will and pleasure, that in the things aforesaid all your officers and ministers shall serve you, according to the laws and statutes of this realm, as they tender the honour of your Majesty, and the prosperity of this kingdom.

Which Petition being read the 2nd of June 1628, the King's answer was thus delivered unto it:

The King willeth that right be done according to the laws and customs of the realm; and that the statutes be put in due execution, that his subjects may have no cause to complain of any wrong or oppressions, contrary to their just rights and liberties, to the preservation whereof he holds himself as well obliged as of his prerogative.

On June 7 the answer was given in the accustomed form, **Soit droit fait comme il est désiré.**

The document, though lengthy, was simple. First, the statute of

Edward III was cited to show that no man could be compelled to loan money to the king, while Clause II recalled that many had been so compelled by the king's officers. Clause III recalled the Great Charter, still vividly in men's minds after four centuries, and sought ratification of that part of it whereby no free man (and since the Statute of Elizabeth I this now meant no Englishman whatsoever) could be imprisoned except by process of law.

Clause V showed that the king's officers, and indeed the king himself, had brushed aside writs of *Habeas Corpus*. These writs, issued by the king at the plea of men illegally imprisoned, demanded that such prisoners should be brought before a justice of the peace for lawful trial. Under Charles it had been customary for his magistrates simply to report that these men were detained by the king's command and so to hustle them unceremoniously back to prison.

Clause VI, VII and VIII dealt with the billeting of soldiers and the use made by the king's commissioner of martial law to execute civilians without trial.

For all the humility of the wording, Charles was being clearly warned that he must govern within the law and in accordance with the solemn undertakings given by his predecessors. He gave a conciliatory answer, promising 'that the statutes be put in due execution, that his subjects may have no cause to complain of any wrong or oppressions, contrary to their rights and liberties . . .' So the Petition of Right, by receiving the royal assent, became law and parliament was quick to exploit its advantage.

Less than three weeks later the Commons submitted a Remonstrance to the king on the subject of tonnage and poundage, the duties imposed upon trade which formed a large part of the royal revenues. It opened with the usual expression of loyalty:

THE REMONSTRANCE AGAINST TONNAGE

AND POUNDAGE—1628

Most Gracious Sovereign, your Majesty's most loyal and dutiful subjects, the Commons in this present Parliament assembled, being in nothing more careful than of the honour and prosperity of your Majesty, and the kingdom, which they know do much depend upon that happy union and relation betwixt your Majesty and your people, do with much sorrow apprehend, that by reason of the incertainty of their continuance together, the unexpected interruptions which have been cast upon them, and the shortness of time in which your Majesty hath determined to end this Session, they cannot bring to maturity and perfection divers businesses of weight, which they have taken into their consideration and resolution, as most important for the common good . . .

These protestations were a prelude to an even sterner statement than the Petition of Right. In the Remonstrance the Commons recalled that the king had already ordered the dissolution of parliament and that accordingly they had no time to pass a Bill. They warned him that it would be more 'prejudicial to the right of the subject if your Majesty should continue to receive [tonnage and poundage] without authority of law, after the determination of a Session, than if there had been a recess by adjournment only.' They were questioning his wisdom in dissolving parliament and almost his right to do so, thus directly challenging the royal power. The Remonstrance reiterated that there should be no taxes on exports or imports 'without common consent by Act of Parliament, 'which is the right and inheritance of your subjects.' Indeed no taxes or subsidies could be claimed by the crown as of right, but all came 'from the free gift of the subjects.' Earlier kings and queens had been voted such monies for life 'by the free love and good will of the subjects'. Charles was reminded of his father's offer never to lay any other impositions without consent. Then, after further protestations of loyalty, the Commons said bluntly :

Nevertheless, your loyal Commons in this Parliament, out of their especial zeal to your service, and especial regard of your pressing occasions, have taken into their consideration, so to frame a grant of subsidy of Tonnage or Poundage to your Majesty, that both you might have been the better enabled for the defence of your realm, and your subjects, by being secure from all undue charges, be the more encouraged cheerfully to proceed in their course of trade; by the increase whereof your Majesty's profit, and likewise the strength of the kingdom would be very much augmented.

III.   But not now being able to accomplish this their desire

111

there is no course left unto them, without manifest breach of their duty, both to your Majesty and their country, save only to make this humble declaration, 'That the receiving of Tonnage and Poundage, and other impositions not granted by Parliament, is a breach of the fundamental liberties of this kingdom, and contrary to your Majesty's royal answer to the said Petition of Right'. And therefore they do must humbly beseech your Majesty to forbear any further receiving of the same, and not to take it in ill part from those of your Majesty's loving subjects, who shall refuse to make payment of any such charges, without warrant of law demanded.

The king furiously ignored the protest against the dissolution and, to show who was master, dissolved parliament a few hours earlier than he had planned! For eleven years he ruled without parliament and governed largely through the Archbishop of Canterbury, William Laud. His other chief instrument was Thomas Wentworth, former member of the House of Commons, whom he created Earl of Strafford.

Charles had two problems—the raising of revenue and the punishment of those who disobeyed him. The jury system made the latter difficult. Where that system prevails the sad and forgotten figure of the political prisoner is rare. Twelve ordinary men, conscious of their rights and duties, could prevent the courts from becoming mere places of punishment. So the king and his ministers made use of the Royal Courts, where no jury sat and where their own decisions went unchallenged. In the Court of Star Chamber, the High Commission Court and the Exchequer Court, men were tried not for breaking the law, but for disobeying the king and the king's men.

When Laud used these courts to suppress the Puritans, many of them left for America, preferring exile to the loss of their ancient liberties. In a far land their descendants a century later were to resume the same struggle against another king of England who, like the Stuarts, had forgotten the old lessons.

To solve the problem of revenue, King Charles turned to an ancient tax called Ship Money. He may have believed that this tax would cause less resentment than any other. Armed ships on blue water, swaying masts and a salt wind, are part of England's heritage. One of the criticisms levelled against Charles's father was that he had woefully neglected the navy. Charles was resolved to refurbish England's proudest weapon and must have felt that a tax directed to that end would surely be acceptable.

In 1634 Charles levied the tax in a writ over the Great Seal, witnessed by himself. Pirates were abroad, robbing not only 'our subjects but also the subjects of our friends in the sea, which hath been accustomed anciently to be defended by the English nation . . .' (The *pax Brittanica* was no nineteenth-century invention.) The writ stressed the king's desire 'by the help of God chiefly to provide for the defence of the kingdom . . .' It contained a trumpet blast of pride, to challenge all foreigners and to delight all Englishmen : 'forasmuch as we and our progenitors, kings of England, have been always heretofore masters of the aforesaid sea . . .' Fine words! But the vital words (stating that parliament had consented) were missing.

Thirty years earlier, when John Bates had refused to pay the customs duties which James I had imposed without parliament's consent, he had been taken before the Court of Exchequer. The judges had ruled in James's favour. One had said 'the revenue of the crown is the very essential part of the crown, and he who rendeth that from the king pulleth also his crown from his head.' (James had seen the judgement as a triumph, but these were ominous words.) Another, Chief Baron Fleming, had distinguished between common law which 'cannot be changed without Parliament' on the one hand, and 'rules of policy' on the other. In the latter case, the king's power was 'absolute'.

Now John Hampden, a well-to-do squire (to whom the ship-money of 20 shillings was nothing) refused to pay and was taken before the same court as Bates. Five of the judges ruled in his favour, seven for the king. The majority was slender and a wiser man than Charles might have heeded the warning.

Archbishop Laud had attempted to impose the English prayer book upon Scotland. Great numbers of Scots signed a solemn covenant to defend their religion. War broke out and although a treaty was signed, in 1640 Charles thought it prudent to call parliament. The new parliament had forgotten nothing and Charles remembered nothing. Again they demanded a redress of all their grievances, and again Charles dissolved parliament.

In the summer the Scots invaded England and occupied much of the North. Charles summoned a fresh parliament which lost no time in establishing its ascendancy over the king. Strafford and Laud were both imprisoned and later executed. Members of Parliament who had been imprisoned by the Royal Courts were released.

There followed a series of Acts defining and extending the powers of parliament, which Charles was compelled to accept. First in 1641 parliament passed an ACT FOR A PARLIAMENT EVERY THREE YEARS, whether the king would or no; the king was not again to rule without regular consultations with his subjects. A further Act was passed ordering that parliament could be dissolved only by a vote of parliament itself, and that 'whatever was done or to be done for the adjournment, proroguing, or dissolving of this present Parliament, contrary to this Act, shall be utterly void and of none effect.' No more was the king to go down to Westminster and by mere command dissolve parliament. To Charles this was a direct usurpation of the sovereign powers of the monarch, who summoned parliament and who alone could dissolve it. (This is the doctrine still followed today. A prime minister must seek a dissolution from his sovereign. He cannot command it, nor can parliament vote in the matter.)

Having thus taken from the king his hitherto legal right to govern without a parliament, the next step was to prevent him from trying men in his own Royal Courts. The Court of Star Chamber was abolished and its authority, in the words of the Act, 'clearly and absolutely dissolved, taken away and determined.' Its abolition was based on the Great Charter and the preamble to the Act reads :

ACT FOR THE ABOLITION OF THE COURT OF STAR CHAMBER—1641

Whereas by the Great Charter many times confirmed in parliament, it is enacted that no freeman shall be taken or imprisoned, or disseised of his freehold or liberties or free customs, or be outlawed or exiled or otherwise destroyed, and that the king will not pass upon him or condemn him but by lawful judgment of his peers or by the law of the land; and by another statute made in the fifth year of the reign of King Edward the Third, it is enacted that no man shall be attached by any accusation nor forejudged of life or limb, nor his lands, tenements, goods nor chattels seised into the King's hands against the form of the Great Charter and the law of the land; and by another statute made in the five-and-twentieth year of the reign of the same King Edward the Third, it is accorded, assented and established, that none shall be taken by petition or suggestion made to the King or to his Council, unless it be by indictment or presentment of good and lawful people of the same neighbourhood where such deeds be done, in due manner or by process made by writ original at the common law, and that none be put out of his franchise or freehold unless he be duly brought in to answer and fore-judged of the same by the course of the law, and if anything be done against the same, it shall be redressed and holden for none; and by another statute made in the eight-and-twentieth year of the reign of the same King Edward the Third, it is amongst other things enacted, that no man of what estate or condition soever he be shall be put out of his lands or tene-ments, nor taken nor imprisoned nor disinherited without being brought in to answer by due process of law; and by another statute made in the two-and-fortieth year of the reign of the said King Edward the Third, it is enacted, that no man be put to answer without presentment before Justices or matter of record, or by due process and writ original accord-ing to the old law of the land, and if anything be done to the contrary, it shall be void in law and holden for error . . .

The fifth clause restated the old doctrine that it was the independent courts, and not the king or his officers, who should have jurisdiction over property :

V. Be it likewise declared and enacted by authority of this present Parliament, that neither His Majesty nor his Privy Council have or ought to have any jurisdiction, power or authority by English bill, petition, articles, libel, or any other arbitrary way whatsoever, to examine or draw into question, determine or dispose of the lands, tenements, hereditaments, goods or chattels of any the subjects of this kingdom, but that the same ought to be tried and determined in the ordinary Courts of Justice and by the ordinary course of the law.

Later, all the other Royal Courts were abolished so that the jury system was firmly entrenched, and arbitrary trial by the king's officers finally outlawed. Charles himself, when the hour of his doom struck, was denied the right enjoyed by all other Englishmen (but by defini-tion impossible in the case of a king) of trial by his peers.

Then, in December 1641 the House of Commons submitted its Grand Remonstrance. As always, the document began with protestations of loyalty and humility:

THE GRAND REMONSTRANCE—1641

Most Gracious Sovereign,

Your Majesty's most humble and faithful subjects the Commons in this present Parliament assembled, do with much thankfulness and joy acknowledge the great mercy and favour of God, in giving your Majesty a safe and peaceable return out of Scotland into your kingdom of England, where the pressing dangers and distempers of the State have caused us with much earnestness to desire the comfort of your gracious presence, and likewise the unity and justice of your royal authority, to give more life and power to the dutiful and loyal counsels and endeavours of your Parliament, for the prevention of that eminent ruin and destruction wherein your kingdoms of England and Scotland are threatened. The duty which we owe to your Majesty and our country, cannot but make us very sensible and apprehensive, that the multiplicity, sharpness and malignity of those evils under which we have now many years suffered, are fomented and cherished by a corrupt and ill-affected party, who amongst other their mischievous devices for the alteration of religion and government, have sought by many false scandals and imputations, cunningly insinuated and dispersed amongst the people, to blemish and disgrace our proceedings in this Parliament, and to get themselves a party and faction amongst your subjects, for the better strengthening themselves in their wicked courses, and hindering those provisions and remedies which might, by the wisdom of your Majesty and counsel of your Parliament, be opposed against them.

For preventing whereof, and the better information of your Majesty, your Peers and all other your loyal subjects, we have been necessitated to make a declaration of the state of the kingdom, both before and since the assembly of this Parliament, unto this time, which we do humbly present to your Majesty, without the least intention to lay any blemish upon

your royal person, but only to represent how your royal
authority and trust have been abused, to the great prejudice
and danger of your Majesty, and of all your good subjects . . .

Though the demands were preceded by the sentence 'We, your most
humble and obedient subjects, do with all faithfulness and humility
beseech your Majesty . . .', the demands themselves were uncompromising. The king was to deprive the bishops of their votes in parliament;
to remove from his council those men to whom parliament objected;
and 'to employ such counsellors; ambassadors and other ministers, in
managing his business at home and abroad, as the Parliament may have
cause to confide in.' There followed the threat that unless this were
done 'we cannot give His Majesty such supplies for support of his own
estate . . .'

The Remonstrance was passed by the House of Commons with a
majority of only nine votes. The majority was narrow enough, and the
speeches on the king's side were staunch enough, to encourage Charles
to believe that all was not lost. In 1642 he felt sufficiently strong to
attempt the arrest of five members of the House of Commons for
treason. He personally went into the House to effect the arrest, but
the five members had already gone by boat down the Thames to the
City of London. Since then, no sovereign has ever been permitted to
enter the House.

For a short while Charles tried a policy of conciliation. He abolished
the rights of bishops to sit in the House of Lords, a right which went
back over a thousand years and appointed as councillors two men pleas-
ing to the Commons.

But this was in vain; and in 1642 the House of Commons went beyond the mere defence of ancient rights and sought new powers, setting
their authority above the king's. They demanded not only that parliament was to approve the appointment of all privy councillors, ministers
and judges, but that it should also control the education and marriages
of the king's children.

War was inevitable. Then in December 1648 troops under Colonel
Pride arrested nearly fifty members of the Commons and ejected a hundred more. The rump that was left, with unconscious irony declared
that the Commons 'being chosen by and representing the people, have
the supreme power in this nation.' (The extinction of democracy by
colonels is not an exclusively modern phenomenon.) It was this rump
too, representing less than half the nation, which tried the king,

sentenced him to death, and caused him to be beheaded on a winter's morning in December of 1649. He died bravely, protesting to the last the beliefs which he so sincerely held and which were the curse of his dynasty. 'For the people . . . their liberty and freedom consists in having government . . . A subject and a sovereign are clear different things.'

For eleven years England tried to live without a king. The experiment failed; and, by a tragic irony, Cromwell was no more successful in his dealings with parliament than Charles had been. Four years after achieving power he dropped all pretence of governing by consultation. He led a troop of armed soldiers into the House of Commons and forcibly put an end to parliament. He was declared Lord Protector by the army and, after one more abortive attempt to govern with parliament, placed England under military rule. King Charles had said 'I desire [the people's] liberty and freedom as much as any man whatsoever, but I must tell you, their liberty and freedom consists in having government . . .' Cromwell is reported as saying 'I am as much for government by consent as any man; but where shall we find that consent?' The ghost of Charles may have smiled sadly in whatever place is reserved for the shades of bewildered and obstinate men.

When Cromwell died in 1658 it was clear that the experiment of an England without a king had failed. Although provision had been made for the election of a new Lord Protector, England applied the familiar principle of hereditary succession, and Cromwell's son Richard was appointed.

Richard carried on ineffectively for a year or so and then in 1660 the dead king's son, who had been living in poverty abroad, was recalled by parliament and the army as King Charles II.

The restoration of the monarchy was greeted with relief and gaiety. The sombre rules of the major-generals were sent spinning into oblivion and all England rejoiced. The new reign opened not merely with delight but in circumstances that went far to resolve the tensions between parliament and the crown—tensions which had grown so disastrously in the reigns of James I and Charles I.

It was parliament which had ordered General Monk to bring back the exiled prince and Charles II knew that he owed his position to the Commons. He knew too that after the first outburst of rejoicing, when the clangour of the bells was stilled and the ashes of the bonfires cold, the people of England would be watching their new king critically. They would not tolerate any infringement of the rights they had so bitterly defended against his father.

Fortunately, the new king was shrewd and the parliament which recalled him was moderate. There were both roundheads and cavaliers among its members and it set about its tasks in a spirit of compromise. Most of the Acts of the Cromwellian period were rescinded, but those which abolished the Court of Star Chamber and the other Royal Courts remained. There was to be no taxation save by the consent of parliament, and the vexed question of Ship Money was finally settled. Besides Ship Money, there were also the feudal dues which the king might have used to raise cash without parliamentary consent—the 'aids' when his daughters were married, or when his sons were made knights and other dues going back over five hundred years to the days of the Normans. All these were abolished by parliament in December 1660, seven months after the king's return. Charles was thus deprived of the courts he might have used for the arbitrary punishment of obdurate subjects, and of the means of raising money without parliament's consent.

We have seen how Charles I had brushed aside writs of *Habeas Corpus*. Parliament was resolved that such writs which had once been safeguards of the subject's liberties, should not again be ignored. If a man had been imprisoned by some local lord, his friends could seek the king's help and the king (or one of his officers) would issue a writ over the Great Seal commanding the man who held the prisoner to 'have the body' (*habeas corpus*) of the prisoner brought before a magistrate for proper trial. Charles I had shown that with a tyrannous king, such writs might be of no avail. Parliament in 1679, resolved to defend the process against future misuse, and passed the Habeas Corpus Act, of which the following are the main provisions :

HABEAS CORPUS ACT—1679

Whereas great delays have been used by sheriffs, gaolers and other officers, to whose custody any of the king's subjects have been committed for criminal or supposed criminal matters, in making returns of writs of Habeas Corpus to them directed by standing out an Alias and Pluries Habeas Corpus and sometimes more, and by other shifts to avoid their yielding obedience to such writs, contrary to their duty and the known laws of the land, whereby many of the king's subjects have been and hereafter may be long detained in prison in such cases where by law they are bailable, to their great charge and vexation.

II.   For the prevention whereof and the more speedy relief of all persons imprisoned for any such criminal or supposed criminal matters; be it enacted by the king's most excellent Majesty, by and with the advice and consent of the lords spiritual and temporal and commons in this present parliament assembled, and by the authority thereof, that whensoever any person or persons shall bring any habeas corpus directed unto any sheriff or sheriffs, gaoler, minister or other person what-soever for any person in his or their custody, and the said writ shall be served upon the said officer or left at the gaol or prison with any of the under officers, under keepers or deputy of the said officers or keepers, that the said officer or officers, his or their under officers, under keepers or deputies shall within three days after service thereof as aforesaid (unless the commitment aforesaid were for treason or felony, plainly and specially expressed in the warrant of commitment) upon payment or tender of the charges of bringing the said prisoner, to be ascertained by the judge or court that awarded the same and endorsed upon the said writ, not exceeding twelve pence per mile, and upon security given by his own bond to pay the charges of carrying back the prisoner, if he shall be remanded by the court or judge to which he shall be brought according to the true intent of this present act, and that he will not make any escape by the way, make return of such writ; and bring or cause to be brought the body of the party so committed or restrained unto or before the lord chancellor, or lord keeper of the great seal of England, for the time being, or the judges or barons of the said court from whence the said writ shall issue, or unto and before such other person or persons before whom the said writ is made returnable, according to the command thereof; and shall then likewise certify the true causes of his detainer or imprisonment; unless the commitment of the said party be in any place beyond the distance of twenty miles from the place or places where such court or person is or shall be residing, and if beyond the distance of twenty miles and not above one hundred miles then within the space of ten days after such delivery afore-said, and not longer.

III.   And to the intent that no sheriff, gaoler or other

officer may pretend ignorance of the import of any such writ; be it enacted by the authority aforesaid, that all such writs shall be marked in this manner, Per statutum tricesimo primo Caroli Secundi regis, and shall be signed by the person that awards the same; and if any person or persons shall be or stand committed or detained as aforesaid, for any crime, unless for treason or felony plainly expressed in the warrant of commitment, in the vacation time, and out of term, it shall and may be lawful to and for the person or persons so committed or detained (other than persons convict or in execution by legal process) or any one on his or their behalf to appeal or complain to the lord chancellor or lord keeper or any one of His Majesty's justices, either of the one bench or of the other, or the barons of the exchequer of the degree of the coif[20]; and the said lord chancellor, lord keeper, justices or barons or any of them, upon view of the copy or copies of the warrant or warrants of commitment and detainer, or otherwise upon oath made that such copy or copies were denied to be given by such person or persons in whose custody the prisoner or prisoners is or are detained, are hereby authorised and required, upon request made in writing by such person or persons or any on his, her or their behalf, attested and subscribed by two witnesses who were present at the delivery of the same, to award and grant an habeas corpus, under the seal of such court whereof he shall then be one of the judges, to be directed to the officer or officers in whose custody the party so committed or detained shall be, returnable immediate before the said lord chancellor or lord keeper, or such justice, baron or any other justice or baron of the degree of the coif of any of the said courts; and upon service thereof as aforesaid, the officer or officers, his or their under officer or under officers, under keeper or under keepers, or deputy, in whose custody the party is so committed or detained, shall within the times respectively before limited bring such prisoner or prisoners before the said lord chancellor or lord keeper or such justices, barons or one of them, before whom the said writ is made returnable, and in case of his absence before any other of them, with the return of such writ and the true causes of the commitment and detainer; and thereupon within two days after the party shall be brought before them, the said lord chancellor or lord keeper, or such

121

justice or baron before whom the prisoner shall be brought as aforesaid, shall discharge the said prisoner from his imprisonment, taking his or their recognisance with one or more surety or sureties in any sum according to their discretions, having regard to the quality of the prisoner and nature of the offence, for his or their appearance in the court of king's bench the term following or at the next assizes, sessions or general gaol-delivery of and for such county, city or place where the commitment was, or where the offence was committed, or in such other court where the said offence is properly cognisable, as the case shall require, and then shall certify the said writ with the return thereof and the said recognisance or recognisances into the said court where such appearance is to be made; unless it shall appear unto the said lord chancellor or lord keeper, or justice or justices, or baron or barons, that the party so committed is detained upon a legal process, order or warrant out of some court that hath jurisdiction of criminal matters, or by some warrant signed and sealed with the hand and seal of any of the said justices or barons, or some justice or justices of the peace, for such matters or offences for the which by the law the prisoner is not bailable.

IV.   Provided always, and be it enacted, that if any person shall have wilfully neglected by the space of two whole terms after his imprisonment to pray a habeas corpus for his enlargement, such person so wilfully neglecting shall not have any habeas corpus to be granted in vacation time in pursuance of this act.

V.   And be it further enacted by the authority aforesaid, that if any officer or officers, his or their under-officer or under-officers, under-keeper or under-keepers, or deputy, shall neglect or refuse to make the returns aforesaid, or to bring the body or bodies of the prisoner or prisoners according to the command of the said writ, within the respective times aforesaid, or upon demand made by the prisoner or person in his behalf shall refuse to deliver, or within the space of six hours after demand shall not deliver, to the person so demanding, a true copy of the warrant or warrants of commitment and detainer of such prisoner, which he and they are hereby required to deliver accordingly; all and every the head gaolers and keepers of such prisons, and such other person in whose custody the prisoner shall be detained, shall for the first offence forfeit to the prisoner or party grieved the sum of one hundred pounds; and for the second offence the sum of two hundred pounds and shall and is hereby made incapable to hold or execute his said office; the said penalties to be recovered by the prisoner or party grieved, his executors or administrators, against such offender, his executors or administrators, by any action of debt, suit, bill, plaint or information, in any of the king's courts at Westminster, wherein no essoin[21], protection, privilege, injunction wager of laws or stay of prosecution by Non vult ulterious[22] prosequi or otherwise shall be admitted or allowed, or any more than one imparlance; and any recovery or judgment at the suit of any party grieved shall be a sufficient conviction for the first offence; and any after recovery or judgment at the suit of a party grieved for any offence after the first judgment shall be a sufficient conviction to bring the officers or person within the said penalty for the second offence.

VI. And for the prevention of unjust vexation by re-iterated commitments for the same offence; be it enacted by the authority aforesaid, that no person or persons, which shall be delivered or set at large upon any habeas corpus, shall at any time hereafter be again imprisoned or committed for the same offence by any person or persons whatsoever, other than by the legal order and process of such court wherein he or they shall be bound by recognisance to appear or other court having jurisdiction of the cause; and if any other person or persons shall knowingly contrary to this act recommit or imprison or knowingly procure or cause to be recommitted or imprisoned for the same offence or pretended offence any person or persons delivered or set at large as aforesaid, or be knowingly aiding or assisting therein, then he or they shall forfeit to the prisoner or party grieved the sum of five hundred pounds, any colourable pretence or variation in the warrant or warrants or commitment notwithstanding, to be recovered as aforesaid.

VII. Provided always, and be it further enacted, that if any person or persons shall be committed for high treason or felony, plainly and specially expressed in the warrant of commitment, upon his prayer or petition in open court the first week of the term or first day of the sessions of oyer and terminer[23] or general gaol delivery to be brought to his trial, shall not be indicted sometime in the next term, sessions of oyer and terminer or general gaol delivery after such commitment; it shall and may be lawful to and for the judges of the court of king's bench and justices of oyer and terminer or general gaol delivery and they are hereby required, upon motion to them made in open court the last day of the term, sessions or gaol delivery, either by the prisoner or any one in his behalf, to set at liberty the prisoner upon bail, unless it appear to the judges and justices upon oath made, that the witnesses for the king could not be produced the same term, sessions or general goal delivery; and if any person or persons, committed as aforesaid, upon his prayer or petition in open court the first week of the term or first day of the sessions of oyer and terminer or general goal delivery to be brought to his trial, shall not be indicted and tried the second term, sessions of oyer and terminer or general gaol delivery after his commitment, or upon his trial shall be acquitted, he shall be discharged from his imprisonment.

VIII.　Provided always, that nothing in this act shall extend to discharge out of prison any person charged in debt or other action or with process in any civil cause, but that after he shall be discharged of his imprisonment for such his criminal offence, he shall be kept in custody according to law for such other suit.

IX.　Provided always, and be it enacted by the authority aforesaid, that if any person or persons, subjects of this realm, shall be committed to any prison or in custody of any officer or officers whatsoever for any criminal or supposed criminal matter, that the said person shall not be removed from the said prison and custody into the custody of any other officer or officers; unless it be by habeas corpus or some other legal writ, or where the prisoner is delivered to the constable or other inferior officer to carry such prisoner to some common gaol, or where any person is sent by order of any judge of assize or justice of the peace to any common work-house or house of correction, or where the prisoner is removed from one prison or place to another within the same county, in order to his or her trial or discharge in due course of law, or in case of sudden fire or infection or other necessity; and if any person or persons shall after such commitment aforesaid make out and sign or countersign any warrant or warrants for such removal aforesaid, contrary to this act, as well he that makes or signs or countersigns such warrant or warrants as the officer or officers that obey or execute the same shall suffer and incur the pains and forfeitures in this act beforementioned, both for the first and second offence respectively, to be recovered in manner aforesaid by the party grieved.

X.   Provided also, and be it further enacted by the authority aforesaid, that it shall and may be lawful to and for any prisoner and prisoners as aforesaid to move and obtain his or their habeas corpus as well out of the high court of chancery or court of exchequer as out of the court of king's bench or common pleas or either of them; and if the said lord chancellor or lord keeper, or any judge or judges, baron or barons for the time being of the degree of the coif, of any of the courts aforesaid, in the vacation time upon view of the copy or copies of the warrant or warrants of commitment or detainer, or upon oath made that such copy or copies were denied as aforesaid, shall deny any writ of habeas corpus by this act required to be granted being moved for as aforesaid, they shall severally forfeit to the prisoner or party grieved the sum of five hundred pounds, to be recovered in manner aforesaid.

XI.   And be it enacted and declared by the authority aforesaid, that an habeas corpus according to the true intent and meaning of this act may be directed and run into any county palatine, the Cinque ports, or other privileged places within the kingdom of England, dominion of Wales or town of Berwick upon Tweed, and the islands of Jersey or Guernsey, any law or usage to the contrary notwithstanding.

XII.   And for preventing illegal imprisonments in prisons beyond the seas; be it further enacted by the authority aforesaid, that no subject of this realm that now is or hereafter shall be an inhabitant or resident of this kingdom of England, dominion of Wales or town of Berwick upon Tweed shall or may be sent prisoner into Scotland, Ireland, Jersey, Guernsey, Tangier or into any parts, garrisons, islands or places beyond the seas, which are or at any time hereafter shall be within or without the dominions of his majesty, his heirs or successors; and that every such imprisonment is hereby enacted and

125

adjudged to be illegal; and that if any of the said subjects now is or hereafter shall be so imprisoned every such person and persons so imprisoned shall and may for every such imprisonment maintain by virtue of this act an action or actions of false imprisonment in any of his majesty's courts of record against the person or persons by whom he or she shall be so committed, detained, imprisoned, sent prisoner or transported, contrary to the true meaning of this act, and against all or any person or persons that shall frame, contrive, write, seal or countersign any warrant or writing for such commitment, detainer, imprisonment or transportation, or shall be advising, aiding or assisting in the same or any of them; and the plaintiff in every such action shall have judgment to recover his treble costs, besides damages, which damages so to be given shall not be less than five hundred pounds; in which action no delay, stay or stop of proceeding by rule, order or command, nor no injunction, protection or privilege whatsoever, nor any more than one imparlance, shall be allowed, excepting such rule of the court wherein the action shall depend, made in open court, as shall be thought in justice necessary, for special cause to be expressed in the said rule; and the person or persons who shall knowingly frame, contrive, write, seal or countersign any warrant for such commitment, detainer or transportation, or shall so commit, detain, imprison or transport any person or persons, contrary to this act, or be any ways advising, aiding or assisting therein, being lawfully convicted thereof, shall be disabled from thenceforth to bear any office of trust or profit within the said realm of England, dominion of Wales or town of Berwick upon Tweed, or any of the islands, territories or dominions thereunto belonging; and shall incur and sustain the pains, penalties and forfeitures limited, ordained and provided in and by the statute of provision and præmunire, made in the sixteenth year of King Richard the Second; and be incapable of any pardon from the king, his heirs or successors, of the said forfeitures, losses or disabilities, or any of them.

XIII. Provided always, that nothing in this act shall extend to give benefit to any person who shall by contract in writing agree with any merchant or owner of any plantation, or other person whatsoever, to be transported to any parts beyond seas, and receive earnest upon such agreement, although that afterwards such person shall renounce such contract.

XIV.   Provided always, and be it enacted, that if any person or persons lawfully convicted of any felony shall in open court pray to be transported beyond the seas, and the court shall think fit to leave him or them in prison for that purpose, such person or persons may be transported into any parts beyond the seas, this act or anything therein contained to the contrary notwithstanding.

XV.   Provided also, and be it enacted, that nothing herein contained shall be deemed, construed or taken to extend to the imprisonment of any person before the first day of June one thousand six hundred seventy and nine, or to anything advised, procured or otherwise done relating to such imprisonment, anything herein contained to the contrary notwithstanding.

XVI.   Provided also, that if any person or persons at any time resident in this realm shall have committed any capital offence in Scotland or Ireland or any of the islands or foreign plantations of the king, his heirs or successors, where he or she ought to be tried for such offence, such person or persons may be sent to such place there to receive such trial in such manner as the same might have been used before the making of this act, anything herein contained to the contrary notwithstanding.

XVII.   Provided also, and be it enacted, that no person or persons shall be sued, impleaded, molested or troubled for any offence against this act, unless the party offending be sued or impleaded for the same within two years at the most after such time wherein the offence shall be committed, in case the party grieved shall not be then in prison; and if he shall be in prison, then within the space of two years after the decease of the person imprisoned, or his or her delivery out of prison, which shall first happen.

XVIII.   And to the intent no person may avoid his trial at the assizes or general gaol delivery by procuring his removal before the assizes, at such time as he cannot be brought back to receive his trial there; be it enacted, that after the assizes proclaimed for that county where the prisoner is detained, no person shall be removed from the common gaol upon any habeas corpus granted in pursuance of this act, but upon any such habeas corpus shall be brought before the judge of assize in open court, who is thereupon to do what to justice shall appertain.

XIX. Provided nevertheless, that after the assizes are ended any person or persons detained may have his or her habeas corpus according to the direction and intention of this act.

XX. And be it also enacted by the authority aforesaid, that if any information, suit or action shall be brought or exhibited against any person or persons for any offence committed or to be committed against the form of this law, it shall be lawful for such defendants to plead the general issue that they are not guilty, or that they owe nothing, and to give such special matter in evidence to the jury that shall try the same, which matter being pleaded had been good and sufficient matter in law to have discharged the said defendant or defendants against the said information, suit or action, and the said matter shall then be as available to him or them to all intents and purposes, as if he or they had sufficiently pleaded, set forth or alleged the same matter in bar or discharge of such information, suit or action.

XXI. And because many times persons charged with petty treason or felony or as accessories thereunto are committed upon suspicion only, whereupon they are bailable or not according as the circumstances making out that suspicion are more or less weighty, which are best known to the justices of peace that committed the persons, and have the examinations before them, or to other justices of the peace in the county; be it therefore enacted, that where any person shall appear to be committed by any judge or justice of the peace and charged as accessory before the fact to any petty treason or felony or upon suspicion thereof, or with suspicion of petty treason or felony which petty treason or felony shall be plainly and specially expressed in the warrant of commitment, that such person shall not be removed or bailed by virtue of this act, or in any other manner than they might have been before the making of this act.

Clauses XIII and XIV were drafted with the overseas dominions in mind and remind us that the old liberties were strengthened not merely in England; they were also reinforced in the American colonies overseas. Just as the Puritan fugitives from Laud's tyranny had taken their inheritance of freedom to the New World, so later settlers carried with them the new spirit of achievement in rights defended and liberties restored. The Petition of Rights, the supremacy of the representative assembly, and the provision of the Great Charter, were now in all men's minds. It was supremely fortunate that so many of England's colonies were planted during this age of awareness and that the old rights and liberties thus became the heritage of a new nation overseas.

One basic liberty had still not developed—the liberty to follow any religion or none. Charles II, although unsuccessful, did much to further this concept. Early in his reign parliament passed several Acts to ensure that all men should worship in accordance with the teachings of the Church of England. In 1664 it was forbidden, under the Conventicle Act, for more than five people to worship together other than by Church of England rites. The Five Mile Act of the following year banned nonconformist ministers from coming within 5 miles of any town.

Then in 1673 King Charles, without consulting parliament, issued a DECLARATION OF INDULGENCE. Here is the text of the first serious attempt to introduce a measure of religious tolerance:

Our care and endeavours for the preservation of the rights and interests of the Church have been sufficiently manifested to the world by the whole course of our government, since our happy restoration, and by the many and frequent ways of coercion that we have used for reducing all erring or dissenting persons, and for composing the unhappy differences in matters of religion, which we found among our subjects upon our return. But it being evident by the sad experience of twelve years, that there is very little fruit of all those forcible courses, we think ourselves obliged to make use of that supreme power in ecclesiastical matters, which is not only inherent in us but hath been declared and recognised to be so by several statutes and acts of parliament. And therefore we do now accordingly issue out this our royal declaration, as well for the quieting the minds of our good subjects in these points, for inviting strangers in this conjuncture to come and live under us, and for the better encouragement of all to a cheerful following of their trades and callings, from whence we hope, by the blessing of God, to have many good and happy advantages to our government; as also for preventing for the future the danger that might otherwise arise from private meetings, and seditious conventicles. And in the first place, we declare our express resolution, meaning, and intention to be, that the Church of England be preserved, and remain entire in its doctrine, discipline, and government, as now it stands established by law: and that this be taken to be, as it is, the basis, rule and standard of the general and public worship of God, and that the orthodox comfortable clergy do receive and enjoy the revenues belonging thereunto; and that no person, though of different opinion and persuasion, shall be exempt from paying his tithes, or other dues whatsoever. And further, we declare, that no person shall be capable of holding any benefice, living, or ecclesiastical dignity or preferment of any kind in this kingdom of England, who is not exactly conformable. We do in the next place declare our will and pleasure to be, that the execution of all and all manner of penal laws in matters ecclesiastical, against whatsoever sort of non-conformists, or recusants, be immediately suspended, and they are hereby suspended. And all judges of assize and gaol-delivery, sheriffs, justices of the peace, mayors, bailiffs, and other officers whatsoever, whether ecclesiastical or civil, are to take notice of it, and pay due obedience thereunto. And that there may be no pretence for any of our subjects to continue their illegal meetings and conventicles, we do declare, that we shall from time to time allow a sufficient number of places, as shall be desired, in all parts of this our kingdom, for the use of such as do not conform to the Church of England, to meet and assemble in, in order to their public worship and devotion; which places shall be open and free to all persons. But to prevent such disorders and inconveniences as may happen by this our indulgence, if not duly regulated, and that they may be the better protected by the civil magistrate, our express will and pleasure is, that none of our subjects do presume to meet in any place, until such place be allowed, and the teacher of that congregation be approved by us. And lest any should apprehend, that this restriction should make our said allowance and approbation difficult to be obtained, we do further declare, that this our indulgence, as to the allowance of public places of worship and approbation of teachers, shall extend to all sorts of non-conformists and recusants, except the recusants of the Roman Catholic religion, to whom we shall no ways allow in public places of worship, but only indulge them their share in the common exemption from the executing the penal laws, and the exercise of their worship in their private houses only. And if after this our clemency and indulgence, any of our subjects shall presume to abuse this liberty, and shall preach seditiously, or to the derogation of the doctrine, discipline, or government of the established church, or shall meet in places not allowed by us; we do hereby give them warning, and declare, we will proceed against them with all imaginable severity: and we will let them see, we can be as severe to punish such offenders, when so justly provoked, as we are indulgent to truly tender consciences.

The most liberal sentence was that 'all manner of penal laws in matters ecclesiastical, against whatsoever sort of nonconformists, or recusants, be immediately suspended.'

But although this declaration explicitly excluded 'the recusants of the Roman Catholic religion,' Charles's subjects were suspicious. Many saw this as opening the door to toleration for the Roman Catholics. Moreover parliament challenged the king's right to suspend Acts which it had passed. Charles, remembering to what sad end obstinacy had led his father, graciously accepted the advice and the declaration was annulled.

Later in the same year parliament, to prevent the appointment of Catholics to high office, insisted that all who held office under the crown should take the oaths of supremacy and allegiance, and should receive the sacrament 'according to the usage of the Church of England.' The possibility of a return to Rome was very real. The eleven-year marriage of Charles to Catherine of Braganza (a Portuguese princess) had produced no children. The heir was the king's brother James, Duke of York, himself a Roman Catholic. He was in charge of the Royal Navy (working with that busiest of secretaries, Samuel Pepys) and the protestant party was apprehensive. Courteously, James was specifically excluded from the provisions of the Act. However, he took the hint and gave up his work at the admiralty.

In 1677 James's daughter Mary was married to William, Prince of Orange, one of the champions of protestantism in Europe. In the following year Titus Oates, a former Church of England clergyman, claimed to have found evidence on the continent of a Catholic plot. True or false (and Oates was not a very reputable witness), the story threw the country into turmoil. Many suspects were imprisoned and some hanged. James was banished by Act of Parliament and removed from the succession : 'That in case his Majesty should happen to die, or resign his Dominions, they should devolve to the person next in succession, in the same manner as if the Duke were dead.' For three years James dwelt in exile, legally no more than a dead man.

Charles's reign had been distinguished and successful. Parliament and the crown worked together in harmony and ancient liberties were restored. The first faint dawn of religious freedom had been seen and, although obscured by the clouds of prejudice, was ultimately to break into full day. Charles seemed to take after his Tudor ancestors rather than his Stuart father and grandfather. He had the administrative skills of Henry VII, the common touch of Henry VIII, and the same deft understanding of his people which Elizabeth had shown. Like Henry VIII he was something of a womaniser, but he did not confuse the issue by divorce, nor seek to legitimise his many unions. He left a brood of illegitimate children whom he ennobled, and the people loved him none the less.

He died in February 1685 and James, who had been restored to the succession and had returned from exile three years earlier, succeeded to a golden inheritance as James II.

Notes p 222

DOCUMENTS QUOTED:

1 The Petition of Right—1628 [*3 Charles I. c. 1.*]
2 The Remonstrance Against Tonnage and Poundage—1628
3 Act for a Parliament every Three Years—1641 [*16 Charles I. c. 1.*]
4 Act for the Abolition of the Court of Star Chamber—1641 [*16 Charles I. c. 10*]
5 The Grand Remonstrance—1641
6 Habeas Corpus Act—1679 [*31 Charles II. c. 2.*]
7 Charles II's Declaration of Indulgence—1673

CHAPTER VII

The Revolution and After
(1685-1714)

KING James II inherited all his father's faults and very few of his virtues. Neither his own exile by parliament nor the terrible example of his father taught him any lasting lesson. Immediately after his accession parliament met, ready to welcome their new Catholic monarch. He was voted a generous income and undertook to govern by the constitution and to support the Church of England.

Within a few months he met his first challenge. The Duke of Monmouth, one of the illegitimate sons of Charles II, set up his standard in the west country, declared himself champion of all good Protestants and proclaimed himself king of England. He and his pathetic army were defeated and James treated the rising with the deadly seriousness of a weak man. Some 250 of Monmouth's followers were executed in the notorious Bloody Assizes of Judge Jeffreys. Hundreds were transported to the West Indies, paying a terrible price for their loyalty to the Protestant cause and to the Merry Monarch's handsome son, who was executed later.

If James had hoped to ensure by terror that none should henceforth challenge his authority, he was mistaken. Even his supporters were shocked by the number of executions, so horribly reminiscent of Mary's persecutions of a hundred years earlier.

Within parliament there was now growing a two party system. The Church of England had been built by Elizabeth on a spirit of compromise and it included men of varying beliefs. Some saw it as representing no revolutionary break with the past : the Church of England was still a Catholic church and they themselves good Catholics. Such men had tended to support Charles I in his struggle with parliament. They were constitutionalists, believed in the natural authority of the king and, while prepared to defend the ancient rights of the subject, opposed any radical change in the structure of society. The Irish had given them the derisory nickname of Tories[24]. This party, High Church, naturally loyal to the crown, might have been James's allies, had he been a wiser man. There were others who saw the Church of England as an out-and-out Protestant institution, set up to defend the new faith and to eradicate all traces of Rome. From these were largely drawn parliament's supporters during the civil war. But they and their successors had now had their bellyful of republicanism and were ready to work with the king. They had been nicknamed the 'Whigamores'[25], and went by the name of Whigs.

James succeeded in alienating both parties. In doing so he unwittingly did the country a service. Whigs and Tories were united in their resentment of the king and came to understand that there was no quarrel between them when it came to the defence of liberty. It was this underlying unity of purpose which made possible the final establishment, after James's pathetic reign was over, of a constitutional monarchy and of the two-party system, a rivalry within a framework of unity, which our own age has inherited.

James, perhaps scared by Monmouth's Protestant rising, began to appoint Catholic officers in the army in direct violation of the Test Act which, without approval of parliament, he simply suspended. By the following year James had dismissed most of his Privy Council, his magistrates and sheriffs (most of whom were Tories) and was putting Catholics in their place. Parliament, which was largely Tory, was furious and Whigs and Tories moved still closer together.

In 1686, James re-established the Court of High Commission, one of the Royal Courts, and mutterings of discontent grew. Whigs and Tories alike began to look towards the king's heir, his daughter Mary, who was married to William of Orange, the Dutch champion of Protestantism. Many began to look forward to the king's death, so that England might once more have a Protestant monarch.

Then in France there was a renewed persecution of the Huguenots, the French Protestants. Refugees from the terror came to England with tales of slaughter and cruelty. The ghosts of Mary's martyrs haunted men's minds and the Pope again became a bogey.

In this atmosphere James sought to legalise his appointment of Catholics. In April 1687 he issued a DECLARATION OF INDULGENCE by which nonconformists and Catholics both became eligible to hold office under the crown. James's motives were to facilitate the creation of a Catholic army and council, the inclusion of Protestant dissenters in the declaration being merely a sop to his political opponents. The document might nevertheless have been an important move towards religious tolerance had the omens been more favourable. But James's subjects were too suspicious of their king and too overwrought by the French persecutions for them to accept the declaration. The opening sentences of the document were inauspicious, emphasising not merely the divine right of kings but God's special protection for James in particular, and the stress on the subject's duty seemed an ill-chosen phrase :

It having pleased Almighty God not only to bring us to the imperial crown of these kingdoms through the greatest difficulties, but to preserve us by a more than ordinary providence upon the throne of our royal ancestors, there is nothing now that we so earnestly desire as to establish our government on such a foundation as may make our subjects happy, and unite them to us by inclination as well as duty.

In the following year, 1688, James issued a second Declaration of Indulgence and ordered it to be read in every church. James, as head of the church, was theoretically entitled to do this but politically he was woefully wrong. The people, whatever their feelings on the merits of religious tolerance, were not prepared to accept government by declaration. The Archbishop of Canterbury and six other bishops submitted a humble petition of protest to the king. James promptly imprisoned them and brought them before the judges of the King's Bench on a charge of issuing a seditious libel. The judges, to London's delirious delight, declared them not guilty. There were wild celebrations with bonfires and junketing in the streets.

On 10 June 1688 a son was born to the king. What should have been an occasion of rejoicing caused widespread dismay; for Protestant Mary was no longer heir to the throne and the crown of England would pass to a Catholic prince, with the reforming work of 150 years permanently undone.

No one wanted another civil war, a sovereign made captive, a trial of doubtful legality, and the public execution of an anointed king. But the time had come to bring James to his senses. The leaders of the Whigs and Tories consulted, and jointly drew up an invitation to William, Mary's husband and himself a grandson of Charles I, to land in England to save the Protestant religion and the constitutional liberties of England.

By November William of Orange had mobilised an army of Protestants from many nations. He landed at Torbay on 5 November, the eighty-third anniversary of the Gunpowder Plot. His declared aim was the summoning of a free parliament and the defence of the Protestant religion. The local people flocked to him as did many of the officers of the king's army, including John Churchill, later to win immortal glory as the first Duke of Marlborough.

With his chief officers deserting him, and the ranks of his armies divided, James prepared to flee the country and William made no haste to prevent him. In December James sent his wife and baby son to France and followed them a few days later. But his ship was intercepted and he was compelled to return. William, somewhat embarrassed, let it be known that James would not be prevented if he should again try to leave. So on Christmas day James left St James's Palace and drove post haste to Rochester. On the way, in what seems a pettish attempt to impede the government of the realm, he threw the Great Seal of England into the Thames. As the wintry waters closed over the seal, the reign of James II ended. Ended too was the Stuart conception of the monarchy, of a king above the law, supreme over parliament and possessing the power to suspend or apply any Act of Parliament at will. From Rochester, James took ship to France where he remained until his death thirteen years later, progenitor of the romantic Stuart pretenders who were to advance their claims to the English throne for another fifty-seven years.

William of Orange entered London and was received as a deliverer. Parliament could not meet for there was no king to summon it and the men of 1688 were as keen to preserve old forms as they were to maintain ancient liberties. Accordingly, early in the new year a body was convened, which, though in essence a Parliament, was called simply the Convention. This assembly declared that the throne was vacant; that it should be offered to Mary, the heir, and to her husband William of Orange who should be joint sovereigns; and that they should accept a Declaration of Rights which the Convention had drawn up, listing the breaches which James had effected in the liberties of his subjects.

William and Mary accepted and the manner of England's government was never thereafter the same.

Twice within a generation the people's representatives had selected their sovereign. The old partnership between crown and parliament was resumed; but now parliament was the senior partner. Formerly, parliament gave its consent to the wishes of the king. Now it was for the king to give his assent to the wishes of parliament. True, William refused his consent five times, but on each occasion the measures were later enacted. The power of the crown to withold assent still exists, but it has not been exercised since 1708. True the crown can still summon or dismiss parliament at will, but the summoning has become automatic and dissolution is normally, but not always, granted at the request of the prime minister.

The 'Glorious Revolution' was glorious because it was bloodless. It was revolutionary not because it introduced, like the Civil War, a total change in the form of government, but because it sharply defined those liberties which had already been won, and finally recorded the rights which the people had gained over seven centuries and more. It was the climax of an evolutionary process, during which the dialogue between sovereign and subject had gone on continually, sometimes violently, more often with mutual affection and respect. A constitutional monarchy had thus developed, under which liberty, and later democracy, could be safeguarded. The winter of 1688–9 was the moment when this new monarchy attained a recognisable identity.

Parliament met and one of its first acts was to vote an annual income of £1,200,000 for William and Mary and a sum of £700,000 for the navy, thus settling the vexed question of Ship Money. In 1689 parliament passed the MUTINY ACT, ostensibly to fix punishments for mutiny, and to regularise courts martial. But the preamble laid down the important new principle that only parliament could authorise the maintenance of an army in time of peace :

Whereas the raising or keeping a standing army within this kingdom in time of peace, unless it be with consent of parliament, is against law; and whereas it is judged necessary by their majesties and this present parliament that during this time of danger several of the forces which are now on foot should be continued, and others raised, for the safety of the kingdom, for the common defence of the Protestant religion and for the reducing of Ireland; . . .

The new monarchy was shedding the last remnants of feudalism. The king still had the theoretical right to call upon the subject for military service, but henceforth only with the consent of the subject's

137

representatives. The Act, almost in parenthesis, was creating a new liberty—freedom from military rule.

In the same year the TOLERATION ACT finally gave freedom of worship to all Protestant nonconformists—provided they met openly and did not lock the doors of their churches and chapels. Moreover all such could now hold office:

Forasmuch as some ease to scrupulous consciences in the exercise of religion may be an effectual means to unite Their Majesties' Protestant subjects in interest and affection:

II. Be it enacted by the king and queen's most excellent Majesties, by and with the advice and consent of the lords spiritual and temporal and the commons in this present parliament assembled, and by the authority of the same, that neither the statute made in the three and twentieth year of the reign of the late Queen Elizabeth, entitled, An Act to Retain the Queen's Majesty's Subjects in their due Obedience; nor the statute made in the twenty ninth year of the said queen, entitled, An Act for the more speedy and due Execution of certain Branches of the Statute made in the three and twentieth year of the Queen's Majesty's Reign, viz. the aforesaid act; nor that branch or clause of a statute made in the first year of the reign of the said queen, entitled, An Act for [the] Uniformity of Common Prayer and Service in the Church and Administration of the Sacraments, whereby all persons having no lawful or reasonable excuse to be absent are required to resort to their parish church or chapel or some usual place where the common prayer shall be used upon pain of punishment by the censures of the church and also upon pain that every person so offending shall forfeit for every such offence twelve pence; nor the statute made in the third year of the reign of the late King James the First, entitled, An Act for the better Discovering and Repressing Popish Recusants; nor that other statute made in the same year, entitled, An Act to Prevent and Avoid Dangers which may grow by Popish Recusants; nor any other law or statute of this realm made against papists or popish recusants, except the statute made in the five and twentieth year of King Charles the Second, entitled, An Act for Preventing Dangers which may happen from Popish Recusants; and except also the statute made in the thirtieth year of the said King Charles the Second, entitled, An Act for the more effectual preserving the King's Person and Government by disabling Papists from sitting in either House of Parliament shall be construed to extend to any person or persons dissenting from the Church of England, that shall take the oaths mentioned in a statute made this present parliament, entitled, An Act for removing and preventing all Questions and Disputes concerning the assembling and sitting of this present Parliament; and shall make and subscribe the declaration mentioned in a statute made in the thirtieth year of King Charles the Second, entitled, An Act to prevent Papists from sitting in either House of Parliament, which oaths and declaration the justices of peace at the general sessions of the peace to be held for the county or place, where such person shall live, are hereby required to tender and administer to such persons as shall offer themselves to take, make and subscribe the same and thereof to keep a register; and likewise none of the persons aforesaid shall give or pay as any fee or reward to any officer or officers belonging to the court aforesaid above the sum of six pence, nor that more than once, for his or their entry of his taking the said oaths, and making and subscribing the said declaration nor above the further sum of six pence for any certificate of the same to be made out and signed by the officer or officers of the said court.

III. And be it further enacted by the authority aforesaid, all and every person and persons already convicted, or prosecuted in order to conviction, of recusancy by indictment, information, action of debt or otherwise grounded upon the aforesaid statutes or any of them, that shall take the said oaths mentioned in the said statute made this present parliament, and make and subscribe the declaration aforesaid, in the court of exchequer or assizes or general or quarter sessions to be held for the county where such person lives, and to be thence respectively certified into the exchequer, shall be thenceforth exempted and discharged from all the penalties, seizures, forfeitures, judgments and executions incurred by force of any the aforesaid statutes without any composition, fee or further charge whatsoever.

IV. And be it further enacted by the authority aforesaid, that all and every such person and persons that shall as aforesaid take the said oaths, and make and subscribe the

139

declaration aforesaid, shall not be liable to any pains, penalties or forfeitures mentioned in an act made in the five and thirtieth year of the reign of the late Queen Elizabeth, entitled, An Act to retain the Queen's Majesty's Subjects in their due Obedience; nor in an act made the two and twentieth year of the reign of the late King Charles the Second, entitled, An Act to prevent and suppress seditious Conventicles; nor shall any of the said persons be prosecuted in any ecclesiastical court for or by reason of their nonconforming to the Church of England.

V.   Provided always, and be it enacted by the authority aforesaid, that if any assembly of persons dissenting from the Church of England shall be had in any place for religious worship with the doors locked, barred or bolted during any time of such meeting together, all and every person or persons that shall come to and be at such meeting shall not receive any benefit from this law, but be liable to all the pains and penalties of all the aforesaid laws recited in this act for such their meeting, notwithstanding his taking the oaths and his making and subscribing the declaration aforesaid.

VI.   Provided always, that nothing herein contained shall be construed to exempt any of the persons aforesaid from paying of tithes or other parochial duties or any other duties to the church or minister, nor from any prosecution in any ecclesiastical court or elsewhere for the same . . .

VIII.   And be it further enacted by the authority aforesaid, that no person dissenting from the Church of England in holy orders or pretended holy orders or pretending to holy orders, nor any preacher or teacher of any congregation of dissenting Protestants, that shall make and subscribe the declaration aforesaid and take the said oaths at the general or quarter sessions of the peace to be held for the county, town, parts or division where such person lives, which court is hereby impowered to administer the same, and shall also declare his approbation of and subscribe the articles of religion mentioned in the statute made in the thirteenth year of the reign of the late Queen Elizabeth, except the thirty-fourth, thirty-fifth and thirty-sixth and these wards of the twentieth article, viz., . . . the

Church hath power to decree rights or ceremonies and authority in controversies of faith and yet . . ., shall be liable to any of the pains or penalties mentioned in an act made in the seventeenth year of the reign of King Charles the Second, entitled, An Act for restraining Nonconformists from inhabiting in Corporations; nor the penalties mentioned in the aforesaid act, made in the two and twentieth year of his said late majesty's reign, for or by reason of such persons preaching at any meeting for the exercise of religion, nor to the penalty of one hundred pounds mentioned in an act made in the thirteenth and fourteenth of King Charles the Second, entitled, An Act for the Uniformity of Public Prayers and Administration of Sacraments and other Rites and Ceremonies, and for establishing the Form of making, ordaining and consecrating of Bishops, Priests and Deacons in the Church of England, for officiating in any congregation for the exercise of religion permitted and allowed by this act . . .

XVI.   Provided always, and it is the true intent and meaning of this act, that all the laws made and provided for the frequenting of divine service on the Lord's day, commonly called Sunday, shall be still in force and executed against all persons that offend against the said laws, except such persons come to some congregation or assembly of religious worship allowed or permitted by this act.

XVII.   Provided always, and be it further enacted by the authority aforesaid, that neither this act nor any clause, article or thing herein contained shall extend or be construed to extend to give any ease, benefit or advantage to any papist or popish recusant whatsoever, or any person that shall deny in his preaching or writing the doctrine of the Blessed Trinity, as it is declared in the aforesaid articles of religion . . .

XIX.   Provided always, that no congregation or assembly for religious worship shall be permitted or allowed by this act, until the place of such meeting shall be certified to the bishop of the diocese, or to the arch-deacon of that archdeaconry, or to the justices of the peace at the general or quarter sessions of the peace for the county, city or place in which such meeting shall be held, and registered in the said bishop's or arch-deacon's court respectively, or recorded at the said general or quarter sessions; the register or clerk of the peace whereof respectively is hereby required to register the same, and to give certificate thereof to such person as shall demand the same, for which there shall be no greater fee nor reward taken than the sum of six pence.

Civil rights were thus given to all Protestants whether belonging to the Church of England or not; but Clause XVII denied 'any ease, benefit or advantage' to any Catholic. Nevertheless, the Act represented a step towards religious tolerance.

In December 1689 parliament passed the BILL OF RIGHTS, based upon the Convention's Declaration of Rights which William and Mary had accepted as the basis of their reign. The following is the text:

Whereas the lords spiritual and temporal and commons assembled at Westminster lawfully, fully and freely representing all the estates of the people of this realm, did upon the thirteenth day of February in the year of our Lord one thousand six hundred eighty-eight, present unto Their Majesties, then called and known by the names and style of William and Mary, prince and princess of Orange, being present in their proper persons, a certain declaration in writing made by the said lords and commons in the words following viz:

Whereas the late king James the Second by the assistance of divers evil counsellors, judges and ministers employed by him did endeavour to subvert and extirpate the Protestant religion and the laws and liberties of this kingdom.

By assuming and exercising a power of dispensing with and suspending of laws, and the execution of laws, without consent of parliament.

By committing and prosecuting divers worthy prelates for humbly petitioning to be excused from concurring to the said assumed power.

By issuing and causing to be executed a commission under the great seal for erecting a court, called the court of commissioners for ecclesiastical causes.

By levying money for and to the use of the crown, by

pretence of prerogative, for other time and in other manner than the same was granted by parliament.

By raising and keeping a standing army within this kingdom in time of peace, without consent of parliament, and quartering of soldiers contrary to law.

By causing several good subjects being Protestants to be disarmed, at the same time when papists were both armed and employed, contrary to law.

By violating the freedom of election of members to serve in parliament.

By prosecutions in the court of king's bench for matters and causes cognisable only in parliament, and by divers other arbitrary and illegal courses.

And whereas of late years partial, corrupt and unqualified persons have been returned and served on juries in trials, and particularly divers jurors in trials for high treason, which were not freeholders.

And excessive bail hath been required of persons committed in criminal cases, to elude the benefit of the laws made for the liberty of subjects.

And excessive fines have been imposed.

And illegal and cruel punishments have been inflicted.

And several grants and promises made of fines and forfeitures before any conviction or judgment against the persons upon whom the same were to be levied.

All of which are utterly and directly contrary to the known laws and statutes and freedom of this realm.

And whereas the said late king James the Second having abdicated the government and the throne being thereby vacant. His Highness the prince of Orange (whom it hath pleased Almighty God to make the glorious instrument of delivering this kingdom from popery and arbitrary power) did (by the advice of the lords spiritual and temporal and divers principal persons of the commons) cause letters to be written to the lords spiritual and temporal, being Protestants; and other letters to the several counties, cities, universities, boroughs and Cinque ports for the choosing of such persons to represent them, as were of right to be sent to parliament, to meet and sit at Westminster upon the two and twentieth day of January in this year one thousand six hundred eighty and eight, in order to such an establishment as that their religion, laws and liberties might not again be in danger of being subverted; upon which letters elections having been accordingly made,

And thereupon the said lords spiritual and temporal and commons pursuant to their respective letters and elections being now assembled in a full and free representative of this nation, taking into their most serious consideration the best means for attaining the ends aforesaid, do in the first place (as their ancestors in like cases have usually done) for the vindicating and asserting their ancient rights and liberties, declare:

That the pretended power of suspending of laws or the execution of laws by regal authority without consent of parliament is illegal.

That the pretended power of dispensing with laws or the execution of laws by regal authority as it hath been assumed and exercised of late is illegal.

That the commission for erecting the late court of commissioners for ecclesiastical causes and all other commissions and courts of like nature are illegal and pernicious.

That the levying money for or to the use of the crown by pretence of prerogative without grant of parliament for a longer time or in other manner than the same is or shall be granted is illegal.

That it is the right of the subjects to petition the king and all commitments and prosecutions for such petitioning are illegal.

That the raising or keeping a standing army within the kingdom in time of peace unless it be with consent of parliament is against law.

That the subjects which are Protestants may have arms for their defence suitable to their conditions and as allowed by law.

That election of members of parliament ought to be free.

That the freedom of speech and debates or proceedings in parliament ought not to be impeached or questioned in any court or place out of parliament.

That excessive bail ought not to be required nor excessive fines imposed nor cruel and unusual punishments inflicted.

That jurors ought to be duly impanelled and returned and

jurors which pass upon men in trials for high treason ought to be freeholders.

That all grants and promises of fines and forfeitures of particular persons before conviction are illegal and void.

And that for redress of all grievances and for the amending, strengthening and preserving of the laws parliaments ought to be held frequently.

And they do claim, demand and insist upon all and singular the premises as their undoubted rights and liberties and that no declarations, judgments, doings or proceedings to the prejudice of the people in any of the said premises ought in any wise to be drawn hereafter into consequence or example. To which demand of their rights they are particularly encouraged by the declaration of His Highness the prince of Orange as being the only means for obtaining a full redress and remedy therein. Having therefore an entire confidence that His said Highness the prince of Orange will perfect the deliverance so far advanced by him, and will still preserve them from the violation of their rights, which they have here asserted, and from all other attempts upon their religion, rights and liberties, the said lords spiritual and temporal and commons assembled at Westminster do resolve, that William and Mary, prince and princess of Orange, be and be declared king and queen of England, France and Ireland and the dominions thereunto belonging, to hold the crown and royal dignity of the said kingdoms and dominions to them the said prince and princess during their lives and the life of the survivor of them; and that the sole and full exercise of the regal power be only in and executed by the said prince of Orange in the names of the said prince and princess during their joint lives; and after their deceases the said crown and royal dignity of the said kingdoms and dominions to be to the heirs of the body of the said princess; and for default of such issue to the princess Anne of Denmark and the heirs of her body; and for default of such issue to the heirs of the body of the said prince of Orange. And the lords spiritual and temporal and commons do pray the said prince and princess to accept the same accordingly. And that the oaths hereafter mentioned to be taken by all persons of whom the oaths of allegiance and supremacy might be required by law instead of them; and that the said oaths of allegiance and supremacy be abrogated.

"I, A.B., do sincerely promise and swear, that I will be faithful and bear true allegiance to Their Majesties King William and Queen Mary."

"I, A.B., do swear, that I do from my heart abhor, detest and abjure as impious and heretical this damnable doctrine and position, that princes excommunicated or deprived by the pope or any authority of the see of Rome may be deposed or murdered by their subjects or any other whatsoever. And I do declare that no foreign prince, person, prelate, state or potentate hath or ought to have any jurisdiction, power, superiority, preeminence or authority, ecclesiastical or spiritual, within this realm. So help me God."

Upon which Their said Majesties did accept the crown and royal dignity of the kingdoms of England, France and Ireland and the dominions thereunto belonging, according to the resolution and desire of the said lords and commons, contained in the said declaration. And thereupon Their Majesties were pleased, that the said lords spiritual and temporal and commons being the two houses of parliament should continue to sit, and with Their Majesties' royal concurrence make effectual provision for the settlement of the religion, laws and liberties of this kingdom, so that the same for the future might not be in danger again of being subverted, to which the lords spiritual and temporal and commons did agree and proceed to act accordingly. Now in pursuance of the premises, the lords spiritual and temporal and commons in parliament assembled for the ratifying, confirming and establishing the said declaration and the articles, clauses, matters and things therein contained, by the force of a law made in due form by authority of parliament, do pray that it may be declared and enacted, that all and singular the rights and liberties asserted and claimed in the said declaration are the true, ancient and indubitable rights and liberties of the people of this kingdom, and so shall be esteemed, allowed, adjudged, deemed and taken to be, and that all and every the particulars aforesaid shall be firmly and strictly holden and observed, as they are expressed in the said declaration; and all officers and ministers whatsoever shall serve Their Majesties and their successors according to the same in all times to come. And the said lords spiritual and temporal and commons, seriously considering how it hath pleased Almighty God in His marvellous provid-

ence and merciful goodness to this nation to provide and
preserve Their said Majesties' royal persons most happily to
reign over us upon the throne of their ancestors, for which they
render unto Him from the bottom of their hearts their humblest
thanks and praises, do truly, firmly, assuredly and in the sin-
cerity of their hearts think, and do hereby humbly recognise,
acknowledge and declare, that King James the Second having
abdicated the government and Their Majesties having
accepted the crown and royal dignity [as] aforesaid, Their
said Majesties did become, were, are and of right ought to be
by the laws of this realm our sovereign liege lord and lady,
king and queen of England, France and Ireland and the dominions thereunto belonging, in and to whose princely persons the
royal state, crown and dignity of the said realms, with all
honours, styles, titles, regalities, prerogatives, powers, jurisdictions and authorities to the same belonging and appertaining, are most fully, rightfully and entirely invested and incor-
porated, united and annexed; and for preventing all questions
and divisions in this realm by reason of any pretended titles to
the crown and for preserving a certainty in the succession
thereof, in and upon which the unity, peace, tranquillity and
safety of this nation doth under God wholly consist and depend, the said lords spiritual and temporal and commons do
beseech Their Majesties, that it may be enacted, established
and declared, that the crown and regal government of the said
kingdom and dominions, with all and singular the premises
thereunto belonging and appertaining, shall be and continue to
Their said Majesties and the survivor of them during their lives
and the life of the survivor of them; and that the entire, perfect
and full exercise of the regal power and government be only
in and executed by His Majesty, in the names of both Their
Majesties, during their joint lives; and after their deceases the
said crown and premises shall be and remain to the heirs of
the body of Her Majesty; and for default of such issue to Her
Royal Highness the princess Anne of Denmark and the heirs
of her body; and for default of such issue to the heirs of the
body of His said Majesty; and thereunto the said lords
spiritual and temporal and commons do in the name of all the
people aforesaid most humbly and faithfully submit themselves, their heirs and posterities forever; and do faithfully
promise that they will stand to, maintain and defend Their

said Majesties, and also the limitation and succession of the crown herein specified and contained, to the utmost of their powers with their lives and estates against all persons whatsoever that shall attempt anything to the contrary. And whereas it hath been found by experience, that it is inconsistent with the safety and welfare of this Protestant kingdom to be governed by a popish prince or by any king or queen marrying a papist, the said lords spiritual and temporal and commons do further pray, that it may be enacted, that all and every person and persons that is, are or shall be reconciled to or shall hold communion with the See or Church of Rome, or shall profess the popish religion, or shall marry a papist, shall be excluded and be forever incapable to inherit, possess or enjoy the crown and government of this realm and Ireland and the dominions thereunto belonging, or any part of the same, or to have, use or exercise any regal power, authority or jurisdiction within the same; and in all and every such case or cases the people of these realms shall be and are hereby absolved of their allegiance; and the said crown and government shall from time to time descend to and be enjoyed by such person or persons, being Protestants, as should have inherited and enjoyed the same, in case the said person or persons so reconciled, holding communion, or professing, or marrying, as aforesaid, were naturally dead; and that every king and queen of this realm, who at any time hereafter shall come to and succeed in the imperial crown of this kingdom, shall on the first day of the meeting of the first parliament, next after his or her coming to the crown, sitting in his or her throne in the house of peers, in the presence of the lords and commons therein assembled, or at his or her coronation, before such person or persons who shall administer the coronation oath to him or her at the time of his or her taking the said oath, (which shall first happen), make, subscribe and audibly repeat the declaration mentioned in the statute made in the thirtieth year of the reign of King Charles the Second, entitled, An Act for the more effectual preserving the King's Person and Government by disabling Papists from sitting in either House of Parliament; but if it shall happen that such king or queen upon his or her succession to the crown of this realm shall be under the age of twelve years, then every such king or queen shall make, subscribe and audibly repeat the said declaration at his or her coronation, or the first day of the meeting of the first parliament as aforesaid, which shall first happen after such king or queen shall have attained the said age of twelve years. All which Their Majesties are contented and pleased shall be declared, enacted and established by authority of this present parliament, and shall stand, remain and be the law of this realm forever; and the same are by Their said Majesties, by and with the advice and consent of the lords spiritual and temporal and commons in parliament assembled, and by the authority of the same, declared, enacted and established accordingly.

II.   And be it further declared and enacted by the authority aforesaid, that, from and after this present session of parliament, no dispensation by **non obstante**[26] of or to any statute or any part thereof shall be allowed, but that the same shall be held void and of no effect, except a dispensation be allowed of in such statute, and except in such a case as shall be specially provided for by one or more bill or bills to be passed during this present session of parliament.

III.   Provided that no charter or grant or pardon, granted before the three and twentieth day of October in the year of our Lord one thousand six hundred eighty-nine, shall be any ways impeached or invalidated by this act, but that the same shall be and remain of the same force and effect in law and no other than as if this act had never been made.

The Bill of Rights recorded the Convention's earlier Declaration, setting out all that James had done contrary to the liberties of the realm : his claim to have the power to suspend or dispense with Acts of Parliament, his imprisonment of the bishops because they had petitioned him, his levying of taxes without parliament's consent, his re-establishing the Royal Courts. All had earlier been matters of contention between kings and their subjects. After the Bill of Rights they lay finally beyond dispute and no later king could ever again attempt them.

The old conventions were maintained. Not the exiled James but 'divers evil counsellors, judges and ministers' are responsible for the wrongs done. Even in disgrace, the king can do no wrong. The Bill, by defining what acts are unlawful even if the crown performs them, finally established that kings must govern within the law.

The document stated that the throne should pass in default of heirs of the body of Mary, to her sister Anne. James and his son were thus excluded and parliament's right to select the king was re-affirmed. The Bill also excluded any Catholic from the throne. It was the chief document of the revolution, and gathered together the main principles of all the earlier charters and statutes of liberty. Freedom of worship was still absent; but with that exception the Bill of Rights offers definitions of civil liberties which any state could still take as a pattern.

The Bill of Rights had restated the doctrine that election of members of parliament ought to be free, and that members should enjoy freedom of speech, but had not laid down that parliament should meet regularly. This was put right in 1694 by the TRIENNIAL ACT of which the following is an extract :

Whereas by the ancient laws and statutes of this kingdom frequent parliaments ought to be held, and whereas frequent and new parliaments tend very much to the happy union and good agreement of the king and people, we Your Majesties' most loyal and obedient subjects, the lords spiritual and temporal and commons in this present parliament assembled, do most humbly beseech Your most excellent Majesties, that it may be declared and enacted in this present parliament, and it is hereby declared and enacted by the king and queen's most excellent Majesties, by and with the advice and consent of the lords spiritual and temporal and commons in this present parliament assembled and by the authority of the same, that from henceforth a parliament shall be holden once in three years at the least.

II. And be it further enacted by the authority aforesaid, that within three years at the farthest from and after the dissolution of this present parliament, and so from time to time forever hereafter within three years at the farthest from and after the determination of every other parliament, legal writs under the great seal shall be issued by directions of Your Majesties, your heirs and successors, for calling, assembling and holding another new parliament.

In the same year Mary died and William reigned alone. There
150

was a growing awareness that England had a foreign king. Although William chose his ministers according to the majority in the Commons—Whig or Tory as each election decided—it was he who decided foreign policy. Many, particularly the Tories, felt that Dutch rather than English interests sometimes guided the king. There was some risk that this situation might be perpetuated; for Anne's only surviving son had died in 1700 and the next heir was Sophia, daughter of James II's aunt Elizabeth. Sophia had married a German and her son who would succeed her was a German prince, George the Elector of Hanover.

In 1701 parliament passed the Act of Settlement defining the succession and took the opportunity to strengthen its own position. The following is the text of the Act:

THE ACT OF SETTLEMENT—1701

Whereas in the first year of the reign of Your Majesty and of our late most gracious sovereign lady queen Mary (of blessed memory) an act of parliament was made, entitled, An Act for declaring the Rights and Liberties of the Subject and for settling the Succession of the Crown, wherein it was (amongst other things) enacted, established and declared, that the crown and regal government of the kingdoms of England, France and Ireland, and the dominions thereunto belonging, should be and continue to Your Majesty and the said late queen during the joint lives of Your Majesty and the said queen and to the survivor; and that after the decease of Your Majesty and of the said queen the said crown and regal government should be and remain to the heirs of the body of the said late queen; and for default of such issue to Her Royal Highness the princess Anne of Denmark and the heirs of her body; and for default of such issue to the heirs of the body of Your Majesty. And it was thereby further enacted, that all and every person and persons that then were or afterwards should be reconciled to or should hold communion with the See or Church of Rome, or should profess the popish religion, or marry a papist, should be excluded, and are by that act made forever incapable to inherit, possess or enjoy the crown and government of this realm and Ireland and the dominions

151

thereunto belonging or any part of the same, or to have, use or exercise any regal power, authority or jurisdiction within the same; and in all and every such case and cases the people of these realms shall be and are thereby absolved of their allegiance; and that the said crown and government shall from time to time descend to and be enjoyed by such person or persons, being Protestants, as should have inherited and enjoyed the same, in case the said person or persons so reconciled, holding communion, professing or marrying as aforesaid, were naturally dead. After the making of which statute and the settlement therein contained, Your Majesty's good subjects, who were restored to the full and free possession and enjoyment of their religion, rights and liberties by the providence of God giving success to Your Majesty's just undertakings and unwearied endeavours for that purpose, had no greater temporal felicity to hope or wish for, than to see a royal progeny descending from Your Majesty, to whom (under God) they owe their tranquillity, and whose ancestors have for many years been principal assertors of the reformed religion and the liberties of Europe and from our said most gracious sovereign lady, whose memory will always be precious to the subjects of these realms; and it having since pleased Almighty God to take away our said sovereign lady, and also the most hopeful prince William, duke of Gloucester, (the only surviving issue of Her Royal Highness the princess Anne of Denmark), to the unspeakable grief and sorrow of Your Majesty and your said good subjects, who, under such losses being sensibly put in mind, that it standeth wholly in the pleasure of Almighty God to prolong the lives of Your Majesty and of Her Royal Highness, and to grant to Your Majesty or to Her Royal Highness such issue as may be inheritable to the crown and regal government aforesaid, by the respective limitations in the said recited act contained, do constantly implore the divine mercy for those blessings; and Your Majesty's said subjects having daily experience of your royal care and concern for the present and future welfare of these kingdoms, and particularly recommending from your throne a further provision to be made for the succession of the crown in the Protestant line, for the happiness of the nation and the security of our religion; and it being absolutely necessary for the safety, peace and quiet of this realm, to obviate all doubts and contentions in the same, by reason of any pretended title to the crown and to maintain a certainty in the succession thereof, to which your subjects may safely have recourse for their protection, in case the limitations in the said just recited act should determine: Therefore for a further provision of the succession of the crown in the Protestant line, we Your Majesty's most dutiful and loyal subjects, the lords spiritual and temporal and commons in this present parliament assembled, do beseech Your Majesty that it may be enacted and declared, and be it enacted and declared by the king's most excellent Majesty by and with the advice and consent of the lords spiritual and temporal and commons in this present parliament assembled, and by the authority of the same, that the most excellent princess Sophia, electress and duchess dowager of Hanover, daughter of the most excellent princess Elizabeth, late queen of Bohemia, daughter of our late sovereign lord king James the First, of happy memory, be and is hereby declared to be the next in succession in the Protestant line to the imperial crown and dignity of the said realms of England, France and Ireland, with the dominions and territories thereunto belonging, after His Majesty and the princess Anne of Denmark, and in default of issue of the said princess Anne and of His Majesty respectively; and that from and after the deceases of His said Majesty our now sovereign lord and of Her Royal Highness the princess Anne of Denmark, and for default of issue of the said princess Anne and of His Majesty respectively, the crown and legal government of the said kingdoms of England, France and Ireland and of the dominions thereunto belonging, with the royal state and dignity of the said realms and all honours, styles, titles, regalities, prerogatives, powers, jurisdictions and authorities to the same belonging and appertaining, shall be, remain and continue to the said most excellent princess Sophia and the heirs of her body, being Protestants; and thereunto the said lords spiritual and temporal and commons shall and will, in the name of all the people of this realm, most humbly and faithfully submit themselves, their heirs and posterities, and do faithfully promise that after the deceases of His Majesty and Her Royal Highness, and the failure of the heirs of their respective bodies, to stand to, maintain and defend the said princess Sophia and the heirs of her body, being Protestants, according

153

to the limitation and succession of the crown in this act specified and contained, to the utmost of their powers, with their lives and estates, against all persons whatsoever that shall attempt anything to the contrary.

II.   Provided always, and it is hereby enacted, that all and every person and persons, who shall or may take or inherit the said crown, by virtue of the limitation of this present act, and is, are or shall be reconciled to or shall hold communion with the See or Church of Rome, or shall profess the popish religion, or shall marry a papist, shall be subject to such incapacities, as in such case or cases are by the said recited act provided, enacted and established; and that every king and queen of this realm, who shall come to and succeed in the imperial crown of this kingdom by virtue of this act, shall have the coronation oath administered to him, her or them, at their respective coronations, according to the act of parliament made in the first year of the reign of His Majesty and the said late queen Mary, entitled, An Act for establishing the Coronation Oath, and shall make, subscribe and repeat the declaration in the act first above recited, mentioned or referred to, in the manner and form, thereby prescribed.

III.   And whereas it is requisite and necessary that some further provision be made for securing our religion, laws and liberties, from and after the death of His Majesty and the princess Anne of Denmark, and in default of issue of the body of the said princess and of His Majesty respectively; be it enacted by the king's most excellent Majesty, by and with the advice and consent of the lords spiritual and temporal and commons in parliament assembled, and by the authority of the same:

That whosoever shall hereafter come to the possession of this crown shall join in communion with the Church of England as by law established.

That in case the crown and imperial dignity of this realm shall hereafter come to any person, not being a native of this kingdom of England, this nation be not obliged to engage in any war for the defence of any dominions or territories which do not belong to the crown of England, without consent of parliament.

That no person who shall hereafter come to the possession of this crown shall go out of the dominions of England,

154

Scotland or Ireland, without consent of parliament.

That from and after the time that the further limitation by this act shall take effect, all matters and things relating to the well governing of this kingdom, which are properly cognisable in the privy council by the laws and customs of this realm, shall be transacted there; and all resolutions taken thereupon shall be signed by such of the privy council as shall advise and consent to the same.

That after the said limitation shall take effect as aforesaid, no person born out of the kingdoms of England, Scotland or Ireland or the dominions thereunto belonging (although he be naturalised or made a denizen, except such as are born of English parents) shall be capable to be of the privy council, or a member of either house of parliament, or to enjoy any office or place of trust, either civil or military, or to have any grant of lands, tenements or hereditaments from the crown to himself or to any other or others in trust for him.

That no person who has an office or place or profit under the king or receives a pension from the crown shall be capable of serving as a member of the house of commons.

That after the said limitation shall take effect as aforesaid, judges commissions be made **quam diu se bene gesserint**[27], and their salaries ascertained and established, but upon the address of both houses of parliament it may be lawful to remove them.

That no pardon under the great seal of England be pleadable to an impeachment by the commons in parliament.

IV.   And whereas the laws of England are the birthright of the people thereof, and all the kings and queens who shall ascend the throne of this realm ought to administer the government of the same according to the said laws, and all their officers and ministers ought to serve them respectively according to the same; the said lords spiritual and temporal and commons do therefore further humbly pray, that all the laws and statutes of this realm for securing the established religion and the rights and liberties of the people thereof, and all other laws and statutes of the same now in force, may be ratified and confirmed, and the same are by His Majesty, by and with the advice and consent of the said lords spiritual and temporal and commons, and by authority of the same, ratified and confirmed accordingly.

The Act was the final document of the revolution. Clause I did not merely lay down the succession, it finally recorded parliament's power to decide who should wear the crown—a right first seen in the Witan of the Saxon Kings and exercised as recently as 1936. Moreover it was made clear that all kings and queens should be Protestants and that all Catholics should be automatically excluded. Realising that the crown would pass to Princess Sophia's son, who was a foreigner, parliament laid down in Clause III that no foreign king was to exploit the resources of England in the interests of his overseas kingdom, nor could he be an absentee monarch. So, while *Magna Carta* had guaranteed the right of the subject freely to leave and re-enter the kingdom (except in times of war), the monarch might travel abroad only with parliament's consent. Kings, by the Act, became the acknowledged servants of parliament. In theory they were still sovereign so that lords and commons, in the Act itself, are said to 'beseech' the king. The paradox is now formally defined.

Parliament was now supreme in all fields of government and the king's powers had henceforth to be exercised in accordance with its will. It needed only the gradual improvement of the methods of election, ensuring that parliament reflected the people's will, to bring about a democracy operating within the social stability provided by a constitutional monarchy.

In 1702 William died and Mary's sister Anne, the last Stuart to rule over England, came to the throne. Her reign was marked by the triumph of English arms abroad and the development of England's position as a world power. Churchill, Duke of Marlborough, led her armies to victory and the new parliamentary machine worked fairly efficiently.

For many years Queen Anne was influenced by Churchill's wife Sarah with whom she had a deep and somewhat eccentric relationship. The Churchills were Whigs and Whig policy at first prevailed. Later when the relationship with Sarah cooled and Anne came under the influence of her new friend, Mrs Masham, it was the turn of the Tories. Churchill was dismissed and later retired to the continent. Harley, Earl of Oxford, and St John, Viscount Bolingbroke, replaced the Whig ministers; Robert Walpole, a leading Whig, was expelled from the Commons and imprisoned for corruption. The novel game of party politics was being played with a vengeance. As the queen grew older, Bolingbroke planned the restoration of the Stuarts, for whom the

Tories always had a sneaking sympathy. He opened negotiations with James II's son in France, but his colleague Harley would have none of it.

In the summer of 1714, when Anne lay dying, she appointed the Earl of Shrewsbury, a leading Whig, as Lord Treasurer. He alerted the Fleet to prevent any Stuart landing, and a message was sent to Anne's cousin in Hanover inviting him to England. When Anne died on 1 August, all was prepared and George succeeded to the throne.

England thus had a foreign king and, as a result, the power of parliament and of ministers was still further to increase and the forms of government as we know them were to be finally established.

Notes p 222

DOCUMENTS QUOTED:

1 James II's Declaration of Indulgence—1687 [*AS*]
2 The Mutiny Act—1689 [*1 William and Mary. c. 5*]
3 The Toleration Act—1689 [*1 William and Mary. c. 18*]
4 The Bill of Rights—1689 [*1 William and Mary. c. 36*]
5 The Triennial Act—1694 [*6 & 7 William and Mary. c. 2*]
6 The Act of Settlement—1701 [*12 & 13 William III. c. 2*]

CHAPTER VIII

Georgian England
(1714-1829)

IT must have been a very bewildered George who landed at Greenwich after the death of his cousin Anne. Fifty-four years old, set in his ways, he had been the absolute monarch of his native Hanover. Suddenly he was king of a rich country, with a navy that was the fear and envy of the world, and an army which had proved itself invincible at Oudenarde, Malplaquet and Blenheim. He had subjects across the Atlantic where prosperous colonies came under the sweep of his new sceptre. His subjects were established in India and his flag was seen in every sea. A new grandeur surrounded his middle-aged and somewhat uncomprehending figure. Yet behind the deference shown to him by powerful men who in his land might have been accounted princes, he found himself the servant as well as the master of his new subjects.

This was not England's first experience of a king who had been a monarch in another land. James I had long experience as king of Scotland, with disastrous results for himself and his descendants. King George was never dazzled by the glories of his new kingdom and made no such blunders as did James. He was too old or too idle to study the character of his new subjects and the language barrier prevented him from taking an active part in government. Because of the accident of inheritance, the doctrines of the revolution were thus reinforced. More power passed to parliament and the concept that the king reigns but does not govern began to be formed.

The function of the king's ministers also underwent a change, and the powers and duties of ministers today were basically shaped 'when George in pudding time came o'er.'

Before, the king's ministers had been the king's servants, partly secretaries and partly advisers. Even after the revolution this was still largely true and the monarch still presided over the meetings of ministers. George's English was so poor that he could understand little of what went on and was unable to take part in—let alone guide—the discussions. Instead, a senior minister took the chair and reported to the king. So the office of *premier ministre,* prime minister, was born by accident, and the office grew without formal definition. The other ministers and secretaries of state quietly looked after their departments, reporting to the prime minister rather than to the German-speaking king.

George chose his ministers from among the Whigs and Sir Robert Walpole, their leading spokesman, became England's first prime minister. The Whigs, traditional supporters of parliamentary power, enjoyed a long ascendancy.

Eighteenth-century England suffered from two evils, of which the first was corruption. Almost everything could be bought—power, influence, seats in the Commons, and high office. The salaried positions which lay in the king's gift gradually became the property of the prime minister. This patronage could be used to influence the House of Commons just as bribery could control its composition. Election of members was by show of hands; landlords and employers could see how men voted and could bring harsh sanctions to bear. Some constituencies had so few voters that to bribe them all cost very little. Pocket Boroughs and Rotten Boroughs abounded. The Tories as landlords, the Whigs as wealthy men, influenced voting in a way that made nonsense of the ancient principle that 'elections ought to be free.'

The second evil was a growing self-consciousness about the 'Constitution.' The old documents of liberty began to be seen not merely as important but as sacrosanct. Some of England's political flexibility began to fade and there was a risk of society setting into rigid and unchanging forms.

King George soon saw possibilities of using the power of his new kingdom to advance the interests of Hanover. An English fleet sailed to the Baltic to reinforce Hanover's claims to Bremen and Verden. The Tories, out of office, looked on with apprehension and resentment. Men began to raise their glasses to the king over the water and Jacobite hopes kindled. Plans were laid for risings in Devonshire, Lancashire and the Scottish Highlands. James, the 'Old Pretender' landed in Scotland, tardily and ineffectually. The Whig administration put down the risings and the Old Pretender returned to France chastened and unsuccessful.

This incident aroused the Whigs' fears of a Tory revival. Under the old Triennial Act of 1694 an election was due in 1717 and this might have resulted in a Tory majority. This could have ended not merely the Whig administration but the Hanoverian succession and all that had been gained in the revolution.

Accordingly, the Whig leaders made use of their majority to pass a Septennial Act, extending the life of parliament to seven years:

THE SEPTENNIAL ACT—1716

Whereas in and by act of parliament made in the sixth year of the reign of their late Majesties king William and queen Mary (of ever blessed memory) entitled, An Act for the frequent Meeting and Calling of Parliaments: it was among other things enacted, that from thenceforth no parliament whatsoever, that should at any time then after be called, assembled or held, should have any continuance longer than for three years only at the farthest, to be accounted from the day on which by the writ of summons the said parliament should be appointed to meet: and whereas it has been found by experience, that the said clause hath proved very grievous and burdensome, by occasioning much greater and more continued expenses in order to elections of members to serve in parliament, and more violent and lasting heats and animosities among the subjects of this realm, than were ever known before the said clause was enacted; and the said provision, if it should continue, may probably at this juncture, when a restless and popish faction are designing and endeavouring to renew the rebellion within this kingdom, and an invasion from abroad, be destructive to the peace and security of the government; be it enacted by the king's most excellent Majesty, by and with the advice and consent of the lords spiritual and temporal, and commons, in parliament assembled, and by the authority of the same, that this present parliament, and all parliaments that shall at any time hereafter be called, assembled or held, shall and may respectively have continuance for seven years, and no longer, to be accounted from the day on which by the writ of summons this present parliament hath been, or any future parliament shall be, appointed to meet, unless this present, or any such parliament hereafter to be summoned, shall be sooner dissolved by His Majesty, his heirs or successors.

This was certainly not intended to increase liberty, but was a piece of party legislation designed to perpetuate a majority. The result however was to increase the power of members of parliament by giving them seven years of independence from their constituents, in which to develop their ideas, shape their policies, and become representatives rather than delegates. The Act remained in force for some 200 years. moulding the character of the Commons and greatly enhancing the dignity and value of their debates.

Despite the corruption and imperfections of the electoral system, parliament now reflected in some measure the feelings of the country. On the whole the nation preferred the unromantic George, who allowed ministers and parliament to get on with the job of government, to the romantic Stuarts in exile and to the risk of their restoration which any Tory victory might carry. George and Walpole both, by the judicious offer of paid jobs or cash to members of parliament, and by the purchase of seats where necessary, assured the survival of a Whig administration.

George died in 1727 with Walpole still in power. The new king, George II, had as Prince of Wales been estranged from his father, and dismissed Walpole, only to reinstate him within a few days.

The new reign was one of growing prosperity. Walpole kept England out of foreign wars until 1739. The new urban poor had not yet multiplied and ninety per cent of the people still drew their living from the land. The rich still counted their wealth in acres rather than in money. Rich and poor therefore shared an interest in the land and each felt that the prosperity of the one depended upon the prosperity of the other. Tension between the classes was slight, and the ghosts of John Ball and Wat Tyler were stilled, exorcised by abundant ale, by good bread, a fat goose, and the savour of frequent meat. Foreign trade was developing and bringing new wealth into the country. It was an age neither of glory nor of great events. People were content with the machinery of government as it had evolved and with the liberties which, since 1688, seemed to be so completely safeguarded.

In 1742 Walpole retired, receiving an earldom and a large pension from his grateful sovereign. For the rest of the reign military events dominated the scene. In 1745 Prince Charles Edward Stuart, son of the

Old Pretender, landed in Scotland, raised the Highlanders, proclaimed himself king, and invaded England. But no rejoicing subjects in England rallied to the advancing standard of the handsome Young Pretender. In Scotland the events left a legacy of romantic legend; in England they left the National Anthem ('God Save the King' was first sung at Covent Garden Theatre during these troubles) and a disenchantment with the Stuart cause.

Abroad, British arms advanced in Canada and in India. The parliamentary system worked as well in war as in peace and when George II died in 1760, there had been nothing to prompt any advances towards new rights and liberties.

He was succeeeded by his grandson, the Prince of Wales having already died. George III's accession was received with delight for he was three generations removed from Hanover and an Englishman born and bred. Unfortunately, his mother, the Dowager Princess of Wales, had taught him the ideas of absolute monarchy that prevailed in the small German court where she herself had been educated. These ideas were reinforced by the tutor she selected for him, the Earl of Bute, who bore the ominous name of James Stuart. Bute based his teaching on Bolingbroke's pamphlet *The Idea of a Patriot King*. The king should govern and should appoint ministers on his own judgement and not at the dictates of parties.

Superficially, there was much to be said for George III's attitude. Two reigns in which the sovereign had depended upon the Whigs had led to an unnatural growth in that party's influence. Government by consent had degenerated into government by corruption; and the limitation of the crown's authority seemed to have placed power permanently into the hands of a privileged minority. George III felt justified in pursuing the doctrine of the Patriot King, defending the people and their liberties against the selfish dictates of party politicians.

He took patronage back into his own hands, appointed ministers of his own choice, formed a mixed administration of Whigs and Tories, and set about establishing a King's Party in the House of Commons.

England's war with France had been vigorously waged by William Pitt, the brilliant parliamentarian whose eloquence dominated the House of Commons. The new king criticised the war—'this bloody and expensive war'—in the Privy Council and within a year had got rid of Pitt and signed a treaty with the French. To destroy the Whig monopoly of parliamentary power, he resorted to massive bribery and began to revive the old pre-revolution conception of monarchy.

In 1765 George became mentally ill. In the same year parliament resolved that all legal documents in the American colonies should bear stamps to raise funds to pay for the garrisons there. It seemed just that the king's colonial subjects should contribute to the cost of the British forces which defended them, but the Stamp Act was bitterly opposed in America and was repealed.

The origins of the United States of America lie in one of the principles established by the Great Charter and by other documents we have examined : no one was to be taxed without consent. The colonists of America had inherited the same unshakeable belief in those rights as their cousins in the homeland. In 1773 the British government arranged that the East India Company, which was going through difficult times, might ship its tea direct to the American colonies where less duty would be paid than in England. How the men of Boston reacted to this we know. It was not that the duty was a bad one, but that it had been levied without their consent.

At first the American subjects did not question the king's ultimate authority. They claimed nothing more than the ancient rights and liberties of their race, and recognition that the charters and statutes of former ages were as binding upon their king in his realms overseas as they were in England.

But the Boston Tea Party was seen in London—even by the Whigs —as a lawless defiance of authority. Attitudes on both sides hardened. Representatives of all the colonies met at a Continental Congress in 1774. The northern colonies, largely peopled by descendants of the Puritans, were now talking of repudiating the crown. The more Tory South (many were descendants of Royalists who had fled the country after Cromwell's triumph) could not agree. Finally the Congress, following ancient tradition, submitted a petition stating their grievances. George, by now almost a believer in the Divine Right of Kings, refused to accept it despite provision for it in the Bill of Rights.

After that, armed conflict was inevitable and the first blood was shed at Lexington in 1775. Even then, and even though men died in other battles, there were still many delegates to Congress who were reluctant to make the final break. Reform under the king, liberty under the crown, these were still the objectives of many. But, just as the Long Parliament in England had finally broken with King Charles I, so now Congress in America finally proclaimed itself, and the people it represented, independent of King George. The document contains harsh strictures upon the king but for this he has only himself to blame. He had treated his subjects with disdain, departed from the ancient principle of taxation by consent and—worst of all—he had refused a traditional petition for the redress of grievances. In all these events it was the American revolutionaries who were the traditionalists and the Tory king who was making a revolutionary break with the ancient duties of his office.

The Declaration of Independence of which the following is the text was the first document of liberty drawn up by Englishmen overseas:

THE DECLARATION OF INDEPENDENCE—1776

When in the Course of human Events, it becomes necessary for one People to dissolve the Political Bands which have connected them with another, and to assume among the Powers of the Earth, the separate and equal Station to which the Laws of Nature and of Nature's God entitle them, a decent Respect to the Opinions of Mankind requires that they should declare the causes which impel them to the Separation.

We hold these Truths to be self-evident, that all Men are created equal, that they are endowed by their Creator with certain unalienable Rights, that among these are Life, Liberty, and the Pursuit of Happiness— That to secure these Rights, Governments are instituted among Men, deriving their just Powers from the Consent of the Governed, that whenever any Form of Government becomes destructive of these Ends, it is the Right of the People to alter or to abolish it, and to institute new Government, laying its Foundation on such Principles, and organising its Powers in such Form, as to them shall seem most likely to effect their Safety and Happiness. Prudence, indeed, will dictate that Governments long established should not be changed for light and transient Causes; and accordingly all experience hath shewn, that Mankind are more disposed to suffer, while Evils are sufferable, than to right themselves by abolishing the Forms to which they are accustomed. But when a long Train of Abuses and Usurpations, pursuing invariably the same Object, evinces a Design to reduce them under absolute Despotism, it is their Right, it is their Duty, to throw off such Government, and to provide new Guards for their future Security. Such has been the patient Sufferance of these Colonies; and such is now the Necessity which constrains them to alter their former Systems of Government. The History of the present King of Great Britain is a History of repeated Injuries and Usurpations, all having in direct Object the Establishment of an absolute Tyranny over these States. To prove this, let Facts be submitted to a candid World.

He has refused his Assent to Laws, the most wholesome and necessary for the public Good.

He has forbidden his Governors to pass Laws of immediate and pressing Importance, unless suspended in their Operation till his Assent should be obtained; and when so suspended, he has utterly negelected to attend to them.

He has refused to pass other Laws for the Accommodation of large Districts of People, unless those People would relinquish the Right of Representation in the Legislature, a Right inestimable to them, and formidable to Tyrants only.

He has called together Legislative Bodies at Places unusual, uncomfortable, and distant from the Depository of their public Records, for the sole Purpose of fatiguing them into Compliance with his Measures.

He has dissolved Representative Houses repeatedly, for opposing with manly Firmness his Invasions on the Rights of the People.

He has refused for a long Time, after such Dissolutions, to cause others to be elected; whereby the Legislative Powers, incapable of Annihilation, have returned to the People at large for their exercise; the State remaining in the mean time exposed to all the Dangers of Invasion from without, and Convulsions within.

He has endeavoured to prevent the Population of these States; for that Purpose obstructing the Laws for Naturalization of Foreigners; refusing to pass others to encourage their Migrations hither, and raising the Conditions of new Appropriations of Lands.

He has obstructed the Administration of Justice, by refusing his Assent to Laws for establishing Judiciary Powers.

He has made Judges dependent on his Will alone, for the Tenure of their Offices, and the Amount and Payment of their Salaries.

He has erected a Multitude of new Offices, and sent hither

Swarms of Officers to harrass our People, and eat out their Substance.

He has kept among us, in Times of Peace, Standing Armies, without the consent of our legislatures.

He has affected to render the Military independent of and superior to the Civil Power.

He has combined with others to subject us to a Jurisdiction foreign to our Constitution, and unacknowledged by our Laws; giving his Assent to their Acts of pretended Legislation:

For quartering large Bodies of Armed Troops among us:

For protecting them, by a mock Trial, from Punishment for any Murders which they should commit on the Inhabitants of these States:

For cutting off our Trade with all Parts of the World:

For imposing Taxes on us without our Consent:

For depriving us, in many Cases, of the Benefits of Trial by Jury:

For transporting us beyond Seas to be tried for pretended Offences:

For abolishing the free System of English Laws in a neighbouring Province, establishing therein an arbitrary Government, and enlarging its Boundaries, so as to render it at once an Example and fit Instrument for introducing the same absolute Rule into these Colonies:

For taking away our Charters, abolishing our most valuable Laws, and altering fundamentally the Forms of our Governments:

For suspending our own Legislatures, and declaring themselves invested with Power to legislate for us in all Cases whatsoever.

He has abdicated Government here, by declaring us out of his Protection and waging War against us.

He has plundered our Seas, ravaged our Coasts, burnt our Towns, and destroyed the Lives of our People.

He is, at this Time, transporting large Armies of foreign Mercenaries to complete the Works of Death, Desolation, and Tyranny, already begun with circumstances of Cruelty and Perfidy, scarcely paralleled in the most barbarous Ages, and totally unworthy the Head of a civilised Nation.

He has constrained our fellow Citizens taken Captive on the high Seas to bear Arms against their Country, to become the

Executioners of their Friends and Brethren, or to fall themselves by their Hands.

He has excited domestic Insurrections amongst us, and has endeavoured to bring on the Inhabitants of our Frontiers, the merciless Indian Savages, whose known Rule of Warfare, is an undistinguished Destruction, of all Ages, Sexes and Conditions.

In every stage of these Oppressions we have Petitioned for Redress in the most humble Terms: Our repeated Petitions have been answered only by repeated Injury. A Prince, whose Character is thus marked by every act which may define a Tyrant, is unfit to be the Ruler of a free People.

Nor have we been wanting in Attentions to our British Brethren. We have warned them from Time to Time of Attempts by their Legislature to extend an unwarrantable Jurisdiction over us. We have reminded them of the Circumstances of our Emigration and Settlement here. We have appealed to their native Justice and Magnanimity, and we have conjured them by the Ties of our common Kindred to disavow these Usurpations, which, would inevitably interrupt our Connections and Correspondence. They too have been deaf to the Voice of Justice and of Consanguinity. We must, therefore, acquiesce in the Necessity, which denounces our Separation, and hold them, as we hold the rest of Mankind, Enemies in War, in Peace, Friends.

We, therefore, the Representatives of the **United States of America**, in General Congress Assembled, appealing to the Supreme Judge of the World for the Rectitude of our Intentions, do, in the Name, and by Authority of the good people of these Colonies, solemnly Publish and Declare, That these United Colonies are, and of Right ought to be, **Free and Independent States;** that they are absolved from all Allegiance to the British Crown, and that all political Connection between them and the State of Great Britain, is and ought to be totally dissolved; and that as **Free and Independent States,** they have full Power to levy War, conclude Peace, contract Alliances, establish Commerce and to do all other Acts and Things which **Independent States** may of right do. And for the support of this Declaration, with a firm Reliance on the Protection of divine Providence, we mutually pledge to each other our Lives, our Fortunes, and our sacred Honor.

The Declaration was in the mainstream of those earlier documents of liberty which we have examined and from which the criticisms of the king's actions were almost wholly derived. To declare that he had been guilty of 'imposing taxes on us without our consent' and of 'depriving us . . . of the Benefits of Trial by Jury' was to declare him in breach of the Great Charter. The maintaining of a standing army in times of peace without consent was an infringement of the Mutiny Act of 1689; his 'quartering of large Bodies of Armed troops among us' was an infringement of the Bill of Rights; while his refusal of 'Assent to Laws, the most wholesome and necessary for the public Good' was a failure to comply with the practices of the post-revolutionary monarchy. The American War of Independence was fought, as was the civil war in England, by men who were prepared to defend their inherited and inalienable rights against the armies of an arbitrary king.

The ideas formulated in the Witan, at Runnymede, in the Grand Council, in parliament, and on the battlefields of the civil war, had crossed the Atlantic with the ships of the adventurous settlers. Folk from many other lands were later to join the new nation, bringing their own customs and beliefs. But the theme of government by consent was central to the new United States of America and remains so to this day.

At home, liberty of worship was advanced in 1778 by an Act permitting Catholic services to be held. In London the mob rose in violent protest and for three or four days the streets witnessed scenes of unchecked lawlessness. It was the king who called out the troops, ensured that order (not without bloodshed) was restored, and who made the Act effective.

By now the American war was going badly for England. A new government was formed under Lord Shelbourne which took from the king the instruments he had used for purchasing parliamentary votes. Sinecures were abolished and the Secret Service Fund was limited to £10,000 a year. The new Chancellor of the Exchequer, William Pitt, son of the great statesman, was only 21 when he became a Tory member of parliament.

The king, after a short-lived coalition between Lord North and Charles James Fox, the Whig leader, appointed young Pitt (now twenty-three years old) as prime minister. Pitt won the election of 1784 and gave a new look to the Tory party, attracting many of the wealthy middle class who had hitherto supported the Whigs. He moved to-wards reform and the abolition of corrupt practices in the parliamentary system, and he tried unsuccessfully to end the slave trade.

Towards the end of the century, the French Revolution again shattered the peace of Europe. In 1793 England and the new France were at war, and at Westminster horror at the excesses carried out by the French in the name of liberty caused a reaction against reform. Many Whigs joined Pitt's ministry and it was Fox, with a handful of supporters, who kept alive the now unpopular spirit of liberty and reform.

In 1797 Britain's fortunes were at their lowest ebb. There was a financial crisis, and a mutiny of the Royal Navy (very reasonable in its demands) at Spithead, and a more disorderly one at the Nore. Napoleon had conquered Italy, and the British fleet had been driven out of the Mediterreanan. The Irish problem was reaching new proportions, with the French actively assisting the Irish.

Meanwhile the nonconformists, whose own civic rights had already been secured, were advancing the liberties of all those who had not shared in the enlargement of freedom. John Wesley's preaching had re-vitalised the puritan movement, bringing a return to the teachings of the New Testament, which had been in danger of being lost among the political considerations that had so dominated religion. Men and women began to be increasingly concerned with the underprivileged. Elizabeth Fry and John Howard strove to improve conditions in the prisons, where filth and degradation, squalor and disease had hitherto been taken for granted. Others looked overseas, and during the last ten years of the eighteenth century, William Wilberforce was working for the abolition of slavery. The slave trade had reached vast propor-tions as cotton plantations in America increased; and it was ships from Britain—land of liberty—which carried most of the slaves to the New World. Wilberforce succeeded in awakening the conscience of parlia-ment, and in 1807 Fox and his friends put through a Bill making un-lawful the transportation of and traffic in slaves.

ACT ABOLISHING THE NEGRO SLAVE TRADE—1807

Whereas the two houses of Parliament did, by their resolu-tions of the tenth and twenty-fourth days of July one thousand eight hundred and six, severally resolve, upon certain grounds therein mentioned, that they would, with all practicable expedition, take effectual measures for the abolition of the African slave trade, in such manner, and at such period, as might be deemed advisable; and whereas it is fit upon all and each of the grounds mentioned in the said resolutions, that the same should be forthwith abolished and prohibited, and declared to be unlawful: be it therefore enacted by the king's most excellent Majesty, by and with the advice and consent of the lords spiritual and temporal, and commons, in this present parliament assembled, and by the authority of the same, that from and after the first day of May one thousand eight hundred and seven, the African slave trade, and all and all manner of dealing and trading in the purchase, sale, barter, or transfer of slaves, or of persons intended to be sold, transferred, used, or dealt with as slaves, practised or carried on, in, at, to, or from any part of the coast or countries of Africa, shall be, and the same is hereby utterly abolished, prohibited, and declared to be unlawful; and also that all and all manner of dealing, either by way of purchase, sale, barter, or transfer, or by means of any other contract or agreement whatever, relating to any slaves, or to any persons intended to be used or dealt with as slaves, for the purpose of such slaves or persons being removed or transported either immediately or by transhipment at sea or otherwise, directly or indirectly from Africa, or from any island, country, territory, or place whatever, in the West Indies, or in any other part of America, not being in the dominion, possession, or occupation of His Majesty, to any other island, country, territory, or place whatever, is hereby in like manner utterly abolished, prohibited, and declared to be unlawful . . .

Slavery was to remain legal for another thirty years. But the first step had been taken to end it. The rights which Englishmen had gained for themselves were beginning to be seen as the birthright of all mankind.

In 1811 George III's mental illness grew acute and the Prince of Wales became Regent. For nine years George III lived in the sad shadows of his disease and 'Prinny' reigned over an elegant and changing England, succeeding his father in 1820 as George IV. During the Regency the long wars against Napoleon were victoriously ended on the plains of Waterloo—a battle which won a century's reputation of invincibility for British arms. The Industrial Revolution developed apace. Goods were abundant, the population increased and the towns grew.

A new class came into being—that of the urban poor. Villeinage had ended in the days of Elizabeth. Now there was a new multitude of dispossessed and deprived. But overall there was a new gaiety, a new sense of reason, new aspirations towards social justice, and a realisation that the new wealth ought to be more equitably shared. London extended into new semi-rural suburbs, with open squares and classically designed houses for the rich and humbler but still finely proportioned houses for the middle classes. It was an age of new thinking and of a search for new forms of liberty to match the new society which had developed.

Under Pitt, the Combination Acts had made trade unionism illegal, but men were combining together nonetheless. There was an increasing belief that every man should be entitled to vote without any property qualification. In 1819 workers from the cotton industry demonstrated in St Peter's Fields, Manchester, demanding manhood suffrage. They were dispersed by a cavalry charge ordered by panic-stricken magistrates. Many died and the tragic incident was long remembered as the 'Peterloo Massacre'—a mocking reference to the great victory won four years earlier at Waterloo.

In the field of religion there was a new spirit of rationality. Men were beginning to claim that true religion lay in the service of mankind—particularly the dispossessed or the uncivilised; whilst others were not ashamed to question the existence of God nor to profess atheism. Young Shelley had published his pamphlet on the need for atheism and suffered no worse punishment than to be sent down from Oxford. The only two universities in England, Oxford and Cambridge, were closely identified with the established Church. Attendance at chapel was compulsory and this meant that Catholics, the stricter nonconformists, and such groups as the Quakers (to say nothing of the Jews), were effectively denied a university education. It is indicative of the new spirit of reason that in 1826 Jeremy Bentham the philosopher, with a group which included Thomas Campbell the poet, founded University College London. It had no chapel and was open to all. Its motto was *Cuncti adsint meritaeque expectent praemia palmae,* which roughly translated means 'Let 'em all come and may the best man win'. This was the beginning of universal opportunity for university education and the results of Bentham's great stride towards liberty are with us still.

In 1825 trade unions were made legal, long before they were permitted in any other country. It was laid down that men might consult together upon wages or prices or withhold their labour by concerted action, but they were not to obstruct or molest employers or fellow workmen. So the liberty to strike was secured.

George IV did not support these radical movements, but he was far less bigoted than his autocratic father, and was a friend of the Whigs, the party of reform.

So when in 1828 parliament removed the Corporation Act and the Test Act, King George did not explode with anger as his father had done when parliament had tried to make it possible for Catholics to sit as members. The old Acts were repealed and Catholics could now hold office. Finally in 1829 came the Catholic Emancipation Act (of which the following are extracts) permitting Catholics to sit in parliament. Only the high offices of state were closed to them and priests in holy orders could not sit.

CATHOLIC EMANCIPATION ACT (EXTRACTS)

Whereas by various acts of parliament certain restraints and disabilities are imposed on the Roman Catholic subjects of His Majesty, to which other subjects of His Majesty are not liable: and whereas it is expedient that such restraints and disabilities shall be from henceforth discontinued: and whereas by various acts certain oaths and certain declarations, commonly called the declaration against transubstantiation, and the declaration against transubtantiation and the invocation of saints and the sacrifice of the mass, as practised in the Church of Rome, are or may be required to be taken, made, and subscribed by the subjects of His Majesty, as qualifications for sitting and voting in parliament, and for the enjoyment of certain offices, franchises, and civil rights: be it enacted by the king's most excellent Majesty, by and with the advice and consent of the lords spiritual and temporal, and commons, in this present parliament assembled, and by the authority of the same, that from and after the commencement of this act all such parts of the said acts as require the said declarations, or either of them, to be made or subscribed by any of His Majesty's subjects, as a qualification for sitting and voting in

172

parliament, or for the exercise or enjoyment of any office, franchise, or civil right, be and the same are (save as hereinafter provided and excepted) hereby repealed.

II. And be it enacted, that from and after the commencement of this act it shall be lawful for any person professing the Roman Catholic religion, being a peer, or who shall after the commencement of this act be returned as a member of the house of commons, to sit and vote in either house of parliament respectively, being in all other respects duly qualified to sit and vote therein, upon taking and subscribing the following oath, instead of the oaths of allegiance, supremacy, and abjuration:

' I, A.B., do sincerely promise and swear, that I will be faithful and bear true allegiance to His Majesty King George the Fourth, and will defend him to the utmost of my power against all conspiracies and attempts whatever, which shall be made against his person, crown, or dignity; and I will do my utmost endeavour to disclose and make known to His Majesty, his heirs and successors, all treasons and traitorous conspiracies which may be formed against him or them: and I do faithfully promise to maintain, support, and defend, to the utmost of my power, the succession of the crown, which succession, by an act, entitled, An Act for the further Limitation of the Crown, and better securing the Rights and Liberties of the Subject, is and stands limited to the princess Sophia, electress of Hanover, and the heirs of her body, being Protestants; hereby utterly renouncing and abjuring any obedience or allegiance unto any other person claiming or pretending a right to the crown of this realm; and I do further declare, that it is not an article of my faith, and that I do renounce, reject, and abjure the opinion, that princes excommunicated or deprived by the pope, or any other authority of the see of Rome, may be deposed or murdered by their subjects, or by any person whatsoever: and I do declare, that I do not believe that the pope of Rome, or any other foreign prince, prelate, person, state, or potentate, hath or ought to have any temporal or civil jurisdiction, power, superiority, or preeminence, directly or indirectly, within this realm. I do swear, that I will defend to the utmost of my power the settlement of property within this realm, as established by the laws: and I do hereby disclaim, disavow, and solemnly abjure any intention to subvert the present church establishment, as settled by law within this realm: and I do solemnly swear, that I will never exercise any privilege to which I am or may become entitled, to disturb or weaken the Protestant religion or Protestant government in the united kingdom: and I do solemnly, in the presence of God, profess, testify, and declare, that I do make this declaration, and every part thereof, in the plain and ordinary sense of the words of this oath, without any evasion, equivocation, or mental reservation whatsoever.

So help me God.'

III.   And be it further enacted, that wherever, in the oath here appointed and set forth, the name of His present Majesty is expressed or referred to, the name of the sovereign of this kingdom for the time being, by virtue of the act for the further limitation of the crown and better securing the right and liberties of the subject, shall be substituted from time to time, with proper words of reference thereto.

IV.   Provided always, and be it further enacted, that no peer professing the Roman Catholic religion, and no person professing the Roman Catholic religion, who shall be returned a member of the house of commons after the commencement of this act, shall be capable of sitting or voting in either house of parliament respectively, unless he shall first take and subscribe the oath hereinbefore appointed and set forth, before the same persons, at the same times and places, and in the same manner as the oaths and the declaration now required by law are respectively directed to be taken, made, and subscribed; and that any such person professing the Roman Catholic religion, who shall sit or vote in either house of parliament, without having first taken and subscribed, in the manner aforesaid, the oath in this act appointed and set forth, shall be subject to the same penalties, forfeitures, and disabilities, and the offence of so sitting or voting shall be followed and attended by and with the same consequences, as are by law enacted and provided in the case of persons sitting or voting in either house of parliament respectively, without the taking, making, and subscribing the oaths and the declaration now required by law.

V.   And be it further enacted, that it shall be lawful for persons professing the Roman Catholic religion to vote at elections of members to serve in parliament for England and for

Ireland, and also to vote at the elections of representative peers of Scotland and of Ireland, and to be elected such representative peers, being in all other respects duly qualified, upon taking and subscribing the oath hereinbefore appointed and set forth, instead of the oaths of allegiance, supremacy, and abjuration, and instead of the declaration now by law required, and instead also of such other oath or oaths as are now by law required to be taken by any of His Majesty's subjects professing the Roman Catholic religion, and upon taking also such other oath or oaths as may now be lawfully tendered to any persons offering to vote at such elections.

IX.   And be it further enacted, that no person in holy orders in the Church of Rome shall be capable of being elected to serve in parliament as a member of the house of commons; and if any such person shall be elected to serve in parliament as aforesaid, such election shall be void; and if any person, being elected to serve in parliament as a member of the house of commons, shall, after his election, take or receive holy orders in the Church of Rome, the seat of such person shall immediately become void; and if any such person shall, in any of the cases aforesaid, presume to sit or vote as a member of the house of commons, he shall be subject to the same penalties, forfeitures, and disabilities as are enacted by an act passed in the forty-first year of the reign of King George the Third, entitled An Act to remove Doubts respecting the Eligibility of Persons in Holy Orders to sit in the House of Commons; and proof of the celebration of any religious service by such person, according to the rites of the Church of Rome, shall be deemed and taken to be **prima facie** evidence of the fact of such person being in holy orders, within the intent and meaning of this act.

X.   And be it enacted, that it shall be lawful for any of His Majesty's subjects professing the Roman Catholic religion to hold, exercise, and enjoy all civil and military offices and places of trust or profit under His Majesty, his heirs or successors, and to exercise any other franchise or civil right, except as hereinafter excepted, upon taking and subscribing, at the times and in the manner hereinafter mentioned, the oath hereinbefore appointed and set forth, instead of the oaths of allegiance, supremacy, and abjuration, and instead of such oath or oaths as are or may be now by law required to be taken for the purpose aforesaid by any of His Majesty's subjects professing the Roman Catholic religion.

XI.   Provided always, and be it enacted, that nothing herein contained shall be construed to exempt any person professing the Roman Catholic religion from the necessity of taking any oath or oaths, or making any declaration, not hereinbefore mentioned, which are or may be by law required to be taken or subscribed by any person on his admission into any such office or place of trust or profit as aforesaid.

XII.   Provided also, and be it further enacted, that nothing herein contained shall extend or be construed to extend to enable any person or persons professing the Roman Catholic religion to hold or exercise the office of guardians and justices of the united kingdom, or of regent of the united kingdom, under whatever name, style, or title such office may be constituted; nor to enable any person, otherwise than as he is now by law enabled, to hold or enjoy the office of lord high chancellor, lord keeper or lord commissioner of the great seal of Great Britain or Ireland; or the office of lord lieutenant, or lord deputy, or other chief governor or governors of Ireland; or His Majesty's high commissioner to the General Assembly of the Church of Scotland.

So the old feud was ended after nearly 300 years of bitter strife between the two creeds, beginning with such cruelty under the Tudors. Freedom of worship had almost been won. The Jews had to wait nearly another thirty years, but the Catholic Emancipation Act made total religious toleration inevitable.

George IV died in 1830, unpopular and unloved. His fashionable friends, whose leader he had once been in such matters as the cut of a waistcoat, the knotting of a cravat, or the proper use of hair pomade, despised him in his fat old age. The common people hated him because of his shabby treatment of his wife, who was shut out of Westminster Abbey at his coronation; and they disliked him because they were impatient for reform, manhood suffrage, the right to form trade unions, and the acquiring of civil rights by every section of the people, against all of which they saw the king as the chief obstruction.

Mud was thrown at his funeral procession. The crown was never in greater disrepute nor, since the days of Charles I, was the institution of monarchy in greater danger.

DOCUMENTS QUOTED:

1 The Septennial Act—1716 [*1 George I. stat 2, c. 38*]
2 American Declaration of Independence—1776
3 Act Abolishing the Negro Slave Trade—1807 [*47 George III. c. 36*]
4 Catholic Emancipation Act—1829 [*10 George IV. c. 7*]

CHAPTER IX

Universal Suffrage
(1829-1969)

GEORGE IV left no legitimate children and the crown passed to his younger brother William IV, who had no great aspirations or abilities.

Protected by the crown, the Tories had stood stubbornly against the forces of change. The shift from agriculture to industry, the growth of the towns and cities, the increase in population, had brought the poorer people together in larger numbers than ever before. When men met only the folk in their own village, when the genial ale-house and the accustomed church or chapel were the only meeting places, they were content for the world to jog along unchanged. But when they met in factories or crowded streets, saw one another's poverty, knew that the factory-owners and great landowners lived a life as different from theirs as theirs was from that of the beasts, they realised their deprivation. The artisan, no longer completely deferential, wanted the vote so that he too might enjoy government by consent and the right to form his own associations.

Under the Georges little advance had been made. Now the pressures were mounting and the choice, realised by the Whigs and by the new progressive Tories, lay starkly between reform or revolution. The character of the Tory party had changed during the last years of George IV. New men, coming not from the landed aristocracy but from those whose wealth was drawn from the Industrial Revolution, had joined them.

One of them, Robert Peel, reduced the number of offences for which men might be hanged, leaving only murder, treason and arson. He abolished the use of government spies, who had been sent to industrial areas to watch for unrest and to smell out the 'reformers'. Oppression by harsh and unreasonable laws is itself a loss of liberty. It is for the winning of liberty from this kind of oppression that Peel

178

deserves to be remembered as much as for his better known work in founding the police force.

In 1828 Lord Wellington, victor of Waterloo, was appointed prime minister with instructions from the king to form a ministry including both Whigs and Tories. Wellington was a Tory of the old school and very quickly got rid of his progressive colleagues, so William IV faced a political crisis at the outset of his reign. Melbourne, Palmerston and their friends wanted the more glaring injustices of the parliamentary system to be put right. Parliamentary boroughs were still the same as in the reign of James I, and this was clearly wrong. Tudor monarchs had ensured a friendly Commons by summoning many members from Cornwall (a royal Duchy) and now it returned more than the whole of Scotland! Over the centuries some towns had grown and some villages were deserted. Some constituencies now had five or ten voters, and a few none at all. In such places the landlord could send whom he wished as member and the great landowner could dictate the composition of the Commons. The Industrial Revolution had vastly increased the population of the northern counties, but they still sent no more members to parliament than when they were sparsely populated pastoral areas under the Tudors. Finally, there was no uniformity about the vote. Franchise varied from constituency to constituency. In some places all ratepayers, in some only those living in certain houses, had the vote.

The growing clamour for reform had been resisted by succeeding governments as mere sedition, an attack on the constitution. But now the demand was growing from several quarters. The new class of factory workers was increasingly impatient of methods which denied to them all civil rights. At the other end of the scale, the new class of the wealthy, who had achieved their riches through commerce and industry were also frustrated. It was the landowners, not they, who could operate the electoral system. There were also the progressive Tories who knew that their party could not survive if it continued to resist reasonable improvements. But Wellington would not budge. In December 1830 the progressive Tories joined the Whig opposition. Wellington was defeated and resigned.

King William appointed the Whig leader, Earl Grey, as prime minister. The progressive Tories supported him and two, Melbourne and Palmerston, joined the cabinet. A committee was appointed and drafted a Reform Bill, introduced by Lord John Russell. It passed its second reading by one vote and was defeated on the third reading. Grey obtained a dissolution and a general election was fought on the issue of the Bill. The Tory-owned constituences could not be moved. But wherever there was a free electorate, members were returned who supported the measure. The new Commons passed the Bill by a substantial majority, only to have the Lords amend it to the point of destruction. Grey asked the king to create a hundred new Whig peers to overcome the hereditary Tory majority in the upper house. King William refused and Grey resigned. The Duke of Wellington again became prime minister, but a wave of demonstrations and violence swept the country. In the north, thousands of working men drilled in order to fight for the Bill. There were riots in Bristol and in Derby. Wellington's cabinet itself was divided. Peel made it clear that he would not help Wellington in introducing repressive measures. Wellington resigned and the king invited Grey to form a government. Grey agreed, but only after he had obtained William's written promise that he would create the new peers if necessary.

The Lords decided to yield rather than to become a predominantly Whig body. They withdrew their amendments and the Reform Bill become The Reform Act in 1832. It reads in part as follows:

REFORM ACT—1832

Whereas it is expedient to take effectual measures for correcting divers abuses that have long prevailed in the choice of members to serve in the commons house of parliament, to deprive many inconsiderable places of the right of returning members, to grant such privilege to large, populous, and wealthy towns, to increase the number of knights of the shire, to extend the elective franchise to many of His Majesty's subjects who have not heretobefore enjoyed the same, and to diminish the expense of elections: Be it therefore enacted by the king's most excellent Majesty, by and with the advice and consent of the lords spiritual and temporal, and commons, in this present parliament assembled, and by the authority of the same, that each of the boroughs enumerated in the Schedule marked A (56 in all) shall from and after the end of this present parliament cease to return any member or members to serve in parliament.

Clauses II to XVII list the constituencies and the numbers of members to be returned.

XVIII. That no person shall be entitled to vote in the election of a knight or knights of the shire to serve in any future parliament, or in the election of a member or members to serve in any future parliament for any city or town being a county of itself, in respect of any freehold lands or tenements whereof such person may be seised for his own life, or for the life of another, or for any lives whatsoever, except such person shall be in the actual and **bona fide** occupation of such lands or tenements, or except the same shall have come to such person by marriage, marriage settlement, devise, or promotion to any benefice or to any office, or except the same shall be of the clear yearly value of not less than 10 £ above all rents and charges payable out of or in respect of the same; any statute or usage to the contrary notwithstanding: provided always, that nothing in this act contained shall prevent any person now seised for his own life, or for the life of another, or for any lives whatsoever, of any freehold lands or tenements in respect of which he now has, or but for the passing of this act might acquire, the right of voting in such respective elections, from retaining or acquiring, so long as he shall be so seised of the same lands or tenements, such right of voting in respect thereof, if duly registered according to the respective provisions hereinafter contained.

XIX. That every male person of full age, and not subject to any legal incapacity, who shall be seised at law or in equity of any land or tenements of copyhold or any other tenure whatever except freehold, for his own life, or for the life of another, or for any lives whatsoever, or for any larger estate, of the clear yearly value of not less than 10 £ over and above all rents and charges payable out of or in respect of the same, shall be entitled to vote in the election of a knight or knights of the shire to serve in any future parliament for the county, or for the riding, parts, or division of the county, in which such lands or tenements shall be respectively situate.

XX. That every male person of full age, and not subject to any legal incapacity, who shall be entitled, either as lessee or assignee, to any lands or tenements, whether of freehold or of

181

any other tenure whatever, for the unexpired residue, whatever it may be, of any term originally created for a period of not less than sixty years, (whether determinable on a life or lives, or not,) of the clear yearly value of not less than 10 £ over and above all rents and charges payable out of or in respect of the same, or for the unexpired residue, whatever it may be, of any term originally created for a period of not less than twenty years, (whether determinable on a life or lives, or not,) of the clear yearly value of not less than 50 £ over and above all rents and charges payable out of or in respect of the same, or who shall occupy as tenant any lands or tenements for which he shall be **bona fide** liable to a yearly rent of not less than 50 £, shall be entitled to vote in the election of a knight or knights of the shire to serve in any future parliament for the county, or for the riding, parts, or division of the county, in which such lands or tenements shall be respectively situate: provided always, that no person, being only a sublessee, or the assignee of any under-lease, shall have a right to vote in such election in respect of any such term of sixty years or twenty years as aforesaid, unless he shall be in the actual occupation of the premises.

XXI. That no public or parliamentary tax, nor any church rate, county rate, or parochial rate, shall be deemed to be any charge payable out of or in respect of any lands or tenements within the meaning of this act .

XXII. That in order to entitle any person to vote in any election of a knight of the shire or other member to serve in any future parliament, in respect of any messuages, lands, or tenements, whether freehold or otherwise, it shall not be necessary that the same shall be assessed to the land tax; any statute to the contrary notwithstanding.

XXVI. That notwithstanding anything hereinbefore contained no person shall be entitled to vote in the election of a knight or knights of the shire to serve in any future parliament unless he shall have been duly registered according to the provisions hereinafter contained; and that no person shall be so registered in any year in respect of his estate or interest in any lands or tenements, as a freeholder, copyholder, customary tenant, or tenant in ancient demesne, unless he shall have

182

been in the actual possession thereof, or in the receipt of the rents and profits thereof for his own use, for six calendar months at least next previous to the last day of July in such year, which said period of six calendar months shall be sufficient, any statute to the contrary notwithstanding; and that no person shall be so registered in any year, in respect of any lands or tenements held by him as such lessee or assignee, or as such occupier and tenant as aforesaid, unless he shall have been in the actual possession thereof, or in receipt of the rents and profits thereof for his own use, as the case may require, for twelve calendar months next previous to the last day of July in such year: provided always, that where any lands or tenements, which would otherwise entitle the owner, holder, or occupier thereof to vote in any such election, shall come to any person, at any time within such respective periods of six or twelve calendar months, by descent, succession, marriage, marriage settlement, devise, or promotion to any benefice in a church, or by promotion to any office, such person shall be entitled in respect thereof to have his name inserted as a voter in the election of a knight or knights of the shire in the lists then next to be made, by virtue of this act as hereinafter mentioned, and, upon his being duly registered according to the provisions hereinafter contained, to vote in such election.

XXVII. That in every city or borough which shall return a member or members to serve in any future parliament, every male person of full age, and not subject to any legal incapacity, who shall occupy, within such city or borough, or within any place sharing in the election for such city or borough, as owner or tenant, any house, warehouse, counting-house, shop, or other building, being, either separately, or jointly with any land within such city, borough, or place occupied therewith by him as owner, or therewith by him as tenant under the same landlord, of the clear yearly value of not less than 10£, shall, if duly registered according to the provisions hereinafter contained, be entitled to vote in the election of a member or members to serve in any future parliament for such city or borough: provided always, that no such person shall be so registered in any year unless he shall have occupied such premises as aforesaid for twelve calendar months next previous to the last day of July in such year, nor unless such person, where such premises are situated in any parish or township in which there shall be a rate for the relief of the poor, shall have been rated in respect of such premises to all rates for the relief of the poor in such parish or township, made during the time of such his occupation so required as aforesaid, nor unless such person shall have paid, on or before the 20th of July in such year, all the poor's rates and assessed taxes which shall have become payable from him in respect of such premises previously to the 6th April then next preceding: provided also, that no such person shall be so registered in any year unless he shall have resided for six calendar months next previous to the last day of July in such year within the city or borough, or within the place sharing in the election for the city or borough, in respect of which city, borough, or place respectively he shall be entitled to vote, or within seven statute miles thereof or of any part thereof.

XXVIII.   That the premises in respect of the occupation of which any person shall be entitled to be registered in any year, and to vote in the election for any city or borough as aforesaid, shall not be required to be the same premises, but may be different premises occupied in immediate succession by such person during the twelve calendar months next previous to the last day of July in such year, such person having paid on or before the 20th of July in such year, all the poor's rates and assessed taxes which shall previously to the 6th of April then next preceding have become payable from him in respect of all such premises so occupied by him in succession.

XXXVI.   That no person shall be entitled to be registered in any year as a voter in the election of a member or members to serve in any future parliament for any city or borough who shall within twelve calendar months next previous to the last day of July in such year have received parochial relief or other alms, which by the law of parliament now disqualify from voting in the election of members to serve in parliament.

XXXVII.   That the overseers of the poor of every parish and township shall, on the 20th day of June in the present and in every succeeding year, cause to be fixed on or near the

184

doors of all the churches and chapels within such parish or township, or if there be no church or chapel therein, then to be fixed in some public and conspicuous situation within the the same respectively, a notice according the form numbered 1. in the schedule (H.) to this act annexed, requiring all persons who may be entitled to vote in the election of a knight or knights of the shire in respect of any property situate wholly or in part in such parish or township, to deliver or transmit to the said overseers on or before the 20th of July in the present and in every succeeding year a notice of their claim as such voters, according to the form numbered 2. in the said schedule (H.), or to the like effect: provided always, that after the formation of the register to be made in each year, as hereinafter mentioned, no person whose name shall be upon such register for the time being shall be required thereafter to make any such claim as aforesaid, so long as he shall retain the same qualification, and continue in the same place of abode described by such register.

XXXVIII.   That the overseer of the poor of every parish and township shall, on or before the last day of July in the present year, make out or cause to be made out, according to the form numbered 3. in the said schedule (H.), an alphabetical list of all persons who shall claim as aforesaid to be inserted in such list as voters in the election of a knight or knights of the shire in respect of any lands or tenements situate wholly or in part within such parish or township; and that the said overseers shall on or before the last day of July in every succeeding year make out or cause to be made out a like list, containing the names of all persons who shall be upon the register for the time being as such voters, and also the names of all persons who shall claim as aforesaid to be inserted in the last-mentioned list as such voters; and in every list so to be made out by the overseers as aforesaid, the Christian name and surname of every person shall be written at full length, together with the place of his abode, the nature of his qualification, and the local or other description of such lands or tenements, as the same are respectively set forth in his claim to vote, and the name of the occupying tenant, if stated in such claim; and the said overseers, if they shall have reasonable cause to believe that any person so claiming as aforesaid, or whose name shall appear in the register for the time being, is not entitled to vote in the election of a knight or knights of the shire . . . shall have power to add the words 'objected to' opposite the name of every such person on the margin of such list; and the said overseers shall sign such list, and shall cause a sufficient number of copies of such list to be written or printed, and to be fixed on or near the doors of all the churches and chapels within their parish or township, or if there be no church or chapel therein, then to be fixed up in some public and conspicuous situation within the same respectively, on the two Sundays next after such list shall have been made; and the said overseers shall likewise keep a true copy of such list, to be perused by any person, without payment of any fee, at all reasonable hours during the first two weeks after such lists shall have been made; provided always that every precinct or place, whether extra-parochial or otherwise, which shall have no overseers of the poor, shall for the purpose of making out such list as aforesaid be deemed to be within the parish or township adjoining thereto, such parish or township being situate within the same county, or the same riding, parts, or division of a county, as such precinct or place; and if such precinct or place shall adjoin two or more parishes or townships so situate as aforesaid, it shall be deemed to be within the least populous of such parishes or townships according to the last census for the time being, and the overseers of the poor of every such parish or township shall insert in the list for their respective parish or township the names of all persons who shall claim as aforesaid to be inserted therein as voters.

XXXIX. That every person who shall be upon the register for the time being for any county, or for any riding, parts, or division of a county, or who shall have claimed to be inserted in any list for the then current year of voters may object to any person as not having been entitled on the last day of July then next preceding to have his name inserted in any list of voters so to be made out as aforesaid; and every person so objecting (save and except overseers objecting in the manner hereinbefore mentioned) shall on or before the 25th of August in the present and in every succeeding year, give or cause to be given a notice in writing according to the form numbered 4. in the said schedule (H.), or to the like effect, to the overseers who shall have made out the list in which the name so objected to shall have been inserted; and the person so objecting shall also, on or before the 25th of August give to the person objected to, or leave at his place of abode as described in such list, or personally deliver to his tenant in occupation of the premises described in such list, a notice in writing according to the form numbered 5. in the said schedule (H.), or to the like effect; and the overseers shall include the names of all persons so objected to in a list according to the form numbered 6. in the said schedule (H.), and shall cause copies of the same to be fixed on or near the doors of all the churches on the two Sundays next preceding the 15th of September in the present and every succeeding year; and the overseers shall likewise keep a copy of the names of all the persons so objected to, to be perused by any person.

XL. That on the 29th of August in the present and in every succeeding year the overseers of every parish and township shall deliver the list of voters so made out as aforesaid, together with a written statement of the number of persons objected to by the overseers and by other persons, to the high constable or high constables of the hundred or other like district in which such parish or township is situate; and such high constable or high constables shall forthwith deliver all such lists, together with such statements as aforesaid, to the clerk of the peace of the county, riding, or parts, who shall forthwith make out an abstract of the number of persons objected to by the overseers and by other persons in each parish or township, and transmit the same to the barrister or barristers appointed as hereinafter mentioned to revise such lists, in order that the said barrister or barristers may fix proper times and places for holding his or their courts for the revision of the said lists.

XLI. That the lord chief justice of the court of king's bench shall, in the month of July or August in the present and in every succeeding year, nominate and appoint for Middlesex, and the senior judge for the time being in the commission of assize for every other county shall, when travelling the summer circuit, nominate and appoint for every such county, or for each of the ridings, parts, or divisions of such county, a barrister or barristers to revise the lists of voters in the election of a knight or knights of the shire; and such barrister

or barristers so appointed as aforesaid shall give public notice,
as well by advertisement in some of the newspapers circu-
lating within the county, riding, parts, or division, as also by
a notice to be fixed in some public and conspicuous situation
to be given three days at the least before the commencement
of his or their circuit,) that he or they will make a circuit of
the county, riding, parts, or division for which he or they
shall be so appointed, and of the several times and places at
which he or they will hold courts for that purpose, such times
being between the 15th of September inclusive and the 25th
of October inclusive in the present and in every succeeding
year, and he or they shall hold open courts for that purpose
at the times and places so to be announced; and where two or
more barristers shall be appointed for the same county, riding,
parts, or division, they shall attend at the same places together, but shall sit apart from each other, and hold separate
courts at the same time for the despatch of business: provided always, that no member of parliament; nor any person
holding any office or place of profit under the crown, shall be
appointed such barrister, and that no barristers so appointed
as aforesaid shall be eligible to serve in parliament for eighteen months from the time of such his appointment.

XLII. That the clerk of the peace shall at the opening of
the first court to be held by every such barrister produce or
cause to be produced before him the several lists of voters for
such county, riding, parts, or division which shall have been
delivered to such clerk of the peace by the high constable as
aforesaid; and the overseers of every parish and township
who shall have made out the lists of voters shall attend the
court to be held by every such barrister at the place appointed
for revising the lists relating to such parish or township
respectively, and shall also deliver to such barrister a copy
of the list of the persons objected to, so made out by them
as aforesaid; and the said overseers shall answer upon oath
all such questions as such barrister may put to them or any of
them touching any matter necessary for revising the lists of
voters; and every such barrister shall retain on the lists of
voters the names of all persons to whom no objection shall
have been made by the overseers, or by any other person, in
the manner hereinbefore mentioned; and he shall also retain
on the list of voters the name of every person who shall have

been objected to by any person other than the overseers, unless the party so objecting shall appear by himself or by someone on his behalf in support of such objection; and where the name of any person inserted in the list of voters shall have been objected to by the overseers, or by any other person in the manner hereinbefore mentioned, and such person so objecting shall appear by himself or by some one on his behalf in support of such objection, every such barrister shall require it to be proved that the person so objected to was entitled on the last day of July then next preceding to have his name inserted in the list of voters in respect of the qualification described in such list; and in case the same shall not be proved to the satisfaction of such barrister, or in case it shall be proved that such person was then incapacitated by any law or statute from voting in the election of members to serve in parliament, such barrister shall expunge the name of every such person from the said lists; and he shall also expunge from the said lists the name of every person who shall be proved to him to be dead; and shall correct any mistake which shall be proved to him to have been made in any of the said lists as to any of the particulars by this act required to be inserted in such lists, and where the Christian name of any person, or his place of abode, or the nature of his qualification, or the local or other description of his property, or the name of the tenant in the occupation therof, as the same respectively are required to be inserted in any such list, shall be wholly omitted therefrom, such barrister shall expunge the name of every such person from such list, unless the matter or matters so omitted be supplied to the satisfaction of such barrister before he shall have completed the revision of such list, in which case he shall then and there insert the same in such list: provided always, that no person's name shall be expunged from any such list, except in case of his death or of his being objected to on the margin of the list by the overseers as aforesaid, or except in case of any such omission or omissions as hereinbefore last-mentioned, unless such notice as is hereinbefore required in that behalf shall have been given to the overseers, nor unless such notice as is hereinbefore required in that behalf shall have been given to such person, or left at his place of abode, or delivered to his tenant as hereinbefore mentioned.

XLIII. Provided also, that if it shall happen than any person who shall have given to the overseers of any parish or township due notice of his claim to have his name inserted in the list of voters in the election of a knight or knights of the shire, shall have been omitted by such overseers from such list, it shall be lawful for the barrister, upon the revision of such list, to insert therein the name of the person so omitted, in case it shall be proved to the satisfaction of such barrister that such person gave due notice of such his claim to the said overseers, and that he was entitled on the last day of July then next preceding to be inserted in the list of voters in the election of a knight or knights of the shire . . .

Clauses XLIV–LII. Regulations for registration of voters for boroughs.

LVI. That for the purpose of defraying the expenses to be incurred by the overseers of the poor and by the clerk of the peace in carrying into effect the several provisions of this act, so far as relates to the electors for any county, or for any riding, parts, or division of a county, every person, upon giving notice of his claim as such elector to the overseers, as hereinbefore mentioned, shall pay or cause to be paid to the said overseers the sum of 1s.; and such notice of claim shall not be deemed valid until such sum shall have been paid; and the overseers of each parish or township shall add all monies so received by them to the money collected or to be collected for the relief of the poor in such parish or townships, and such monies so added shall be applicable to the same purposes as monies collected for the relief of the poor; and that for the purpose of defraying the expenses to be incurred by the returning officer of every city and borough, and by the overseers of the several parishes and townships in every city and borough, and place sharing in the election therewith, in carrying into effect the provisions of this act, so far as relates to the electors for such city or borough, every such elector whose name shall be upon the register of voters for such city or borough for the time being shall be liable to the payment of 1s. annually, which sum shall be levied and collected from each elector in addition to and as a part of the money payable by him as his contribution to the rate for the relief of the poor, and such sum shall be applicable to the same purposes as money collected for the relief of the poor; and that the expenses incurred by the overseers of any parish or township in making out, printing, and publishing the several lists and notices directed by this act, and all other expenses incurred by them in carrying into effect the provisions of this act, shall be defrayed out of the money collected or to be collected for the relief of the poor in such parish or township; and that all expenses incurred by the returning officer of any city or borough in causing the lists of the electors for such city or borough to be copied out and made into a register, and in causing copies of such register to be written or printed, shall be defrayed by the overseers of the poor of the several parishes and townships within such city or borough, or place sharing in the election therewith, out of the money collected or to be collected for the relief of the poor in such parishes and township, in proportion to the number of voters placed on the register of voters for each parish or township; and that all expenses incurred by the clerk of the peace of any county, riding, or parts in causing the lists of the electors for such county, riding, or parts, or for any division of such county, to be copied out and made into a register, and in causing copies of such register to be written or printed, and in otherwise carrying into effect the provisions of this act, shall be defrayed by the treasurer of such county, riding, or parts out of any public money in his hands, and he shall be allowed all such payments in his accounts: provided always, that no expenses incurred by any clerk of the peace under this act shall be so defrayed unless the account shall be laid before the justices of the peace at the next quarter sessions after such expenses shall have been incurred, and allowed by the court.

LVII. That every barrister appointed to revise any list of voters under this act shall be paid at the rate of five guineas for every day that he shall be so employed, over and above his travelling and other expenses; and every such barrister, after the termination of his last sitting, shall lay or cause to be laid before the lords commissioners of His Majesty's treasury for the time being a statement of the number of days during which he shall have been so employed, and an account of the travelling and other expenses incurred by him in respect of such employment; and the said lords commissioners shall make an order for the amount to be paid to such barrister.

LXII. That at every contested election of a knight or knights to serve in any future parliament for any county, or for any riding, parts, or division of a county, the polling shall commence at nine o'clock in the forenoon of the next day but two after the day fixed for the election, unless such next day but two shall be Saturday or Sunday, and then on the Monday following, at the principal place of election, and also at the several places to be appointed as hereinafter directed for taking polls; and such polling shall continue for two days only, such two days being successive days; (that is to say,) for seven hours on the first day of polling, and for eight hours on the second day of polling; and no poll shall be kept open later than four o'clock in the afternoon of the second day; any statute to the contrary notwithstanding.

LXIII. That the respective counties in England and Wales, and the respective ridings, parts, and divisions of counties, shall be divided into convenient districts for polling, and in each district shall be appointed a convenient place for taking the poll at all elections of a knight or knights of the shire to serve in any future parliament, and such districts and places for taking the poll shall be settled and appointed by the act to be passed in this present parliament for the purpose of settling and describing the divisions of the counties enumerated in the schedule marked (F.) to this act annexed; provided that no county, nor any riding, parts, or division of a county, shall have more than fifteen districts and respective places appointed for taking the poll for such county, riding, or division.

LXIV. That at every contested election for any county, riding, parts, or division of a county, the sheriff, under-sheriff, or sheriff's deputy shall, if required thereto by or on behalf of any candidate, on the day fixed for the election, and if not so required may if it shall appear to him expedient, cause to be erected a reasonable number of booths for taking the poll at the principal place of election, and also at each of the polling places so to be appointed as aforesaid, and shall cause to be affixed on the most conspicuous part of each of the said booths the names of the several parishes, townships, and places for which such booth is respectively allotted; and no person shall be admitted to vote at any such election in respect of any property situate in any parish, township, or place, except at the booth so allotted for such parish, township or place, and if no booth shall be so allotted for the same, then at any of the booths for the same district; and in case any parish, township, or place shall happen not to be included in any of the districts to be appointed, the votes in respect of property situate in any parish, township, or places omitted shall be taken at the principal place of election for the county, or riding, parts, or division of the county, as the case may be.

LXXI.   That from and after the end of this present parliament all booths erected for the convenience of taking polls shall be erected at the joint and equal expense of the several candidates, and the same shall be erected by contract with the candidates, if they shall think fit to make such contract, or if they shall not make such contract, then the same shall be erected by the sheriff or other returning officer at the expense of the several candidates as aforesaid, subject to such limitation as is hereinafter next mentioned; (that is to say,) that the expense to be incurred for the booth or booths to be erected at the principal place of election or at any of the polling places so to be appointed as aforesaid, shall not exceed the sum of 40 £ in respect of any one such principal place of election or any one such polling place, and that the expense to be incurred for any booth or booths to be erected for any parish, district, or part of any city or borough shall not exceed the sum of 25 £ in respect of any one such parish district, or part; and that all deputies appointed by the sheriff or other returning officer shall be paid each two guineas by the day, and all clerks employed in taking the poll shall be paid each one guinea by the day, at the expense of the candidates at such election: provided always, that if any person shall be proposed without his consent, then the person so proposing him shall be liable to defray his share of the said expenses in like manner as if he had been a candidate; provided also, that the sheriff or other returning officer may, if he shall think fit, instead of erecting such booth or booths as aforesaid, procure or hire and use any houses or other buildings for the purpose of taking the poll therein, subject always to the same regulations, provisions, liabilities, and limitations of expense as are hereinbefore mentioned with regard to booths for taking the poll.

LXXVIII. Provided always, that nothing in this act contained shall extend to or in any wise affect the election of members to serve in parliament for the universities of Oxford or Cambridge, or shall entitle any person to vote in the election of members to serve in parliament for the city of Oxford or town of Cambridge in respect of the occupation of any chamber or premises in any of the colleges or halls of the universities of Oxford or Cambridge.

The Act was received with nationwide rejoicing, yet for the working man, who had struggled so hard to obtain it, it was but bitter fruit. The qualification for the vote, payment of £10 or more in annual rent, meant that artisans and mechanics were largely excluded from the Act's provisions; and since, under the old happy-go-lucky system, many had been entitled to vote, as a class they were worse off than before.

However, the Act was a great step forward. Influence in the Commons was no longer openly for sale. Elections, which under the old system crudely reflected the mood of the people, were to do so with increasing accuracy. Moreover, as in the case of so many earlier documents, the rights won for one class were soon to be passed to all, and the dream of manhood suffrage was coming to fulfilment.

The first House of Commons to be elected under the new Act was not very different from its predecessor—members were largely drawn from the landed gentry—but its attitude was vastly changed. It took up the task of reform in many fields with enthusiastic vigour. One of its first achievements was to abolish slavery throughout all British territories. The Act of 1833 reads in part as follows:

ACT ABOLISHING NEGRO SLAVERY—1833

Whereas divers Persons are holden in Slavery within divers

194

of His Majesty's Colonies, and it is just and expedient that all such Persons should be manumitted and set free, and that a reasonable Compensation should be made to the Persons hitherto entitled to the Services of such Slaves for the Loss which they will incur by being deprived of their Right to such Services: And whereas it is also expedient that Provision should be made for promoting the Industry and securing the good Conduct of the Persons so to be manumitted, for a limited Period after such their Manumission: And whereas it is necessary that the laws now in force in the said several Colonies should forthwith be adapted to the new State and Relations of Society therein which will follow upon such general Manumission as aforesaid of the said Slaves; and that, in order to afford the necessary Time for such Adaptation of the said Laws, a short interval should elapse before such Manumission should take effect: Be it therefore enacted by the King's most Excellent Majesty, by and with the Advice and Consent of the Lords Spiritual and Temporal, and Commons, in this present Parliament assembled, and by the Authority of the same, That from and after the First Day of August One thousand eight hundred and thirty-four all Persons who in conformity with the Laws now in force in the said Colonies respectively shall on or before the First Day of August One thousand eight hundred and thirty-four have been duly registered as Slaves in any such Colony, and who on the said First Day of August One thousand eight hundred and thirty-four shall be actually within any such Colony, and who shall by such Registries appear to be on the said First Day of August One thousand eight hundred and thirty-four of the full Age of Six Years or upwards, shall by force and virtue of this Act, and without the previous Execution of any Indenture of Apprenticeship, or other Deed or Instrument for that Purpose, become and be apprenticed Labourers; provided that, for the Purposes aforesaid, every Slave engaged in his ordinary Occupation on the Seas shall be deemed and taken to be within the Colony to which such Slave shall belong.

II.   And be it further enacted, That during the Continuance of the Apprenticeship of any such apprenticed Labourer such Person or Persons shall be entitled to the Services of such apprenticed Labourer as would for the Time being have been entitled to his or her Services as a Slave if this Act had not been made.

III.   Provided also, and be it further enacted, That all Slaves who may at any Time previous to the passing of this Act have been brought with the Consent of their Possessors, and all apprenticed Labourers who may hereafter with the like Consent be brought, into any Part of the United Kingdom of Great Britain and Ireland, shall from and after the passing of this Act be absolutely and entirely free to all Intents and Purposes whatsoever.

XXIV.   And whereas, towards compensating the Persons at present entitled to the Services of the Slaves to be manumitted and set free by virtue of this Act for the Loss of such Services, His Majesty's most dutiful and loyal Subjects the Commons of Great Britain and Ireland in Parliament assembled have resolved to give and grant to His Majesty the Sum of Twenty Millions Pounds Sterling; be it enacted, That the Lords Commissioners of His Majesty's Treasury of the United Kingdom of Great Britain and Ireland may raise such Sum or Sums of Money as shall be required from Time to Time under the Provisions of this Act, and may grant as the Consideration for such Sum or Sums of Money Redeemable Perpetual Annuities or Annuities for Terms of Years . . .

XXXIII.   And for the Distribution of the said Compensation Fund, and the Apportionment thereof amongst the several Persons who may prefer Claims thereon, be it enacted, That it shall and may be lawful for His Majesty from Time to Time, by a Commission under the Great Seal of the United Kingdom to constitute and appoint such Persons, not being less than Five, as to His Majesty shall seem meet, to be Commissioners of Arbitration for inquiring into and deciding upon the Claims to Compensation which may be preferred to them under this Act.

XLV.   And be it further enacted, That the said Commissioners shall proceed to apportion the said Sum into Nineteen different Shares, which shall be respectively assigned to the several British Colonies or Possessions hereinafter mentioned; (that is to say,) the Bermuda Islands, the Bahama Islands, Jamaica, Honduras, the Virgin Islands, Antigua, Montserrat, Nevis, Saint Christopher's, Dominica, Barbadoes, Grenada, Saint Vincent's, Tobago, Saint Lucia, Trinidad, British Guiana, the Cape of Good Hope, and Mauritius; and in making such Apportionment of the said Funds between the said several Colonies the said Commissioners shall and are hereby required to have regard to the Number of Slaves belonging to or settled in each of such Colonies as the same may appear and are stated according to the latest Returns made in the Office of the Registrar of Slaves in England, appointed in pursuance and under the Authority of an Act passed in the Fifty-ninth Year of His late Majesty King George the Third, intituled An Act for establishing a Registry of Colonial Slaves in Great Britain, and for making further Provision with respect to the Removal of Slaves from British Colonies; and the said Commissioners shall and they are hereby further required, in making such Apportionment as aforesaid, to have regard to the Prices for which, on an Average of Eight Years ending on the Thirty-first Day of December One thousand eight hundred and thirty, Slaves have been sold in each of the Colonies aforesaid respectively, excluding from Consideration any such Sales in which they shall have sufficient Reason to suppose that such Slaves were sold or purchased under any Reservation, or subject to any express or tacit Condition affecting the Price thereof; and the said Commissioners shall then proceed to ascertain, in reference to each Colony, what Amount of Sterling Money will represent the average Value of a Slave therein for the said Period of Eight Years; and the total Number of the Slaves in each Colony being multiplied into the Amount of Sterling Money so representing such average Value as aforesaid of a Slave therein, the Product of such Multiplication shall be ascertained for each such Colony separately; and the said Twenty Millions of Pounds Sterling shall then be assigned to and apportioned amongst the said several Colonies rateably and in proportion to the Product so ascertained for each respectively.

The Act was a triumph for the humanitarian zeal of the new parliament. England had now made some amends for the part she had taken in selling, like cattle, men, women and children brutally kidnapped from their homes in Africa. Now because her people had grown to value the treasure of their own liberties, she was the first country to grant full liberty to all slaves.

The spread of factories which followed the development of steam power resulted in untold squalor and misery throughout Britain. Families moved into the cities and into the new industrial slum-towns built on the coalfields. Children, scarcely more than babies, were driven by their parents' poverty to work in the cotton mills and other factories for twelve hours a day or more. A large proportion of the population was deprived of rights even more fundamental than those set out in the consitutional documents : the right to enough food, to a normal childhood, and to such basic things as air, sunlight and happiness. The Reform Parliament took steps to safeguard some of these rights. The Factory Act of 1833 forbade the employment of children under nine years old (it is now difficult to conceive a society in which such legislation was necessary) and limited the hours of work for older children. Inspectors were appointed to see that the Act was enforced.

King William had not been happy about the Reform Bill, nor did he much care for the great number of reforming Acts which followed it. He took an early opportunity to appoint Robert Peel as Tory prime minister in 1836. Peel called an election, and fought it on the basis of a manifesto explaining his new conception of Toryism. He accepted the Reform Act of 1832; and, while the Tories still believed in conserving old standards, this 'Conservatism' did not prevent him from being in favour of 'moderate and judicious redress for proved grievances.' Peel's manifesto made little appeal to a nation that was set on wider reform. He lost the election and Melbourne came back as Whig prime minister.

Then in 1837 King William died, leaving no children. His younger brother, the Duke of Kent, the fourth son of George III, had died seventeen years earlier. So the heir was Kent's daughter, Victoria, grand-daughter of George III. She was only nineteen when William died, with no experience of political affairs, and no knowledge of the crown's position other than what she had read in her history books. Lord Melbourne, urbane, kindly and worldly-wise, guided the young queen in her new duties.

Four years after her accession she learned her first hard constitutional lesson. In 1841 there was an election and Peel's new 'Conservative' party came to power. The young queen lost the help of Melbourne and had to accept the austere and aloof Sir Robert Peel. Worse, her ladies-in-waiting resigned with the old government and new ones were appointed. Victoria objected, sulked, and finally agreed to the change.

The early years of Victoria's reign were marked by dramatic technical advances. The steam locomotive made travel speedier than it had ever been in man's long history. The towns of England seemed suddenly very close together so that York and London became neighbouring cities. The new penny post of 1840 made communication by letter widely available. The electric telegraph provided a method of exchanging information at a speed that was miraculous. With all these spectacular advances there was a general progress in the technology of manufacture. Iron was produced more abundantly than ever before. The spinning rooms and weaving sheds of Lancashire hummed and clattered ceaselessly. More and more miners grunted and coughed their grimy way along the low galleries, their limbs glistening in the dim light, coated with a gleaming polish of coal dust and sweat.

Working men saw a country growing immensely wealthy by the toil of their aching muscles and the skill of their scarred hands. When their fathers had worked on the farms, they and their rich landlords both looked on the golden fields of August barley, judging its ripeness for the scythe. Both would taste the beer that foamed from the reaped harvest, and eat the pork and bacon from pigs fattened on the ripe grain. The landlord had more than they but there was some link and kinship. Now they took nothing of what their hands produced. The fine cloths they wove, the intricate ironwork they forged or cast, the furniture upon which they laboured, the ships they built, the opulent first class railway carriages they constructed—none of these things came their way.

They had heard much of the Reform Bill and of the right to vote and sit in parliament. They knew there had been great charters in the past, defining and defending the rights of the subject. They themselves would draw up a charter. It was largely drafted by William Lovett, a cabinet maker, and a leading member of the London Working Men's Association, an organisation founded to improve the lot of working men.

The GREAT CHARTER made six demands :

(1) *Household Suffrage* : whereby the head of every household was to have a vote irrespective of rent or wealth.

(2) *Vote by Ballot*: so that men could vote secretly without intimidation by landlord or employer.

(3) *Equal Electoral Districts*: the Reform Act had left some constituencies with ten times more voters than others.

(4) *The Abolition of the Property Qualification*: thereby giving to all the right of representation.

(5) *Payment of Members of Parliament*: so that working men might become members, representing their own class, as the landowners and businessmen represented theirs.

(6) *Annual Elections*: so that members would have to look continually at their constituents' wishes.

The charter gained enthusiastic support, not only from working men but from an increasing number of Radicals—the extreme Whigs who desired radical reforms. In 1839, mass meetings of working men were held in all the industrial centres, and delegates were elected to attend a national convention. The Chartists (as supporters of the charter were called) resolved to present a petition to parliament. Lovett was anxious that everything should be done in a constitutional manner and the charter is evidence of his moderation.

The charter was presented and parliament rejected it. There were riots in the Midlands and in Wales. The Chartist movement petered out with the arrest of the ringleaders and a despairing lethargy among many of its supporters, but it left its mark. Where the working classes in other countries were seeking violent solutions to their problems, in England men followed traditional methods : the redress of grievances by petition and the production of a charter of rights and liberties.

Lord John Russell, who had introduced the Reform Bill, later became prime minister of a Whig (now Liberal) administration. The foreign secretary was Lord Palmerston, a man whose direct and brutal diplomacy has become a byword. It was not only foreigners whom he treated with disdain. He was in the habit of sending instructions to ambassadors without consulting the queen. Victoria, with some twelve years of experience behind her and very conscious of being the queen, wrote a letter to the prime minister stating roundly that she would insist upon Palmerston's resignation if he did not mend his ways. Palmerston ignored the warning and in 1851 sent certain instructions to the British Ambassador in Paris without consulting either the queen or Lord John. Both were furious and Palmerston was dismissed. In revenge he and his followers voted with the Conservative opposition and Lord John's government fell.

The new government under Lord Derby, with Disraeli as Chancellor of the Exchequer, survived only a year. An election was held and the Liberals again gained a majority. A coalition government was formed of Whigs and moderate Tories one of whom, Lord Aberdeen, became prime minister, with Gladstone as Chancellor of the Exchequer and Palmerston, exiled from the Foreign Office, as Home Secretary.

In 1854 came the Crimean War and when *The Times* published its correspondent's account of the bungling mismanagement of the campaign, the government fell. The obvious choice for prime minister at this crisis was the strong man, Palmerston, but the queen tried her best to avoid him. (There was a remarkable parallel in 1940 : Churchill was the obvious choice when Chamberlain fell, but George VI appointed him with great reluctance, preferring the quieter and more orthodox figure of Lord Halifax.) In the end she bowed to the inevitable and appointed Palmerston.

Peace came in 1856, and in 1858 Palmerston's government fell. Derby again became prime minister, with Disraeli as leader of the House.

Before entering parliament Disraeli had become a Christian. Had he not done so, public life would have been denied to him for no Jew could sit in the House of Commons. It was this government that removed that disability, thus finally establishing the principle of religious liberty. The statute reads :

JEWISH RELIEF ACT—1858

Be it enacted by the Queen's most Excellent Majesty, by and with the Advice and Consent of the Lords Spiritual and Temporal, and Commons, in this present Parliament assembled, and by the Authority of the same, as follows:

1. Where it shall appear to either House of Parliament that a Person professing the Jewish Religion, otherwise entitled to sit and vote in such House, is prevented from so sitting and voting by his conscientious Objection to take the Oath which by an Act passed or to be passed in the present Session of Parliament has been or may be substituted for the Oaths of Allegiance, Supremacy, and Abjuration in the Form therein required, such House, if it think fit, may resolve that thenceforth any Person professing the Jewish Religion, in

taking the said Oath to entitle him to sit and vote as aforesaid, may omit the Words 'and I make this Declaration upon the true Faith of a Christian', and so long as such Resolution shall continue in force the said Oath, when taken and subscribed by any Person professing the Jewish Religion to entitle him to sit and vote in that House of Parliament, may be modified accordingly; and the taking and subscribing by any Person professing the Jewish Religion of the Oath so modified shall, as far as respects the Title to sit and vote in such House, have the same Force and Effect as the taking and subscribing by other Persons of the said Oath in the Form required by the said Act.

II.   In all other Cases, except for sitting in Parliament as aforesaid, or in qualifying to exercise the Right of Presentation to any Ecclesiastical Benefice in Scotland, whenever any of Her Majesty's Subjects professing the Jewish Religion shall be required to take the said Oath, the Words 'and I make this Declaration upon the true Faith of a Christian' shall be omitted.

III.   Nothing herein contained shall extend or be construed to extend to enable any Person or Persons professing the Jewish Religion to hold or exercise the Office of Guardians and Justices of the United Kingdom, or of Regent of the United Kingdom, under whatever Name, Style, or Title such Office may be constituted, or of Lord High Chancellor, Lord Keeper or Lord Commissioner of the Great Seal of Great Britain or Ireland, or the Office of Lord Lieutenant or Deputy or other Chief Governor or Governors of Ireland, or Her Majesty's High Commissioner to the General Assembly of the Church of Scotland.

IV.   Where any Right of Presentation to any Ecclesiastical Benefice shall belong to any Office in the Gift or Appointment of Her Majesty, Her Heirs or Successors, and such Office shall be held by a Person professing the Jewish Religion, the Right of Presentation shall devolve upon and be exercised by the Archbishop of Canterbury for the Time being; and it shall not be lawful for any Person professing the Jewish Religion, directly or indirectly, to advise Her Majesty, Her Heirs or Successors, or any Person or Persons holding or exercising the Office of Guardians of the United Kingdom, or of Regent of the United Kingdom, under whatever Name, Style, or Title such Office may be constituted, or the Lord Lieutenant or Lord Deputy, or any other Chief Governor or Governors of Ireland, touching or concerning the Appointment to or Disposal of any Office or Preferment in the United Church of England and Ireland or in the Church of Scotland; being thereof convicted by due Course of Law, be deemed guilty of a high Misdemeanour, and disabled for ever from holding any Office, Civil or Military, under the Crown.

Lord Derby's government, anxious to find some popular measure upon which to fight the next election, considered widening the scope of the Reform Act of 1832 but before anything could be done the government fell and Palmerston again became prime minister. For Chancellor of the Exchequer he selected Gladstone, a former Peelite Tory.

Gladstone became the spokesman for those who were demanding votes for all men. He spoke of the 'forty-nine-fiftieths of the working classes' who were excluded from the vote. Every man, he argued, was morally entitled to come within the constitution. Just after the 1865 election Palmerston died. Lord John Russell (now Earl Russell) became prime minister, and Gladstone took over the leadership of the Commons.

A Bill was introduced lowering the voting qualification to the payment of an annual rent of £7. This was a very tentative step forward, but the Conservative opposition found it revolutionary. The Radicals on the other hand, who with Gladstone wanted all householders to have the vote, were disappointed. To add to the Bill's difficulties, a group of Whigs voted with the opposition. The government was defeated and the Bill died.

There was no new election and Derby, with Disraeli as his lieutenant, took office without a Commons majority. Meanwhile the disappointed working classes seethed with anger at the Bill's rejection. There were mass meetings up and down the country. In London, crowds stormed Hyde Park from which their demonstration had been excluded and tore down the railings. The shaky government, seeking some popular measure for the next election, decided to make the cause of reform its own. It was Disraeli who persuaded the queen that it was right to reform the electoral system, and carried Lord Derby with him.

In March 1867 he introduced a new Reform Bill giving votes to all rate-paying householders. This was not as far-reaching as it appears, since in the case of poorer tenants the landlords normally paid the rates. Gladstone and John Bright put forward a series of amendments widening the scope of the Bill. The government, lacking a clear majority, could not oppose these amendments without losing the Bill itself. So the Representation of the People Act, 1867, became law. It reads :

REFORM ACT—1867

Whereas it is expedient to amend the laws relating to the representation of the people in England and Wales:

Be it enacted by the queen's most excellent Majesty, by and with the advice and consent of the lords spiritual and temporal, and commons, in this present parliament assembled, and by the authority of the same as follows:

1. This act shall be cited for all purposes as 'The Representation of the People Act, 1867.'

2. This act shall not apply to Scotland or Ireland, nor in any wise affect the election of members to serve in parliament for the universities of Oxford or Cambridge.

PART I

FRANCHISES

3. Every man shall, on and after the year one thousand eight hundred and sixty-eight, be entitled to be registered as a voter, and, when registered, to vote for a member or members to serve in parliament for a borough, who is qualified as follows; (that is to say,)

    1. Is of full age, and not subject to any legal incapacity and

    2. Is on the last day of July in any year, and has during the whole of the preceding twelve calendar months been, an inhabitant occupier, as owner or tenant, of any dwelling house within the borough: and

    3. Has during the time of such occupation been rated as an ordinary occupier in respect of the premises so occupied by him within the borough to all rates

(if any) made for the relief of the poor in respect of such premises; and

4. Has on or before the twentieth day of July in the same year **bona fide** paid an equal amount in the pound to that payable by other ordinary occupiers in respect of all poor rates that have become payable by him in respect of the said premises up to the preceding fifth day of January:

Provided that no man shall under this section be entitled to be registered as a voter by reason of his being a joint occupier of any dwelling house.

4. Every man shall, in and after the year one thousand eight hundred and sixty-eight, be entitled to be registered as a voter, and, when registered, to vote for a member or members to serve in parliament for a borough, who is qualified as follows; (that is to say,)

1. Is of full age and not subject to any legal incapacity, and

2. As a lodger has occupied in the same borough separately and as sole tenant for the twelve months preceding the last day of July in any year the same lodgings, such lodgings being part of one and the same dwelling house, and of a clear yearly value, if let unfurnished, of ten pounds or upwards; and

3. Has resided in such lodgings for the twelve months immediately preceding the last day of July, and has claimed to be registered as a voter at the next ensuing registration of voters.

5. Every man shall, in and after the year one thousand eight hundred and sixty-eight, be entitled to be registered as a voter (and, when registered, to vote for a member or members to serve in Parliament for a county, who is qualified as follows; (that is to say,)

1. Is of full age, and not subject to any legal incapacity, and is seised at law or in equity of any lands or tenements of freehold, copyhold, or any other tenure whatever, for his own life, or the life of another, or for any lives whatsoever, or for any larger estate of the clear yearly value of not less than five pounds over and above all rents and

charges payable out of or in respect of the same, or who is entitled, either as lessee or assignee, to any lands or tenements of freehold or of any other tenure whatever for the unexpired residue, whatever it may be, of any term originally created for a period of not less than sixty years (whether determinable on a life or lives or not), of the clear yearly value of not less than five pounds over and above all rents and charges payable out of or in respect of the same:

Provided that no person shall be registered as a voter under this section unless he has complied with the provisions of the twenty-sixth section of the act of the second year of the reign of His Majesty William the Fourth, Chapter forty-five.

6. Every man shall, in and after the year one thousand eight hundred and sixty-eight, be entitled to be registered as a voter, and, when registered, to vote for a member or members to serve in parliament for a county, who is qualified as follows; (that is to say,)

1. Is of full age, and not subject to any legal incapacity, and

2. Is on the last day of July in any year, and has during the twelve months immediately preceding been, the occupier, as owner or tenant, of lands or tenants within the county of the rateable value of twelve pounds or upwards; and

3. Has during the time of such occupation been rated in respect to the premises so occupied by him to all rates (if any) made for the relief of the poor in respect of the said premises; and

4. Has on or before the twentieth day of July in the same year paid all poor rates that have become payable by him in respect of the said premises up to the preceding fifth day of January.

The right to vote was not yet universal, but the voice of the lower middle classes could now be heard, as well as that of the more prosperous artisans and mechanics in the towns. Since the Act referred only to the boroughs, the farm labourers in the country and working men living outside parliamentary boroughs benefited not at all. Nevertheless, it was a step forward.

In the election which followed, the new electors, recognising that it was Gladstone's amendments which had given force to the new measure, returned the Liberals with a large majority. Gladstone became prime minister and his administration passed the Ballot Act in 1872, of which the following are extracts:

BALLOT ACT—1872

Whereas it is expedient to amend the law relating to procedure at parliamentary and municipal elections:

Be it enacted by the queen's most excellent Majesty, by and with the advice and consent of the lords spiritual and temporal and commons, in this present parliament assembled and by the authority of the same, as follows:

2. In the case of a poll at an election the votes shall be given by ballot. The ballot of each voter shall consist of a paper (in this act called a ballot paper) showing the names and description of the candidates. Each ballot paper shall have a number printed on the back, and shall have attached a counterfoil with the same number printed on the face. At the time of voting, the ballot paper shall be marked on both sides with an official mark, and delivered to the voter within the polling station, and the number of such voter on the register of voters shall be marked on the counterfoil, and the voter having secretly marked his vote on the paper, and folded it up so as to conceal his vote, shall place it in a closed box in the presence of the officer presiding at the polling station (in this act called 'the presiding officer') after having shown to him the official mark at the back.

Any ballot paper which has not on its back the official mark, or on which votes are given to more candidates than the voter is entitled to vote for, or on which anything, except the said number on the back, is written or marked by which the voter can be identified, shall be void and not counted.

After the close of the poll the ballot boxes shall be sealed up, so as to prevent the introduction of additional ballot papers, and shall be taken charge of by the returning officer, and that officer shall, in the presence of such agents, if any, of the candidates as may be in attendance, open the ballot boxes, and ascertain the result of the poll by counting the votes given to each candidate, and shall forthwith declare to be elected the candidates or candidate to whom the majority of votes have been given, and return their names to the clerk of the crown in chancery. The decision of the returning officer as to any question arising in respect of any ballot paper shall be final, subject to reversal on petition questioning the election or return.

Where an equality of votes is found to exist between any candidates at an election for a county or borough, and the addition of a vote would entitle any of such candidates to be declared elected, the returning officer, if a registered elector of such county or borough, may give such additional vote, but shall not in any other case be entitled to vote at an election for which he is returning officer.

At last the old principle that 'elections ought to be free' was properly fulfilled. With elections no longer made openly at the hustings, neither landlord nor employer could browbeat or buy the electors.

Gladstone remained in office until 1873, in which year the electorate returned a Conservative majority and Disraeli became prime minister. In all these events, the figure and influence of Queen Victoria loomed large. She accepted the constitutional position completely, but she nonetheless saw herself as the queen and her ministers as her advisers and helpers, chosen by the electorate certainly, but owing their duty to her as the holder of sovereign power in the kingdom.

Disraeli remained in office for seven successful years. Towards the end, Victoria raised him to the peerage with the title of Earl of Beaconsfield. He had played a large part in building the might of the Empire, had increased Britain's influence on the Continent, and had introduced a great deal of reform. The Employers and Workmen Act gave trade unions the right of peaceful picketing and laid down that no union could be prosecuted for any deed which an individual might lawfully perform. The Factory Acts were revised and modernised, and limits set on the number of hours which women might work (fifty-six in a week).

Difficulties arising from troubles with the Zulus in Africa, from a disaster in Afghanistan and from a series of bad harvests induced Gladstone to come out out of retirement and stand in the election of 1880. He won from the Tories their hitherto safe seat of Midlothian and the Liberals secured a majority of 140 seats. Gladstone—now 'The Grand Old Man'—became prime minister and the following year Disraeli died.

In 1884 the Gladstone government put through a further Reform Act. This gave the same right to householders in the counties as had been given to them in the boroughs by the Act of 1867 and so put right a glaring anomaly. An indication of that anomaly and of the importance of the new Act is that it brought more new voters on to the register than both the two earlier Reform Acts put together. The following are its most important provisions.

REFORM ACT—1884

Be it enacted by the queen's most excellent Majesty, by and with the advice and consent of the lords spiritual and temporal, and commons, in this present parliament assembled, and by the authority of the same, as follows:

PRELIMINARY

1. This act may be cited as the Representation of the People Act, 1884.

EXTENSION OF THE HOUSEHOLD AND LODGER FRANCHISE

2. A uniform household franchise and a uniform lodger franchise at elections shall be established in all counties and boroughs throughout the united kingdom, and every man possessed of a household qualification or a lodger qualification shall, if the qualifying premises be situate in a county in England or Scotland, be entitled to be registered as a voter, and when registered to vote at an election for such county, and if the qualifying premises be situate in a county or borough in Ireland, be entitled to be registered as a voter, and when registered to vote at an election for such county or borough.

o

3. Where a man himself inhabits any dwelling-house by virtue of any office, service, or employment, and the dwelling-house is not inhabited by any person under whom such man serves in such office, service, or employment, he shall be deemed for the purposes of this act and of the representation of the people acts to be an inhabitant occupier of such dwelling house as a tenant.

With the vote now in the hands of every householder in the land, parliament more and more represented the views of the people and this new electoral system was to be used right up to the twentieth century.

In the following year the Liberal government was defeated in the commons by a combination of Conservative and Irish Nationalist MPs. At the election the Liberals came back with a reduced majority but were again defeated on a Bill for Home Rule for Ireland.

A new Conservative administration was formed under Lord Salisbury which governed until the election of 1892, and in 1898 Gladstone died. He had sat in the Commons for some sixty years, had been a towering figure for most of them, and had introduced massive reforms. At the beginning of the century, parliaments were still elected as they had been in Stuart times. By the time Gladstone died every householder in the kingdom participated in the processes of government.

Towards the end of the century the working class movement of trade unions and co-operative societies became more and more identified with socialism—the new theory that mere reform of existing systems was not enough, and that the entire economic structure of society should be changed. There could be no social justice, so it was argued, until the people themselves owned the factories in which they laboured, together with the shops where the goods they had manufactured were sold. Earlier in the century the co-operative movement, which started in Lancashire, began to give practical effect to the latter part of this doctrine.

The ideas of socialism were supported not only by the working class. Men like Charles Kingsley had started the Christian Socialist movement in the middle of the century. Later, William Morris saw socialism as the only way to create the 'Merry England' of the romantic legends.

As a result of all this, and of the beliefs of the more radical members of the Liberal party, the idea began to grow that the labouring classes should themselves sit as members of parliament; the Labour Party was founded in 1900 with this declared purpose.

The century ended dramatically with Queen Victoria's death in 1901.

She had reigned longer than any other English monarch and had become a mother-figure throughout Europe and indeed the world. She symbolised the stability, prosperity, and influence of her kingdom and her death seemed to mark not only the end of a century but of generations of history.

At the time of her death, England was fighting the Boer War and when, after initial setbacks, it ended in expected victory, men looked forward to a resumption of prosperity and happiness under the queen's elderly and somewhat raffish son. Edward VII with his fat cigars, his well-fed figure, his rakish hats, his card-playing, and his handsome mistresses, made his brief and genial reign one of gaiety rather than happiness. The social ferment continued. Keir Hardie, the first Labour MP, spoke for the underprivileged. Education was spreading and the disenfranchised were becoming articulate.

Another portent of change was the claim by women that they too should have the vote. The demand for adult manhood suffrage had been revolutionary enough, but for women to claim a voice in government was considered at best ridiculous and at worst shocking.

In 1905 Mrs Pankhurst began her campaign of dramatic violence to demand votes for women. Suffragettes (as they were derisively called) chained themselves to railings, marched through the streets with banners, shouted slogans, and one was to throw herself to her death beneath the hooves of the king's horse at Epsom.

In 1910 King Edward died. His eldest son, the Duke of Clarence, was already dead, and he was accordingly succeeded by his younger son George V. George had not been brought up in expectation of the crown, but had been a serving naval officer. A bluff, stern, yet kindly man, he was the last king set in the mould of the eighteenth and nineteenth centuries. For those who believe the constitutional myth that in modern times the king is but a figurehead, the career of George V is worthy of study. A conscientious supporter of constitutional and traditional practices, he nevertheless intervened in political matters, playing a full part in governing as well as reigning over his kingdom. He personally called a conference at Buckingham Palace in 1914 in an attempt to solve the intractable problems of Ireland. He played a part in the appointment of Stanley Baldwin as prime minister, in place of the Conservative party's choice of Lord Curzon, since he felt that it was out of keeping with a democratic society to have a prime minister who was not an elected member of parliament. In doing so he established a principle that was to lead to constitutional changes in the House of Lords—the right of a peer to renounce his title and the appointment of life peers. When the Labour Party first came to power he guided his new ministers in their unaccustomed duties. In 1931 he declined to dissolve parliament, arguing that an election would be dangerous at a time of acute financial difficulties, and recommending the formation of a government of all the parties.

The early part of his reign was a continuation of the long Victorian and Edwardian summer. The Royal Navy ruled the seven seas. A sixth of the world's people were King George's subjects and his realms and Empire covered a quarter of the earth's surface. The wealthy lived spacious and leisurely lives, the middle classes were prosperous, and working people were climbing out of poverty.

In 1911 members of parliament were given salaries of £400 a year, so yet another of the demands of the Chartists had been met. Parliament was no longer reserved for the wealthy. Working men and salary-earners could now take their place in the councils of the nation. In the same year a scheme of unemployment and health insurance was introduced and progress towards another freedom—freedom from want—had begun.

Then, in 1914 came the supreme disaster of George V's reign, the Great War, which lasted until 1918. Basically it arose from the growing economic and naval rivalry between Britain and Germany. In so far as personal considerations can play a part in such cataclysmic events, the Kaiser's jealousy of his cousin George was not without influence. After all, if the crown of England passed to the eldest child of the monarch and not to the eldest son, he would himself have sat on the English throne as William V, for his mother had been the eldest of Queen Victoria's many children.

The Great War finally destroyed nineteenth-century Europe. The German, Austrian and Russian Empires fell; new republics replaced old monarchies; the accumulated wealth of generations was used to purchase munitions. A universal madness seized the world, in which all the virtues triumphed—comradeship, unselfishness, endurance, courage, humour and self-sacrifice; but triumphed at the loss of almost a whole generation of the brave young men who possessed those virtues. They died in the mud of Belgium, the fields of France, the sandy ways of the near east, the shores of Turkey and elsewhere; and they drowned in every sea.

England survived, seemingly stronger than ever before, having proved her invincibility in vaster and bloodier battles than Agincourt or Waterloo. In reality she was sorrowfully weakened. Young men were few and leadership scarce for twenty years thereafter. But her institutions remained unshakeable and she began to rebuild a new life. Lloyd George, the Liberal prime minister who led the nation to victory, had promised the soldiers 'a land fit for heroes to live in'.

Immediately after the war, partly in gratitude, and partly because it was logical that all men should participate in the processes of government, since men of every class had fought for their country, manhood suffrage was finally achieved. An Act passed in 1918 gave the vote to all men aged 21 and over. The only exceptions were Church of England clergymen, (since they were already represented in parliament by the bishops in the House of Lords), peers of the realm and lunatics :

REPRESENTATION OF THE PEOPLE ACT—1918

Be it enacted by the King's most Excellent Majesty, by and with the advice and consent of the Lords Spiritual and Temporal, and Commons, in this present Parliament assembled, and by the authority of the same, as follows:

PART I

FRANCHISES

1.—(1) A man shall be entitled to be registered as a parliamentary elector for a constituency (other than a university constituency) if he is of full age and not subject to any legal incapacity, and—

(a) has the requisite residence qualification; or
(b) has the requisite business premises qualification.

(2) A man, in order to have the requisite residence qualification or business premises qualification for a constituency:

(a) must on the last day of the qualifying period be residing in premises in the constituency, or occupying business premises in the constituency, as the case may be; and

Parliamentary franchises (men)

213

(b) must during the whole of the qualifying period have resided in premises, or occupied business premises, as the case may be, in the constituency, or in another constituency within the same parliamentary borough or parliamentary county, or within a parliamentary borough or parliamentary county contiguous to that borough or county, or separated from that borough or county by water, not exceeding at the nearest point six miles in breadth, measured in the case of tidal water from low-water mark.

For the purposes of this subsection the administrative county of London shall be treated as a parliamentary borough.

(3) The expression 'business premises' in this section means land or other premises of the yearly value of not less than ten pounds occupied for the purpose of the business, profession, or trade of the person to be registered.

So at last the dream of the Chartists had been fulfilled. Every Englishman could now freely make his choice as to who should sit in parliament and take part in the king's business. Since in 1911 it had been agreed that members of parliament should be paid, all points of the charter, with the exception of annual elections, had now been met. Somewhere the shades of John Ball, Wat Tyler, Jack Cade and those of a host of forgotten men, nodded their approval. And the more recent ghosts of Lovett the cabinet-maker, John Bright and Gladstone joined them in their rejoicing. Now at last the ancient statutes and royal charters guaranteed the liberties of all men.

Nor were women excluded. The suffragette movement had been suspended during the war. Women had then demonstrated their abilities in more telling ways than during Mrs Pankhurst's militant campaign.

They joined auxiliary units of the armed forces, became bus conductresses, policewomen and—in the catchphrases of the times—did their bit and carried on until the boys came home. And once the boys came home the bustling and efficient wartime women could not go back with quiet docility to the drawing-room, the kitchen or the nursery. The old tribal assembly, ancestor of parliament, had been an assembly of the fighting men. Women, although they had not borne arms, had played their part in the struggle. There was no more any question about equality. The case had been proved and the Act provided for women but only those aged 30 and over, to have the vote :

REPRESENTATION OF THE PEOPLE ACT—1918

4.—(1) A woman shall be entitled to be registered as a parliamentary elector for a constituency (other than a university constituency) if she—

(a) has attained the age of thirty years; and

(b) is not subject to any legal incapacity; and

(c) is entitled to be registered as a local government elector in respect of the occupation in that constituency of land or premises (not being a dwelling-house) of a yearly value of not less than five pounds or of a dwelling-house, or is the wife of a husband entitled to be so registered.

A.D. 1918

(2) A woman shall be entitled to be registered as a parliamentary elector for a university constituency if she has attained the age of thirty years and either would be entitled to be so registered if she were a man, or has been admitted to and passed the final examination, and kept under the conditions required of women by the university the period of

215

residence, necessary for a man to obtain a degree at any university forming, or forming part of, a university constituency which did not at the time the examination was passed admit women to degrees.

(3) A woman shall be entitled to be registered as a local government elector for any local government electoral area—

(a) where she would be entitled to be so registered if she were a man; and

(b) where she is the wife of a man who is entitled to be so registered in respect of premises in which they both reside, and she has attained the age of thirty years and is not subject to any legal incapacity.

For the purpose of this provision, a naval or military voter who is registered in respect of a residence qualification which he would have had but for his service, shall be deemed to be resident in accordance with the qualification.

Universal suffrage had arrived, one of the few benefits won on those ghastly battlefields of the world war. It remained only for successive Acts first in 1928 to give the vote to women at 21 and then, in 1969, to men and women at 18.

REPRESENTATION OF THE PEOPLE ACT—1969

Be it enacted by the Queen's most Excellent Majesty, by and with the advice and consent of the Lords Spiritual and Temporal, and Commons, in this present

216

Parliament assembled, and by the authority of the same, as follows:—

The franchise and its exercise

1.—(1) For purposes of the Representation of the People Acts a person shall be of voting age if he is of the age of eighteen years or over; and, if otherwise qualified, a person who is of voting age on the date of the poll at a parliamentary or local government election shall be entitled to vote as an elector, whether or not he is of voting age on the qualifying date.

Voting age

(2) A person, if otherwise qualified, shall accordingly be entitled to be registered in a register of parliamentary electors or a register of local government electors if he will attain voting age before the end of the twelve months, following the day by which the register is required to be published; but, if he will not be of voting age on the first day of those twelve months—

(a) his entry in the register shall give the date on which he will attain that age; and

(b) until the date given in the entry he shall not by virtue of the entry be treated as an elector for any purposes other than purposes of an election at which the day fixed for the poll is that or a later date.

(3) A person, if otherwise qualified, shall be capable of voting as proxy at parliamentary or local government elections at which he is of voting age on the date of the poll, and of being appointed proxy for that purpose before he is of voting age.

(4) A person shall be qualified under

217

the parliamentary or local elections rules
to assist a blind voter to vote if that person is one of the relatives specified in the
relevant rule and is of voting age.

(5) For purposes of the Representation
of the People Acts a person shall be
deemed, according to the law in Northern
Ireland as well as according to the law in
other parts of the United Kingdom, not to
have attained a given age until the commencement of the relevant anniversary of
the day of his birth.

Parliament was now the representative of all the nation; the right
of participation in government, and those liberties which men and
women alike had yearned and fought for, were thus finally established.

DOCUMENTS QUOTED :

1 The Reform Act—1832 [2 *William IV. c. 45*]
2 Act Abolishing Negro Slavery—1833 [3 & 4 *William IV. c. 73*]
3 The Chartists' 'Charter'—1839
4 The Jewish Relief Act—1858 [21 & 22 *Victoria. c. 49*]
5 The Reform Act—1867 [30 & 31 *Victoria, c. 102*]
6 The Ballot Act—1872 [35 & 36 *Victoria, c. 33*]
7 The Reform Act—1884 [48 *Victoria. c. 3*]
8 Representation of the People Act—1918 [8 *George V. c. 64*]
9 Representation of the People Act—1969 [*Elizabeth II, 1969. c. 15*]

Epilogue

THE constant theme running through all that we have examined is that, however radical the changes which new circumstances or new aspirations may require, these are always most successful when achieved without the destruction of the framework of society.

All forms of government must be efficient. Without efficiency, the justice and liberty which men seek would come to nothing. The total destruction of central authority is too high a price to pay for the introduction of new sociological concepts. Inefficiency, and that type of political chaos which results from the total destruction of the machinery of government, work for the overthrow of liberty as fiercely as any conscious tyranny. Man can be free only within a peaceful environment. So the acceptance—even by the most radical elements of society —of the need for the maintenance of domestic peace is a prerequisite of useful change.

The very English conception of the king's peace and of the overriding loyalty of all men, even the rebels, to the monarch who personifies and protects the state, has rendered it possible to obtain change with stability, and continuity without inflexibility. A subtle balance between uncritical loyalty to the monarch on the one hand, and uninhibited and destructive criticism on the other, has marked all the documents we have studied. Nor has the instinct to act in this way totally vanished in the twentieth century. In 1931 the men of the Royal Navy mutinied at Invergordon in protest against a cut in pay. A manifesto was written by an able seamen serving in HMS *Norfolk*. The manifesto was an ultimatum, containing a refusal to carry out any duties until there was a guarantee from the Admiralty, confirmed by parliament, that the pay cuts would be reviewed. Yet the opening sentence reads :

We the loyal subjects of His Majesty the King do hereby present my
Lords Commissioners of the Admiralty our representations to implore them to amend the drastic cuts in pay . . .

The accuracy with which these words echo those other petitions and
remonstrances, addressed to George V's remoter ancestors, is uncanny.
The phrases reflect the unchanging purpose of rebel and reformer;
namely to achieve redress against tyrannous or unthinking governments
whenever liberty or social justice is in danger; to do so swiftly and
continually, without being overawed by the great or intimidated by the
powerful; but always as members of a united community and with
loyalty to the symbols of that unity.

The past also teaches us that there is a kind of gravitational law
which governs both liberty and justice. Where the common people are
alert, then both liberty and justice seep downwards through society.
Rights that were wrung from the crown by small, privileged groups of
powerful men, are grasped by those below them and in the end spread
throughout the population. The resentment of the barons against King
John's arbitrary taxes and duties led, through a vast complexity of later
events, to the conception of parliament and ultimately to universal
suffrage. But because of the manner in which redress was sought, and
the style adopted in every age by those who demanded justice, a
descendant of John still sits upon the throne of England, still summons
parliament, and still symbolises—and merely by so doing helps to maintain—the unity of the community.

Whether this method and this style will remain of value in the
future is a matter not of history but speculation. During the last fifty
years entirely new forces have come into play. Organised labour has
long ceased only to protect its own interests and working conditions.
By its views on economics and by its judgements on matters political,
it can mightily influence events. Organised capital, either in the form
of the new giant undertakings which now dominate the field of
production, or in the form of associations and confederations, now
wields more power than any duke or earl of days gone by. In a military
society, political power rode with the mounted knight or marched with
the humbler bowman, but today the last vestiges of the old military
society are vanished, erased by two world wars. We now live in an
industrial society, and so far (in terms of the long perspective of
history) have had but brief experience of it. Swords have not been
beaten into ploughshares. Rather the sword, and all that it symbolises,
has become so dangerous as to be irrelevant. Small nations can defy the

super-powers safe in the knowledge that the latter will not use against them the ultimate weapons they possess.

So where, within the new society, does political power now lie? The rebels and radicals, like the small nations in the field of international politics, can defy authority with impunity. Panic-stricken magistrates could order the sabres of the cavalry to be wielded against the demonstrators of Peterloo, but modern weapons are a different matter. Authority is instinctively moving back to the medieval, and arming its forces with helmet and shield and cudgel.

We have traced the growth of liberty from Saxon days to the twentieth century. The rough timbers of the hall where the Witan met heard the same kind of arguments that were advanced in Victorian parliaments and that are amplified through loudspeakers in today's House of Commons. The continuity that we have examined is almost unbelievable, and probably unique in the world's history. The modern insistence upon the necessity of change and the need for participation is not new. Perhaps the solutions, like the problems, are to be found somewhere in the past, however different and remote that past may deceptively appear.

1	SOC	right of local jurisdiction
2	HONOUR	a group of manors held by one lord
3	WAPENTAKE	a subdivision of a county in the North of England or Midlands
4	MARK	worth 13s 4d
5	VILL	a group of houses forming an estate
6	NOVEL DISSESIN	action to recover land of which one was recently dispossessed
7	MORT D'ANCESTOR	action to recover land lost to a stranger on the death of an ancestor
8	DERREIN PRESENTMENT	action for the recovery of the right to appoint a clergyman to a benefice
9	PRECIPE	a writ commanding something to be done or a reason to be given for non-performance
10	HABERJECT	a kind of cloth, possibly with a special finish
11	FEE-FARM	tenure of land at a rent without service
12	SOCAGE	tenure of land by defined services
13	BURGAGE	tenure of land in socage at a yearly rent
14	ESCHEAT	land coming to a lord for want of heirs
15	BAILWICK	district under the jurisdiction of a bailiff or sheriff
16	WHITETAWERS	men who tawed or cured hides into white leather
17	DISHERISON	disinheriting
18	COMPULSORIES	mandates compelling obedience
19	AD SALUTEM	for salvation
20	COIF	a serjeant at law
21	ESSOIN	a lawful excuse
22	NON VULT ULTERIUS	the dropping of a suit
23	OYER AND TERMINER	a commission authorised to 'hear and determine' indictments of treason or felony
24	TORY	Irish for an outlaw
25	WHIGAMORE	Scots for a cattle thief
26	NON OBSTANTE	licence from the king to do something notwithstanding any statute to the contrary
27	QUAM DIU SE BENE GESSERINT	as long as they are of good behaviour